CONNIE HAGEN

Drinking The Cup
You Are Served

THE BIBLE STUDY
Includes access to Streaming Videos

Thrilling Life Publishers
Southlake, TX

Drinking the Cup You Are Served – The Bible Study
Copyright © 2026 Connie Hagen

Publishers by Thrilling Life Publishers
In Association with Let's Write
PO Box 92522, Southlake TX 76092.
ThrillingLife.com

ISBN 979-8-9997169-4-1
Cover Design: StudioAnneli.com
Editor: Jennifer Strickland
Production: Victorya Rogers
Author Photo: Madison Hagen

Unless otherwise noted, Scripture quotations are taken from the Holy Bible, New Living Translation. © 1996, 2004, 2015 by Tyndale House Foundation. Used by permission of Tyndale House Ministries, Carol Stream, Illinois 60188. All rights reserved.

All rights reserved. No portion of this book may be reproduced, stored in a retrieval system, or transmitted in any form or by any means—electronic, mechanical, photocopy, recording, scanning, or other—except for brief quotations in critical reviews or articles without the prior written permission of the publisher.

Printed in the United States of America

CONTENTS

Introduction 4

A Guide For Leaders 6

Weeek One A Cup You Didn't Choose 11

Week Two A Cup of Doubt 43

Week Three A Cup of Perception 77

Week Four A Cup of Shame 116

Week Five A Cup of Fear... 153

Week Six A Cup of Sorrow 192

Week Seven A Cup of Freedom... 232

About the Author 267

Access to Streaming Videos... 269

A Journey Worth Taking

Dear Reader,

I'm so glad you've picked up this study. If you're holding it in your hands, chances are you're carrying something. It could be pain, questions, heartache, or maybe a deep desire to move forward but no idea where to begin. I want to tell you from the very beginning: this journey won't be easy, but it will be worth it. Healing and freedom rarely come without effort. They come when we show up, do the work, and let God meet us in the hard places.

Let me explain what I mean. I am, by all accounts, an amateur tennis player. I've been playing for fun over the last ten years. But recently, I found myself in a lot of pain. I couldn't walk without discomfort, and every step reminded me something wasn't right. It turns out I had plantar fasciitis due to too much tennis. I went to physical therapy for help, and the provider looked me in the eye and said, "If you don't do the exercises, you won't get better. Doing physical therapy only once a week will not be enough."

That was all I needed to hear. Every morning and every night, I faithfully did exactly what I was told. And within a couple of weeks, the pain began to ease. My foot started to heal. The lesson was simple, but powerful: healing often requires more than desire and hope. Healing requires effort and participation.

The same is true when it comes to healing from emotional pain.

Each day of this Bible study, you'll see a section called Faith in Action. Think of it like the exercises I had to do for my foot. These are your practical steps. They may not feel life-changing in the moment, but done consistently, they will strengthen your mind and reshape your beliefs. The suggestions and exercises will help you walk forward with more freedom than you had before. We heal not only from learning, but through doing as well.

Let me also share with you why I wrote this study. Before writing my book *Drinking the Cup You Are Served*, I spent years as a therapist, listening to story after story of pain, loss, betrayal, and sorrow. I sat with women who had experienced unimaginable trauma, and I wrestled deeply with the question: Why would God allow such suffering in the lives of people he loves? The question has haunted me both professionally and personally. To be honest, I couldn't offer a satisfying answer because sometimes there isn't one.

That question set me on a journey. I didn't want to ignore suffering or dismiss it with easy answers. I wanted to understand how to drink a cup that felt too bitter to swallow. This Bible study is a window into what I discovered. It's a blend of my journey, my training as a therapist, and my belief God meets us in our pain.

While this Bible study guide stands on its own, it was designed to work beautifully alongside my book *Drinking the Cup You Are Served*. The book offers a deeper glimpse into my personal journey of learning how to drink the many cups I've been handed. At the beginning of each chapter, I share a personal story about a cup that felt far too bitter to swallow. These stories give context to the themes you'll explore here and will enrich your experience, but reading the book isn't necessary to understand or benefit from this study.

With all my heart I believe healing is possible even when circumstances don't change. I believe you can find peace, strength, and freedom, not by avoiding the hard stuff, but by walking straight through it with God beside you.

So, here's my encouragement to you: keep showing up. Do the work. Engage with the content, and don't skip the Faith in Action exercises. God wants to meet you there. He's not asking you to fix everything, but he is asking you to trust him with the next step.

Let's take the step together. One day at a time.

Connie Hagen

For Group Leaders

HOW TO USE THIS STUDY GUIDE

Thank you for your willingness to serve and lead this group of ladies through *Drinking the Cup You Are Served*. Your commitment to walking alongside others through difficult seasons is a gift to your group and your community. This study explores the cups we didn't ask for but find ourselves holding—those challenging circumstances that test our faith and shape our character.

Drinking the Cup You Are Served is a 7-week journey that examines different "cups" of struggles we encounter: circumstances we didn't choose, seasons of doubt, the weight of others' perceptions, shame, fear, sorrow, and ultimately, the freedom found in surrender. Together, you'll explore how God meets us in these unwanted places and transforms our bitter cups into vessels of grace.

This guide is designed to help you facilitate meaningful discussions and create a safe space where participants can honestly share their struggles. Feel free to adapt these suggestions to fit your group's unique needs and dynamics. Remember, you don't need to have all the answers—your role is to guide the conversation and point people toward hope.

SUGGESTED SCHEDULE FOR WEEKLY MEETINGS
7-8 Group Meetings • Meeting Length: 60-90 minutes

Week One—A Cup You Didn't Choose
Introduce the study, establish group guidelines for sharing, and explore what it means to face circumstances beyond our control.

Week Two—A Cup of Doubt
Examine how doubt can shake our faith and discover how God meets us in our questions.

Week Three—A Cup of Perception
Discuss the burden of others' judgments and finding our identity in God's view of us.

Week Four—A Cup of Shame
Create a safe space to discuss shame's power and the healing found in bringing it to light.

Week Five—A Cup of Fear
Address the paralyzing nature of fear and God's promises in our anxious moments.

Week Six—A Cup of Sorrow
Honor grief and loss while exploring how God comforts us in our deepest pain.

Week Seven—A Cup of Freedom
Celebrate the freedom that comes through surrender and accepting God's will for our lives.

Week Eight (Optional)—Celebration Gathering
Share testimonies, celebrate growth, and commit to continued support.

SUGGESTIONS FOR STRUCTURING GROUP TIME

Open With Prayer: Welcome the ladies, allow 5 minutes for chatting as everyone settles in, then open with prayer.

Watch the Week's Video (10-15 minutes): At the start of each weekly gathering, watch the corresponding teaching video (for example, Week One participants will watch the Week One video) before moving into discussion.

Discuss The Week's Study (45-50 minutes): Group facilitators walk their participants through the previous week's study together. Plan to spend about 8-10 minutes per day, briefly reviewing the Reflection Questions and Faith in Action prompts from each day's reading.

As you go through each day:

- Invite participants to share insights or experiences, but emphasize there's no pressure to share
- Allow space for only one or two ladies to respond to each question (this keeps the discussion moving and prevents anyone from dominating). If no one answers a question, just move on.

- Remind the group there is no pressure to share unless they are comfortable, as some cups are harder to share than others

If you finish before the 50 minutes are up, turn to the Group Discussion Questions at the end of the week's chapter. These guiding questions are designed to spark deeper conversation, encourage spiritual growth, and foster connection among group members.

Share Prayer Requests (15-25 minutes): Go around the room and allow each member to share prayer requests related to their current "cups." Ask the ladies to keep their prayer requests focused on themselves or issues that directly affect their lives. This isn't a time to share requests about neighbors or friends who need prayer; it is for the participants in the group and their own needs. Commit to keep requests confidential within the group and to pray for each other's requests during the week.

Close In Prayer (5 minutes): Close with specific prayer for the group. Consider having members pray for one another by name if you would like.

TIPS FOR LEADING THIS STUDY

Create Safety: This study touches deep wounds. Establish ground rules with your group such as, what's shared during group time stays within group. Please, no trying to fix each other and no offering unsolicited advice. Be gracious, as we all heal at different paces.

Embrace Discomfort: Some weeks will be heavy. Don't rush to make everything feel better. Sometimes sitting with someone in their difficult cup is the most powerful ministry.

Watch For Triggers: Topics like shame, fear, and sorrow can trigger past trauma. Have resources ready (counselor referrals, pastoral care) and be prepared to follow up individually if needed.

Model Vulnerability: Share your own cups when appropriate. Your willingness to be real gives others permission to do the same, but be careful not to overshare. Make sure your group members are given enough time to respond before jumping in with your personal stories.

Celebrate Small Victories: Acknowledge courage—showing up is brave, sharing is brave, continuing when it's hard is brave.

Prepare Personally: Complete each week's study yourself before leading. Pray for your group members by name throughout the week.

Practice Presence: Your greatest tool isn't having the right answers but being fully present. Listen more than you speak.

Remembering Your Purpose: You're not leading this group to fix anyone's problems. You're creating space for people to:

- Feel less alone in their struggles
- Experience God's presence in difficulty
- Find community in vulnerability
- Discover that our unwanted cups can become God's very vessels of grace for us.

Some participants may be in the midst of drinking very bitter cups. Your consistent presence, genuine care, and pointing toward hope may be the very thing that helps them take the next step.

Thank you for saying yes to this sacred work. Trust that God will use your willingness—imperfect as it may feel—to bring healing and hope to your group.

Grace and peace to you as you lead.

Week One

Cup You Didn't Choose

Imagine we are sitting together right now, just the two of us, maybe with a cup of tea. If you asked me how I've made it through the hardest seasons of my life, I wouldn't start with a list of answers. I would pause and take a deep breath. And then I'd tell you the truth. On my own, I would have never survived because there were times when I honestly thought it was too much, and I wondered where God was. I have asked him *why* more times than I can count.

Why did my daughter have to get so sick? Why do bad things keep happening to me? Why did my friend Lisa lose everything she had worked so hard to rebuild? Why did I have to walk through heartbreak after heartbreak when I was doing my best to follow God? Why did it feel like the cup I was handed wasn't just bitter, but to me seemed unbearable?

I've lived those questions. Maybe you have too. Maybe you're living one of them now. Here's what I've come to realize: "Why?" is a very human question. Even Jesus asked it. But it's not the question that will lead us forward. When the answers don't come, and they often don't, we have to ask something else.

What do I believe to be true about God? Who is God in the midst of my pain and suffering? I came to discover God is not defined by our circumstances, but he is defined through them.

In this first week, we're not going to try to explain away suffering or patch up grief as if it doesn't exist. We're going to take the time to sit with our feelings and be honest with them. We're going to walk into the garden with Jesus and watch how he wrestled with the cup he was given, and learn to follow his example.

And together, we're going to shift our question from *why* to *what.*

Instead of asking God, *Why is this happening?,* we are going to ask, *What do I believe about God in the midst of it?*

Asking the right questions keeps us moving forward.

Let's begin the journey!

Day One
I Don't Want To Drink This Cup

Welcome to Day One. Today, we begin by stepping into one of the most honest and vulnerable moments in Scripture when Jesus was in the Garden of Gethsemane. We'll take a closer look at how he responded to sorrow, fear, and the weight of a cup he didn't want. Taking a closer look at how Jesus responded to his grief is where we begin our journey, so we will not start with answers or try to make sense of everything right away. Instead, we'll begin with an honest reflection by acknowledging what hurts and admitting what feels confusing. We will allow ourselves to feel what we feel, regardless of whether we think we should or should not feel a particular way. This kind of honesty and reflection is the starting place, because that is exactly where Jesus began.

Jesus didn't hide his feelings or push them away. He brought them before the Father and chose to surrender. As we open the day, we'll reflect on what it means to trust God not in spite of our pain, but through it.

SCRIPTURE REFLECTION 1
Matthew 26:38-39
"He told them, 'My soul is crushed with grief to the point of death. Stay here and keep watch with me.' He went on a little farther and bowed with his face to the ground, praying, 'My Father! If it is possible, let this cup of suffering be taken away from me. Yet I want your will to be done, not mine'."

UNDERSTANDING THE PASSAGE
Matthew, one of Jesus' disciples, wrote this Gospel primarily for a Jewish audience, portraying Jesus as the long-awaited Messiah. In chapter 26, we find Jesus in the Garden of Gethsemane, moments before his betrayal and arrest. This is a raw, unfiltered scene where Jesus is overwhelmed with sorrow, paralyzed by the fear and agony of bearing the weight of the world's sins as the sacrificial lamb.

We see the depth of his sorrow in his description of his feelings when he tells his disciples, "My soul is crushed with grief to the point of death." His anguish was so deep it pressed down on him physically, emotionally, and spiritually. It's not hard to imagine his body trembling, his chest tight, his face in the dirt as he cried out to his Father.

In the garden, I believe Jesus was gripped by fear. Not because he lacked faith but because he fully understood the suffering to come: the betrayal, the mockery, the beatings, and the cross. In his humanity, it all felt like too much. But in spite of all the overwhelming feelings, he was willing to bring them to the Father with honest desperation.

He didn't hide from his feelings. He didn't suppress them or sanitize them. He let the fear and sorrow rise to the surface and prayed through them. He even asked for a way out: "If it is possible, let this cup of suffering be taken from me." That wasn't weakness. It was vulnerability and it portrays his humanity. This moment in Scripture shows us he is a Savior who feels what we feel.

After he had fully expressed his sorrow and his fear, he surrendered. "Not my will, but yours." This one line holds the tension of heaven and earth and of divinity and humanity. It's the turning point between resistance and obedience.

This intimate encounter with Jesus and his Father is where we begin to understand what supernatural strength really looks like. We see it is not the absence of sorrow, but a soul anchored in our Father's love, even as fear presses in. We see Jesus choosing surrender. We see the first step in what courage through surrender really means. Jesus shows us how to say yes to God.

REFLECTION QUESTIONS

- Name a time you have gone to God in the midst of sorrow and he met you right where you were?

- If you would be totally honest, what are you having a hard time trusting God with today?

When we completely surrender, we position ourselves to receive supernatural strength through the power of the Holy Spirit. I am not talking about the kind of strength coming from our own willpower, or from having all the answers, but in bringing every raw, aching part of ourselves to God and choosing to trust in him.

What gave Jesus the strength to face this moment? I believe it was his absolute trust in the character of God. He knew his father's love and purpose could be trusted even when the path ahead led to suffering.

SCRIPTURE REFLECTION 2
Hebrews 5:7
"While Jesus was here on earth, he offered prayers and pleadings, with a loud cry and tears, to the one who could rescue him from death. And God heard his prayers because of his deep reverence for God."

UNDERSTANDING THE PASSAGE
This passage provides a powerful glimpse into the humanity of Jesus as he prayed in the Garden. The letter to the Hebrews was written to a group of early Jewish believers who were worn down by persecution and were tempted to return to the old covenant.

The early believers were struggling to hold onto their newfound faith in Christ. The author of this passage offers them a clear and urgent declaration of Jesus' deity, revealing him as both fully God and fully human. His goal is to strengthen their faith by teaching them that Jesus understands their suffering because he experienced it himself.

This verse captures the depth of anguish Jesus experienced in the garden, describing how he offered prayers and pleadings with loud cries and tears. This moment was not a composed display of quiet faith but a desperate cry from the depths of his soul. It points us to the Garden of Gethsemane, where the weight of what was coming bore down on him with unbearable intensity.

At first glance, it may sound as if Jesus is asking God to spare him from the cross. However, the Greek phrase "to save him from death" gives us a much deeper insight. In this verse, the word "from" is translated from the Greek word *ek*, which doesn't mean to avoid something, but to be brought out from within it.

In other words, Jesus wasn't asking to escape death. He was asking to be delivered through it. His prayer wasn't to bypass the suffering, but to be brought out to the other side. Jesus knew the reason he came was to be God's sacrificial lamb. He was asking to be delivered out of the paralyzing fear and immense agony that surrounded the cross. He was pleading not for an exit, but for the courage to endure what lay ahead.

This distinction matters. It helps us see the heart of our Savior. He didn't fear obedience; instead, he feared the moments ahead. In the garden, he felt isolated and utterly alone, carrying the heart-wrenching sorrow and the crushing weight of the separation the cross would bring. His cries were not weakness. They were the cries of a fully human son entrusting his grief and fear to his faithful father.

"Then an angel from heaven appeared and strengthened him" (Luke 22:43).

His father heard him. God didn't remove the suffering, nor did he abandon Jesus in the midst of his pain. Luke 22:43 tells us in the midst of his agony, an angel appeared and strengthened him. God showed up! He did not take the cup away because he could see past the cross, but he did equip his Son to drink it, knowing he would be with him.

This wasn't only a divine moment of obedience. It was an intimate, personal moment between the Father and the Son. And it wasn't only for Jesus. What happened in the garden was for us, too.

What God did for his Son, he continues to do for us. He hears our cries. He sees the weight we carry. And he gives us exactly what we need to endure. Because God sees beyond our pain and sees the entirety of our stories, he may not always change the circumstances, but he will always strengthen us in the middle of them.

We may not be spared from walking through the hard places, but we are never asked to walk through them alone. The Holy Spirit, who is our advocate, our comforter, and our helper, dwells within us. What the angel did for Jesus in the garden, the Holy Spirit does for us every single day. When we are overwhelmed, we can cry out with confidence, knowing God will show up. He sees the beginning, the middle, and the end. And he has a plan.

REFLECTION QUESTIONS

- How does knowing God showed up for Jesus in the garden shape the way you view your own moments of surrender?

- What cup are you holding right now that feels too heavy, and how might the Holy Spirit be strengthening you to endure it?

FAITH IN ACTION

Jesus showed us what honest surrender looks like. He didn't hold back his feelings or try to appear strong. He brought his pain to the Father. This is where we begin: by learning to be honest about what hurts, just like Jesus was in the garden. We don't need to hide our feelings or pretend they don't exist. God can handle our grief, our dread, and even our fear.

Take time today to reflect on how you're feeling about your current season. Don't try to fix or explain it, just acknowledge it.

Ask yourself these questions then journal your answers.

1. **Are there any feelings I've been avoiding** or holding back from myself or from God?

2. **What burdens or unspoken struggles** have I been carrying that I need to surrender to God in prayer?

3. **In what ways might I be pushing down** or explaining away pain instead of allowing myself to feel it in God's presence?

4. **What would it look like for me** to bow before God and say, "Not my will, but yours"?

Jesus didn't surrender because he felt strong. He surrendered because he trusted. That's where we begin.

SEEING THE BIGGER PICTURE

God may not always take the cup from our hands, but he never expects us to carry it alone. Jesus' experience in the garden makes it clear surrender isn't the end of the story; rather, it is the turning point. God sent an angel to strengthen Christ while he was praying in the garden, not to take away the cross, but to give Jesus the strength and courage to endure what lay ahead. In our moments of surrender, we can expect the same: for God to show up and give us exactly what we need to keep moving forward in spite of the cup we have been given. He sees beyond what we can see, and just as he did with Jesus, he knows the end of the story and is working out a greater plan.

CLOSING THOUGHT

Surrender doesn't begin with certainty. It begins with honesty by acknowledging what you feel, letting go of control, and choosing to trust God sees what you can't. Even in sorrow, nothing is wasted in the hands of a God who redeems what we do not yet understand.

CLOSING PRAYER

God, I don't always understand the cup I've been given, but I want to trust you with it. Like Jesus in the garden, I bring you my sorrow and my fear and I lay them at your feet. I don't want to run or resist. I want to surrender. Give me the courage to say, "Not my will, but yours." Strengthen me through the power of the Holy Spirit to keep walking, even when the road is hard. Remind me everyday that you see the bigger picture, and you are with me every step.

In Jesus' name,
Amen

Day Two
When Why Doesn't Help

There's something deeply human about the question of why. It tumbles out of us in times of loss, confusion, and grief, often before we even realize we're asking it. *Why did this happen? Why now? Why me?* When life unravels, our hearts reach for meaning and why feels like the most logical place to start. I think knowing why gives us the false idea that we are somehow back in control. We tell ourselves, *If I know why, I can prevent this tragedy from happening again. I will feel some relief if I have someone to blame.* Or *if I can just make sense of what happened, I will feel better.* Sadly, chasing after the why will only spin you in circles because often there is no good answer.

Even Jesus asked why.

On the cross, at the height of his suffering, he cried out, "My God, my God, why have you forsaken me?" That single word reveals the depth of his anguish and the weight of the cup he was given to drink. If Jesus could ask why, surely we are allowed to as well.

But here's where it gets complicated. Answering the question of "why" doesn't always lead us to comfort. Sometimes it turns us inside out. We want answers, thinking they will steady us or make sense of the pain, but the truth is, not every storm comes with an explanation. Not every loss has a reason we can grasp. And chasing why can leave us more disoriented than grounded.

We think understanding will help us heal. If we can just connect the dots, the ache might lessen. But often, there is no satisfying answer. And demanding one can keep us stuck and frozen in our grief. Searching for a reasonable or logical explanation can entangle us in anger and bitterness, leaving us feeling lost and hopeless.

Even though asking why is often not helpful, it doesn't mean the question is wrong. It means the question can only take us so far.

Today, instead of searching for answers we may never get, we're going to explore what it looks like to stop chasing the "why" and start reaching for something more solid through our faith. Not a blind faith that ignores the pain, but a steady trust in the character of God even when we don't understand what he's doing. A trust that anchors us when the waves don't stop. Because it's not knowing *why* that will carry us through; it is God who will carry us through.

SCRIPTURE REFLECTION 1
Job 3:11
"'Why wasn't I born dead? Why didn't I die as I came from the womb'?"

UNDERSTANDING THE PASSAGE
These haunting words come from Job, a man who had lost everything. He lost his children, his health, his wealth, and his sense of purpose. After days of silence, Job finally speaks. He speaks not with a calm reflection, but with a piercing cry that captures the depth of human despair. He doesn't ease into his grief with perspective or theological conclusions. He reaches into the heart of despair and asks: *Why was I even born?* There's no resolution in this moment. No answer. Just pain.

It is important we understand why this response is so significant. By allowing this question to be recorded in Scripture, God clearly wants us to understand he gives us space to feel our feelings and to share them boldly and honestly without correction or condemnation.

Job didn't get punished for feeling devastated or for asking something so bold. Instead, his suffering and his search for understanding became the very place where God would later meet him.

Job's question reveals what sorrow often does to us. It can immobilize us and make it seem as if the rest of the world is moving on, but we can't. Grief can trap us in a mental and emotional space where our sense of time gets warped and we lose track of what's ahead or behind because the pain feels all-consuming. As a result, it often drags us into the depths of why. We may not use Job's exact words, but we've asked similar questions. *Why this diagnosis? Why this loss? Why didn't God stop it?* And like Job, we may sit in the silence. The silence represents our humanness, not our lack of faith.

Scripture doesn't rush to clean up Job's grief, and we shouldn't rush to clean up ours. What Job models for us is this: we can bring our hardest questions to God, including the unspeakable, and still be accepted and loved unconditionally by him.

Job's story is a reminder that asking why isn't always the path to peace. Even though Job cried out for answers, there were none. Finding answers to his questions of *why* was not what led him toward healing and peace; rather, he found healing in knowing *who* God was in the midst of his suffering.

REFLECTION QUESTIONS

- How has the need to understand why kept you from experiencing God's comfort in the midst of pain?

- What has the question "why" cost you emotionally or spiritually in a painful season?

SCRIPTURE REFLECTION 2

Isaiah 55:8–9

"'My thoughts are nothing like your thoughts,' says the Lord. 'And my ways are far beyond anything you could imagine. For just as the heavens are higher than the earth, so my ways are higher than your ways and my thoughts higher than your thoughts'."

UNDERSTANDING THE PASSAGE

This passage shows us how God sees the whole picture when we can only see part of it. His ways are higher, not because he's distant or indifferent, but because he sees from a perspective we cannot yet comprehend. His purposes unfold through a sovereign design that is always consistent with his eternal plan.

Spoken to a weary and discouraged people living in exile, Isaiah's words do not minimize their suffering; they were written to a generation who had lost their homeland and their sense of identity. They could not see any clear path forward. Yet even in their confusion and pain, God informed them his ways were higher. These words do not explain away their grief, but they do invite them to trust in a God who was still writing their story.

Again, Jesus, in the middle of his suffering, cried out, "My God, my God, why have you forsaken me?" (Matthew 27:46). In that moment, he felt the full weight of abandonment. The question he asked echoes every cry we've ever uttered in our own pain. But even as Jesus asked why, he never stepped outside his Father's will. He drank the bitter cup even though, in his humanity, he could not yet see past his pain. He was able to drink that cup because he trusted the one who was still writing his story. He understood his Father could see the whole picture, including the beginning, the middle, and the end.

God did not desert Jesus in his suffering. He gave him supernatural strength to face the cross. God was fulfilling a far greater purpose. He knew, through the anguish and sacrifice of his son, the world would have a Savior.

This passage in Isaiah calls us to trust in God in the same way. Letting go of *why* doesn't mean our pain is ignored. It means we are shifting our focus from the unanswered to the undisputed truth of God's Word, a truth that always holds steady even when everything else feels uncertain. We may not see how all the pieces fit together, but we can trust in the one who does. God didn't abandon Jesus, and he won't abandon us.

God sees the bigger picture. He holds the beginning and the end. And when we choose to surrender what we don't understand, we make room for peace. By letting go of the "why" we trust God to put the pieces back together in a way only he can.

REFLECTION QUESTIONS

- How does Isaiah's declaration that God's ways are higher help us understand the contrast between human perspective and divine purpose?

- How does Isaiah 55:8–9 challenge your assumptions about God's role in your circumstances, especially when the outcome feels unjust or confusing?

FAITH IN ACTION

1. **Shift Your Focus:** Set aside 10 minutes today to turn off distractions and sit in quiet. Ask, *God, what do I need to believe about you today?* Write down what comes to mind.

2. **Pause and Reflect:** Are you asking a "why" question that may never be answered? Write it down, then ask God for the courage to release it.

3. **Anchor Your Belief:** Below are some of the attributes of God given to us in Scripture. Circle the attributes that resonate the most with you today:

| Eternal | Faithful | Good | Holy | Just | Loving | Merciful |

| Omnipotent | Omniscient | Personal | Present | Refuge |

| Righteous | Sovereign | Truthful | Wise |

4. **Now write out these Scriptures:**

- God is faithful – Lamentations 3:22-23

- God is loving – Psalm 103:8

- God is present – Psalm 34:18

- God is our Refuge - Psalm 46:1

Let these verses become the foundation that steadies your heart when your feelings try to tell you otherwise.

SEEING THE BIGGER PICTURE
Releasing the question "why" doesn't mean our pain is dismissed or our confusion is ignored. It means we're choosing to anchor ourselves in what remains steady when everything else feels uncertain. Job never received answers to his questions, yet he encountered God in a way that transformed his suffering. The shift from demanding explanations to trusting God's character is where healing begins. When we stop exhausting ourselves searching for reasons we may never find, we create space for peace to enter. God's ways are higher, not because he's withholding information, but because he sees the complete story while we only see fragments. Trusting his character over our circumstances doesn't erase the ache, but it does redirect our focus toward the one who holds us through it.

CLOSING THOUGHT
Asking why is part of being human. But staying there too long can leave us trapped in a cycle that never brings peace. When we shift our focus from what we can't explain to what we know is true, we begin to let go of control and make room for trust.

CLOSING PRAYER
Dear Jesus,
I don't always understand the path you've allowed me to walk, and I've asked questions that still remain unanswered. I've carried sorrow I didn't know how to release. Help me stop chasing explanations that only leave me more confused or disheartened. Teach me to trust your wisdom, even when it feels out of reach. Quiet the noise in my mind and anchor me in the truth that you are still present, still working, and still writing my story.

In Jesus' name,
Amen

Day Three
Who Is God?

We've spent the last two days sitting with hard questions, wrestling with grief, and beginning to release the need for answers. We've learned the question to ask in the midst of suffering is not *why?* But *who? Who is God? And what do we believe to be true about him when life serves us a bitter cup?*

Today, we begin to answer these questions by focusing on two foundational truths: God is faithful, and God is loving. His faithfulness means he never breaks a promise, even when we can't see the outcome, and his love is not conditional. God loves us no matter what has happened or what we have done. His love is steady and unwavering.

When we know who God is, we stop measuring his goodness by our circumstances. We no longer assume that an easy life means he's near or that hardship means he's absent. His character doesn't shift with our situation. His character holds steady when everything else begins to fall apart. Knowing who he is doesn't take away the pain, but it reshapes how we respond to the pain. And knowing who he is opens our hearts to trust him with a cup we didn't choose.

Today, we will look at how Scripture reveals the faithfulness and unconditional love of God and we will come to understand how his unwavering character equips us with the strength and courage to move forward when life feels too hard.

SCRIPTURE REFLECTION 1
Romans 8:38–39
"And I am convinced that nothing can ever separate us from God's love. Neither death nor life, neither angels nor demons, neither our fears for today nor our worries about tomorrow—not even the powers of hell can separate us from God's love. [39] No power in the sky above or in the earth below—indeed, nothing in all creation will ever be able to separate us from the love of God that is revealed in Christ Jesus our Lord."

UNDERSTANDING THE PASSAGE

This bold declaration from Paul comes at the end of one of the most theologically rich chapters in Scripture. It is not a shallow sentiment meant to make us feel better in the moment. It is a grounded, doctrinal truth that reveals the unchanging nature and character of God. His love doesn't disappear in hardship. It holds steady, even when we can't see it clearly. His love remains a constant we can trust when everything else feels uncertain.

Paul does not say we will not face hardship; in fact, he names it. Death. Fear. Worry. Spiritual attack. These are real. But not one of them, not even the most devastating or painful, has the power to disconnect us from God's love.

Paul wrote this letter to a group of believers in Rome who were facing pressure, uncertainty, and growing tension within their community. Some were struggling with persecution, while others were wrestling with questions about God's presence in their suffering. Paul's words in Romans 8 are both foundational and deeply personal. They are meant to reassure them, and us, that hardship is not a sign of God's absence. Instead, he assures them nothing stands between us and the love of Christ. These were not abstract words for Paul; he had lived through intense trials and could speak with conviction about the unshakable nature of God's love.

The word used for love here is agape, one of several Greek words for love. Agape refers to the unconditional, sacrificial and unearned love of God. It's not based on our goodness or righteousness; it is anchored in the nature of Christ himself. Agape love doesn't shift when we struggle, and it doesn't diminish when we fail. Paul is saying even in our darkest hour, God's love is not up for negotiation. It is fixed. Permanent. Unshakable.

Understanding this kind of love isn't about feeling it all the time. Rather it's about believing it, especially when our feelings do not match what we know to be true. When we know God's love is undeniable, we stop interpreting our suffering as separation. We may not always feel close to God, but our perception does not determine his love. And that love, the kind we can't always feel but can always trust, is what sustains us when everything else falls apart.

REFLECTION QUESTIONS

- How does Romans 8:38–39 shape the way you see God's love when life is hard?

- When have your feelings made it hard to believe God still loves you, and how can you hold onto what's true in those moments?

SCRIPTURE REFLECTION 2

Lamentations 3:21–23

"Yet I still dare to hope when I remember this: The faithful love of the Lord never ends! His mercies never cease. Great is his faithfulness; his mercies begin afresh each morning."

UNDERSTANDING THE PASSAGE

The prophet Jeremiah wrote these words during one of Israel's darkest hours, when Jerusalem fell. Jeremiah had witnessed suffering, devastation, and despair, yet in the middle of deep grief, he speaks these powerful words: "Yet I still dare to hope."

This isn't blind optimism or emotional denial; rather, it is a deliberate choice to remember who God is. Jeremiah doesn't base his hope on what he sees around him, but on what he knows to be true. God's faithful love has not ended. His mercies are still new. And even when life unravels, God remains steady.

The faithfulness Jeremiah speaks of is not tied to emotions or circumstances. It's anchored in who God is. We serve the same God who walked with Jeremiah, delivered the Israelites, and fulfilled every promise throughout the generations. His character doesn't shift with time. God is the same yesterday, today, and forever. When we look back and read the stories in Scripture, we don't just find encouragement, we find evidence. Over and over, we see God's unwavering faithfulness. And that same faithfulness is still at work in our lives today.

When we're walking through our own seasons of grief, confusion, or loss, this passage gives us something to hold onto. Not because it erases the pain, but because it helps us anchor our hearts in what doesn't change. Like Jeremiah, we can dare to hope, not because everything is okay, but because God is still faithful.

REFLECTION QUESTIONS

- What does Lamentations 3:21–23 reveal about how Jeremiah held onto hope, even in deep suffering?

- How have you seen God's faithfulness show up in your life, even when circumstances didn't immediately change?

FAITH IN ACTION

Take time this week to reflect on how God has shown both his unconditional love and his faithfulness in your life. Start by writing down two or three specific moments when he provided for you or sustained you. Think about the time he gave you peace in a difficult season. If you're currently in a hard place, read back over those examples as a reminder that the same God who carried you then is with you now. Consider sharing one of those stories with a friend who could use some encouragement.

SEEING THE BIGGER PICTURE

God's love anchors us, and his faithfulness assures us he will not walk away. Knowing he is loving and faithful is what allows us to keep moving forward. His love is not conditional, and neither his presence nor his help is ever withheld. We see his faithfulness over and over throughout Scripture. Sometimes through provision, sometimes through peace, sometimes through healing, and sometimes through strength. This consistent thread of faithfulness seen across the pages of the Bible points us to a God who does not change.

CLOSING THOUGHT

The Bible declares we serve the same God today, the very same God who revealed himself in both the Old and New Testaments. His character and attributes remain the same, regardless of the generation or circumstance.

I am thankful we serve a God who is the same yesterday, today, and forever. Aren't you?

CLOSING PRAYER

Father,

Thank you for being faithful even when I struggle to see it. When life feels uncertain, help me remember who you are and how you've carried me before. Remind me that your love and faithfulness never run out. I want to trust you not just in the moments that make sense, but in the ones that don't. Anchor my heart in who you are.

In Jesus' name,
Amen

Day Four
The God Who Heals and Provides

I'm so glad you've made it to day four. I know this journey hasn't been a light one. For some of you it has required a great deal of honesty and deep reflection. I want to encourage you. Each step matters. Every moment of showing up is part of the healing God is already working in you.

Today, we're going to take a deeper look at two of the names of God found in the Old Testament: Jehovah Rapha, our Healer, and Jehovah Jireh, our Provider. These names aren't merely theological concepts; they reveal the heart of who God is in the midst of real pain and need.

Maybe you're currently walking through something that feels beyond repair, or maybe you're wondering how provision will come when you can't see a way forward. Learning to identify the names of God can offer hope. These names carry deep meaning. They describe who God is in the midst of our suffering and reflect both his nature and his relationship with us in our time of need. Each name reveals something deeply personal about how God meets us in our brokenness.

Jehovah Jireh means "The Lord Will Provide." This isn't just about material provision. It is about a God who sees our need before we even recognize it ourselves. When we are unsure how we will make it through, Jehovah Jireh reminds us we are not unseen, and we are never left to figure it out alone. He provides in ways we don't expect, with perfect timing and infinite wisdom.

Jehovah Rapha means "The Lord Who Heals." This name speaks to the God who restores us physically, emotionally, mentally, and spiritually. His healing doesn't always happen the way we expect or as quickly as we want, but that doesn't mean it's not happening. Jehovah Rapha assures us that our brokenness is not the end of our story, and healing comes as he walks with us through every layer of our pain.

When we understand the origins of these names and their meanings, we begin to see how they resonate directly with our own stories. They invite us to recognize God's presence in the details of our lives, revealing him as a trustworthy Father who heals our infirmities and provides exactly what we need in times of pain and hardship. He sees every detail of our lives and knows exactly when and how to reveal himself as he walks with us through whatever we face.

Take today to slow down, listen, and look at what Scripture tells us about the God who heals and provides.

SCRIPTURE REFLECTION 1
Exodus 15:25b–26
"It was there at Marah that the Lord set before them the following decree as a standard to test their faithfulness to him. He said, 'If you will listen carefully to the voice of the Lord your God and do what is right in his sight, obeying his commands and keeping all his decrees, then I will not make you suffer any of the diseases I sent on the Egyptians; for I am the Lord who heals you'."

UNDERSTANDING THE PASSAGE
It's hard to talk about healing when healing hasn't come. For the person still waiting, it can feel painful even to hope. Maybe you're there now, trying to trust God in the middle of unanswered prayers, continued doctor visits, or heartache that feels unrelenting. But healing in God's hands is never one-dimensional. He doesn't only mend the body. He restores the soul.

In Exodus 15, the Israelites had just experienced one of the most dramatic rescues in all of Scripture when God parted the Red Sea. But only three days later, their hope gave way to despair when they couldn't find clean water. The water at Marah was bitter, undrinkable. So they started to complain. And God, in his mercy, instructed Moses to throw a piece of wood into the water, and then the water became sweet. It was here, after this moment of provision, that God revealed a new name: Jehovah Rapha, "the Lord who heals you." This new name was not about water. It was a declaration of who God is. He wanted his children to know he was a healer, not just of their bodies, but of nations, fractured relationships, broken hearts, and the deepest places of pain.

This name was not limited to the children in the wilderness. Jehovah Rapha is still our Healer today, even when healing doesn't come in the way or the time we had hoped. For those holding a diagnosis with no improvement, for the individual silently battling trauma or shame, for the one who feels emotionally exhausted or spiritually numb, God's healing is still at work. It may come through medicine, through time, through the support of others, or through the slow mending of a heart that has been shattered. It may manifest as emotional clarity, bringing peace to a confused heart, or mental strength to endure what once felt impossible. Sometimes it takes the form of redemption, where what was meant for harm is used for good, or restoration, where what was broken is gradually rebuilt. Healing doesn't always arrive with a dramatic moment or a clear report. Often, it unfolds slowly and quietly, in places no one sees. It's found in the courage to face another day, the softening of bitterness, the loosening grip of anger, or the ability to forgive.

God's healing is not always a reversal of circumstances; rather, it is a transformation within them. And that kind of healing is no less supernatural. In fact, it often requires more faith to trust the process than to wait for the outcome.

Isaiah 55:8–9 reminds us God's thoughts are not our thoughts, and his ways are not our ways. We may long for resolution, but God is shaping something greater, something eternal. He sees the whole picture, and sometimes what we call unanswered prayer is really an invitation to discover him in a new and deeper way.

When we know God as our healer, we stop asking for quick fixes and start seeking his presence. We begin to see healing in every moment he carries us, in every reminder that we are not alone. His healing may not take away the pain, but it transforms how we live through it. It lifts our eyes from what has not changed to the one who has not left us. That shift changes everything.

If you are still in the middle of it, still aching and still waiting, don't assume God is silent. Don't confuse stillness with absence. Ask him to help you see. Ask him to open your eyes to the subtle, sacred ways he is restoring you. And as you do, let your hope expand. Don't place it solely in the outcome. Let it grow as you trust God to see you through.

And yes! God absolutely continues to heal bodies today. He is Jehovah Rapha, the same healer we read about in Scripture. Sometimes, healing happens suddenly, in a moment that defies explanation. Other times, it comes gradually. And there are also times when the healing we long for doesn't arrive on our timetable, or in the form we expected, but that doesn't mean it won't come. Healing is never out of reach for God, and hope is never misplaced when it's rooted in him. While we wait, he continues to work, strengthening our faith and deepening our trust.

So don't stop believing in the God who heals. Keep your eyes fixed on him. He is the one who sees the whole story. What you experience along the way is not wasted. Your healing may be unfolding even now, piece by piece, in ways you haven't yet recognized. Trust his timing. Trust his heart. The journey may be longer than you wanted, but it is not without purpose. God is still your Healer, body, soul, and spirit, and he has not forgotten you.

REFLECTION QUESTIONS

- How does redefining healing as more than just a physical act change the way you view God's role in your current season?

- In what ways might God be walking with you as Jehovah Rapha, even if the outcome you hoped for hasn't happened yet?

SCRIPTURE REFLECTION 2

Genesis 22:13–14

"Then Abraham looked up and saw a ram caught by its horns in a thicket. So he took the ram and sacrificed it as a burnt offering in place of his son. Abraham named the place Yahweh-Yireh (which means 'the Lord will provide'). To this day, people still use that name as a proverb: 'On the mountain of the Lord it will be provided'."

UNDERSTANDING THE PASSAGE

Abraham's story is one of the most sobering and beautiful accounts in all of Scripture. God had asked the unthinkable. He has asked Abraham to sacrifice the son he had waited a lifetime for. It was a test of both obedience and trust. Abraham didn't know how everything would unfold, but he believed God could be trusted with the outcome. And in the very moment of greatest need, provision appeared. It appeared not before, and not in the way he might have imagined, but exactly when it was needed.

This passage provides the first recorded use of the name Jehovah Jireh, meaning "The Lord will provide." It wasn't declared during a season of abundance or ease; rather, it was spoken from the mountaintop of costly faith, where hope clung to who God is, not to what could be seen. The ram in the thicket was more than a substitution. It was evidence that God saw Abraham. He saw his faith, trust, and obedience. God responded to Abraham's surrender with provision that affirmed his presence and power. It came at just the right moment, revealing a God who sees what we cannot and provides in ways we could never orchestrate on our own.

Knowing God as Jehovah Jireh alters our perspective on our circumstances. Provision doesn't always look like an easy answer or immediate relief. Sometimes it shows up through having enough strength for just today or peace in the waiting. Sometimes he sends people to walk with us through the valley. It may not be what we hoped for, but it is always what we need.

Anchoring ourselves in the character of God as our provider shifts our focus. We no longer equate his goodness with quick solutions or visible results. We learn to trust the quiet ways he meets our deepest needs. We learn to look for his hand in the details, in the delays, and even in the detours. The question is not whether God will provide, but whether we are willing to trust how and when he does.

I've learned the more I trust his timing, the more peace I find in the waiting. Maybe today is an invitation to do the same.

FAITH IN ACTION

1. **Today, reflect on where you need healing or provision.** Be specific. Write down one area of your life where you're asking God to show up either emotionally, spiritually, relationally, or practically. Next to it, write down one of the names of God: Jehovah Rapha or Jehovah Jireh. Then ask: *What would it look like to trust God with this today?*

2. **Take time in prayer and take one small step forward.** Taking one step forward may mean calling a counselor, setting a healthy boundary, reaching out for help, or simply sitting in silence and letting God speak. When you take action aligned with trust, you're walking in faith even if you don't have the full picture.

SEEING THE BIGGER PICTURE

God's sovereignty is the truth that steadies us when life feels most uncertain. It assures us that nothing in our lives has slipped through his hands or caught him by surprise. He isn't scrambling to fix what's broken or trying to figure out what comes next. He sees the entire story. He sees the past, present, and future and works with wisdom we cannot yet comprehend. Surrendering to his sovereignty doesn't mean we stop feeling the weight of our struggles or pretend everything makes sense. It means we choose to trust that the one who holds every detail of our lives is both powerful and good. When we release our need to control outcomes or understand every step, we make room for peace. God's sovereignty reminds us we don't have to see the path ahead to keep walking forward. We're being led by a God who has already gone before us and will never leave us behind.

CLOSING THOUGHT

When we know God as both healer and provider, we stop expecting comfort to come only through outcomes. Instead, we begin to recognize his nearness in our need. His presence is provision. His love is healing. We may not always see the full picture now, but we can be certain he is working in ways we cannot yet see. Healing is happening. Provision is unfolding. And God is with us every step of the way.

CLOSING PRAYER

Dear God,

You are my Healer and my Provider. You see every part of my life, and you know what I need even when I don't. Help me trust you in the places where I feel broken, and in the moments where I cannot see the way forward. Open my heart to your presence and your process. Remind me that I am not alone and that you are not withholding anything good from me. Teach me to walk forward today with confidence in who you are.

In Jesus' name,
Amen

Day Five
The Sovereignty of God

As we close out this first week, I want to pause and say I know these aren't easy conversations to have with yourself, so the fact that you're still here speaks volumes about your willingness to lean in, and I want you to know, I am truly proud of you. You've shown up, opened your heart, and walked through some difficult questions. We've looked honestly at sorrow, wrestled with the ache of unanswered prayers, and started to shift our focus from "why" to "what do I believe?" If you've made it this far, I hope you've started to realize something important: this journey isn't about figuring everything out or having all of the answers. It's about learning to trust in God. He is the one who sees the whole picture and knows the whole story.

Today, we will focus on the sovereignty of God. God's sovereignty is a truth that can be both comforting and complex. It's easy to affirm when life is unfolding the way we hoped. But it becomes more challenging when things begin to unravel, when we're left holding a cup we didn't choose and asking questions that still don't have answers.

God's sovereignty means he sees what we don't. It means he is in control, even when we feel like everything is falling apart. But more than that, it means we are not alone in the middle of what we cannot understand. It means placing our trust in the one who holds every piece of the story, even when the details don't yet make sense.

Let's explore what Scripture tells us about God's sovereignty and what it looks like to surrender our need for control as we learn to rest in the assurance he knows everything, including the smallest details of our lives.

SCRIPTURE REFLECTION 1
Psalm 139:1–6
"O Lord, you have examined my heart and know everything about me. You know when I sit down or stand up. You know my thoughts even when I'm far away. You see me when I travel and when I rest at home. You know everything I do. You know what I am going to say even before I say it, Lord. You go before me and follow me. You place

your hand of blessing on my head. Such knowledge is too wonderful for me, too great for me to understand!"

UNDERSTANDING THE PASSAGE

When we talk about God's sovereignty, we're talking about his complete authority and rule as well as his ability to see everything, know everything, and guide all things according to his perfect will. Sovereignty means nothing slips through his hands. It means there is no part of your story he hasn't already seen and accounted for. He weaves purpose into the tension and silence, into the stretch between what we've prayed for and what we've yet to receive. That space where outcomes are uncertain and the path feels unclear is often where his deepest work unfolds. It is in the unknown when we begin to rely more on who he is than on what we hoped would happen.

David, the shepherd-turned-king of Israel and the writer of many Psalms, often poured his deepest thoughts and emotions into poetic prayers. Psalm 139 brings the truth of God's sovereignty and personal nearness down to a deeply personal level. David isn't making a formal statement about doctrine; rather, he is describing what it feels like to be fully known by God. David doesn't characterize God as distant, watching from above. He shows him as near and deeply involved, a God who sees every movement, hears every unspoken word, and understands the quiet ache beneath the surface. Before a thought forms or a sentence leaves our lips, he knows. He draws near with full attention, never overlooking a single detail of what weighs on our hearts.

David is in awe of a God who is not only sovereign over the universe, but also sovereign over his life. The same God who shaped the heavens is the one who surrounds him with tender awareness and intentional presence. He describes a God who hems him in, who goes before and follows behind laying his hand gently upon him. It's a picture of being completely known and completely seen.

The sovereignty of God does not erase our questions, but it does shift our perspective. It teaches us we don't have to know the outcome to keep walking forward. We are being led by a God who sees beyond what we can see and who will always keep us in his hand.

However, in the midst of a hard season, his nearness can feel hidden beneath the weight of what we're having to carry and walk through. That doesn't mean he's gone; it simply means we're human. What David declared then still holds true that God is involved in every moment of our lives and attentive to every need. He doesn't shift with our circumstances but remains steady through whatever lies ahead.

REFLECTION QUESTIONS

1. How does David describe God's involvement in the details of his life in Psalm 139?

2. What does this passage show us about how God's presence remains steady, even when we can't feel it?

SCRIPTURE REFLECTION 2
Proverbs 16:9
"We can make our plans, but the Lord determines our steps."

UNDERSTANDING THE PASSAGE
Now that we have considered God's complete knowledge of our lives and his constant involvement in every detail, we shift our focus to how we move forward in trust. Proverbs 16:9 speaks to something deeply human. We try to make sense of what's ahead, holding onto hope while building a path we believe will lead us forward. Scripture instructs us it is the Lord, not us, who establishes each step we take.

God's sovereignty invites us to stop trying to manage what only he can carry and to trust his wisdom, which reaches far beyond anything we could piece together on our own. It isn't meant to shut down our response to hardship, but to lead us toward surrender.

When life doesn't go the way we hoped and the waiting feels endless, our natural instinct is to take control. We try to solve the problem ourselves because it feels like nothing is happening. But this passage calls us to a different response. It leads us to release our need for control and trust God's wisdom, even when we don't understand the direction he's taking us. Though the path may look nothing like the story we imagined, his plans remain firm and full of meaning.

God's sovereignty means he holds all authority and nothing lies outside his control. But it also speaks to how personally involved he is in our lives. He sees what we miss and moves through what we struggle to make sense of, guiding every detail with intention and wisdom. His power isn't distant or detached. He is present in the moments that feel uncertain and heavy, working in ways we often won't recognize until much later. We may not understand where he is leading or how the outcome will unfold, but his sovereignty assures us life is not left to chance. We are being led by a God who is actively engaged and completely trustworthy. This is the truth we hold onto when the road feels long and surrender feels costly.

REFLECTION QUESTIONS

- What do these two passages reveal about God's role in both our inner life and the path ahead?

- How can surrendering control become an act of trust rather than a sign of defeat?

FAITH IN ACTION

1. **Take a few moments to write** down something you've been trying to control. It could be an outcome, a person, a diagnosis, or a situation that feels unresolved.

Circle the attribute of God that speaks most directly to what you're facing from the attributes we've studied this week:

| God's Unconditional Love | His Faithfulness |

| God's Provision |

| His Sovereignty | Divine Healing |

2. **Now write a few sentences answering:**
   - How does this specific truth about God address my situation?

   - What changes when I view my struggle through the lens of this attribute?

Practice releasing your need to manage the outcome by inviting God to lead in the way only he can.

SEEING THE BIGGER PICTURE

We don't always get the answer to why. Some situations will never make sense from where we stand. But this is why it is so important we understand the sovereignty of God. He is not just in control. He is trustworthy. He sees the beginning, the middle, and the end. He knows what we cannot begin to comprehend, and he is working in ways we often won't see until much later. That understanding is what keeps us grounded. It becomes the anchor that steadies our boat in the middle of the storm. When we begin to understand God's sovereignty and how he works with wisdom and purpose, we gain something firm to hold onto in the middle of uncertainty. That deeper understanding helps reframe our suffering. We stop asking why and begin asking the better question: *Who is God, and what do I believe to be true about him in the midst of my suffering?*

I've wrestled with these questions too. I've sat in the tension of wanting answers that didn't come and begged God to make something make sense when it just didn't. I know what it's like to feel both faith and frustration at the same time. That is why this week matters so much to me. What we've explored isn't just theological truth; for me, it has been a lifeline during seasons when I felt utterly lost. God's sovereignty and the goodness of his character behind it has been an anchor of truth in the places where I've felt most uncertain. I pray it becomes that for you too.

CLOSING THOUGHT

God's sovereignty reminds us we don't have to see the path ahead to keep walking forward. We're being led by a God who has already gone before us and will never leave us behind.

CLOSING PRAYER

God, thank you for being sovereign over my life. You see what I cannot, and you hold what I've been trying to carry on my own. Help me surrender the parts of my story I've tried to manage. Teach me to trust your wisdom more than my plans and to believe you are good even when I don't understand. When I'm tempted to ask why, help me not to become blind by what I am going through. Instead, help me see who you are in the midst of it. Thank you for your goodness and faithfulness.

In Jesus' name,
Amen

Week One
Group Discussion

Begin by watching the Week One video together. Afterward, ask the group, "What stood out to you most from the video?"

After one or two participants have shared, take time to review last week's study. As a group, flip through each day's reading, briefly noting the Reflection Questions and Faith in Action prompts. Allow time for participants to share their responses to each prompt. If you finish early, use the Group Discussion Questions below to encourage deeper connection.

1. What does Jesus' honesty in the Garden of Gethsemane reveal about his relationship with the Father and his approach to suffering?

2. In what ways does shifting from asking "Why is this happening?" to "Who is God in the middle of this?" change how people walk through suffering?

3. Which attribute of God stood out most clearly to you in this week's passages and why?

4. What do passages like Romans 8:38–39 and Lamentations 3:21–23 reveal about God's love and faithfulness when life feels confusing or painful?

5. How can God's sovereignty, as described in Psalm 139 and Proverbs 16:9, offer steadiness when someone feels handed a "cup" they never would have chosen?

Week Two

A Cup of Doubt

I am so grateful we get to continue walking this journey together. This week, we will peel back the layers of doubt and closely examine the unsettling experiences that lead us to question the very presence of God in our lives.

We will focus on the stories of Joseph and the Israelites, both of whom faced trials that tested their faith. As we reflect on their journeys, we'll explore what it looks like to doubt God's faithfulness and wrestle with the desire to be delivered out of difficult circumstances rather than walk through them.

Together, we will uncover the truths within these powerful narratives, both of which show God's faithfulness even amid doubts. Embrace this chance to deepen your understanding and trust in his plans, knowing he walks with you through every struggle you face.

We all want to be instantly delivered out of our suffering. It is what we hope for and what we pray for. It is natural to yearn for deliverance from pain. However, we must acknowledge while there are times when God will intervene and deliver us directly out of our circumstances, more commonly, he will deliver us through them. In either case, we experience deliverance, but it may not always come in the form we expect.

I've experienced moments when God delivered me out of my pain in ways that were clear and immediate. But I have also walked through seasons where deliverance was more of a journey, where I was slowly delivered through my suffering, taking only one step at a time. Even though the path was long, more often, it was the path that shaped me the most.

Whether God is leading us out or walking us through, he is always present, guiding every step we take. As you engage with Scripture this week, it is my prayer you will find the courage to move beyond your doubts and trust in God's faithfulness to deliver you regardless of what you are going through.

Day One
Acknowledging Doubt

Doubt is a common experience for many believers. Even some of the strongest Christians I know face moments of uncertainty. When life takes an unexpected turn and the answers we seek don't come, we often question if God sees us or if he is truly in control. When we doubt God and his presence in our circumstances, we find ourselves in deep uncertainty. This doubt can feel as though God's love and commitment to our well-being are distant, even unreachable.

Today, we will take a closer look at the Israelites' journey and their struggle to resist doubting God's ability to deliver them. Their story demonstrates God's power and majesty through the miracle he performed. In it, we are able to recognize his ability to deliver his children instantly out of a desperate situation. When the Israelites stood at the edge of the Red Sea with Pharaoh's army closing in, God instantly parted the waters (Exodus 14:21-22). At that moment, God wanted to show the Israelites he was the only one and true God to be served. His glory, power, and majesty were evident in this miracle. However, their journey through the wilderness revealed how they struggled with trust and obedience. Observing their lives teaches us that being delivered directly out of a circumstance does not always equal transformation. Deliverance, however it shows up, is not solely about escaping a circumstance; it is about transforming to be more like Christ, learning to depend fully upon him, and trusting he is faithful in everything.

SCRIPTURE REFLECTION 1

Exodus 14:10-12

"As Pharaoh approached, the people of Israel looked up and panicked when they saw the Egyptians overtaking them. They cried out to the Lord, and they said to Moses, 'Why did you bring us out here to die in the wilderness? Weren't there enough graves for us in Egypt? What have you done to us? Why did you make us leave Egypt? Didn't we tell you this would happen while we were still in Egypt? We said, 'Leave us alone! Let us be slaves to the Egyptians. It's better to be a slave in Egypt than a corpse in the wilderness'!"

UNDERSTANDING THE PASSAGE

The Israelites endured generations of hardship and oppression in Egypt. Because of a famine four hundred years earlier, they had been displaced to a foreign land. Over time, they grew stronger in number and physically stronger, becoming a threat to the Egyptians. As a result, they were enslaved and forced to work under brutal and unimaginable conditions. They were treated harshly and completely stripped of their freedom.

In the midst of their suffering, God heard their cries and sent Moses to lead them to the Promised Land, a new home where they would find peace and freedom. In Exodus 14, the Israelites faced a moment of fear and freedom, standing on the brink of something that would change how they viewed God and themselves forever. After witnessing miraculous signs and plagues that secured their escape, one might believe their faith couldn't have been stronger. Yet, standing there at the edge of the sea, they questioned whether God could truly help them.

As they looked around and saw the Egyptian army approaching, they let fear take control. Instead of trusting in faith, they directed their fear at Moses. They questioned his leadership and even God's plans, accusing him of leading them to destruction. It was raw and emotional. This reaction shows a very human tendency. When faced with an unwanted or painful situation, it's easy to forget God's past faithfulness.

Instead of recalling the miracles that led them out of slavery, the Israelites couldn't see past what was right in front of them. All they could see was their fear and the impossibility of their situation. The Israelites had already forgotten how God had miraculously delivered them out of Egypt.

This passage serves as a strong reminder that we, too, can easily slip into doubt when confronted with a seemingly impossible situation. Life can present us with a cup we never wanted or ever imagined we would have to drink. It could be a cup of unexpected loss, disappointment, or a tragedy that may lead us to question whether God truly cares for us or has a plan for our lives. I encourage you to read the full account of the Red Sea in Exodus 14:1-31 to understand the complete narrative of the Israelites' journey.

REFLECTION QUESTIONS

- Despite witnessing God's miraculous signs and their deliverance from Egypt, the Israelites immediately doubted him when they saw Pharaoh's army approaching. How does this passage illustrate the tension between faith and fear? What does this reveal about the Israelites' spiritual maturity at this point in their journey?

- Despite witnessing God's miracles, the Israelites quickly reverted to fear. What are some ways we can actively remember and hold onto God's past faithfulness when facing new challenges?

SCRIPTURE REFLECTION 2
Isaiah 41:10
"So do not fear, for I am with you; do not be dismayed, for I am your God. I will strengthen you and help you; I will uphold you with my righteous right hand."

UNDERSTANDING THE PASSAGE
These words were spoken through the prophet Isaiah to the people of Israel during a time when they were in great distress and were afraid of what lay ahead. The Israelites were in a season of deep unrest and were uncertain of their future.

This verse was meant to soothe their hearts, as the Israelites faced threats from surrounding nations. They were battling their own doubts about God's faithfulness and were tempted to believe God had abandoned them because their circumstances didn't seem to reflect his promises, and their hearts were burdened with doubt.

In response, God doesn't provide immediate solutions. Instead, he offers himself: "I am with you... I am your God." These words are the core of the entire verse. God wasn't asking his people to ignore their fear; rather, he was inviting them to shift their focus from what felt uncertain to who he had always been. He clarifies that his presence isn't based on their perception but on his unchanging character.

The promise in Isaiah 41:10 speaks directly to those moments when we wonder if God truly sees what we're facing and whether he is capable of doing anything about it. It addresses that quiet fear: Is God still in control? In these moments, this verse becomes a personal reassurance: God sees us, stays with us, and gives us the strength we need to get through.

While Isaiah speaks of God's nearness, Paul echoes this confidence in Romans 8:28 by telling us God is not only present but also purposeful. He is working all things, even the confusing or painful ones, together for good. We may not see how the pieces fit, and we may wrestle with whether he is truly in control, but Scripture invites us to trust God is still active and aware of all our needs. He holds the complete story in his hands.

If you're in a place where you're questioning God's presence or his ability to change the outcome, this verse is for you. It's not a command to feel strong. It's an invitation to lean into the strength of the one who holds you even when your faith feels shaken.

REFLECTION QUESTIONS

- When have you felt unsure if God was truly present in your situation, and how does Isaiah 41:10 speak into that moment?

- What common factors or circumstances tend to challenge a person's belief in God's control, and how does Isaiah 41:10 address those challenges?

FAITH IN ACTION
Today, reflect on how your doubts are interfering with your ability to trust in God's faithfulness in your life through these two exercises.

1. **Journaling:** Take a few minutes to write honestly about your doubts. Ask yourself where they come from and if they are tied to fear, past disappointments, or unmet expectations. Once you identify them, challenge each one by finding a passage of Scripture that speaks directly to that area of fear or uncertainty. Use God's Word to anchor your response.

   Examples:

   Thought: "I am alone in this."
   Scripture: "Never will I leave you; never will I forsake you" (Hebrews 13:15).

   Thought: "I've failed too many times for God to use me."
   Scripture: "His mercies never come to an end; they are new every morning" (Lamentations 3:22-23).

2. **Affirmations:** Create an affirmation based on Scriptures that speak directly to your doubts. These short, truth-filled statements can serve as reminders of who God is and what he has promised. Speak them out loud, write them in your journal, or keep them somewhere visible throughout the week. *Examples:*

- When I feel alone, I will remember:
    "God is with me." (Isaiah 41:10)

- When I feel anxious or out of control:
    "God is not overwhelmed by what overwhelms me." (Psalm 46:1 – "God is our refuge and strength, always ready to help in times of trouble.")

- When I question if things will work out:
    "God is working, even when I can't see it" (Romans 8:28).

- When I feel weak or incapable:
    "God will strengthen and uphold me" (Isaiah 41:10).

- When I wonder if God still cares:
    "Nothing can separate me from his love" (Romans 8:38–39).

   Now write your own affirmation here:

SEEING THE BIGGER PICTURE

As we walk through the story of the Israelites, it's essential to recognize how doubt can hinder us from seeing the hand of God working in our lives. We learn the importance of the rearview mirror. We can recall all the times when God showed up not only in the lives of the Israelites but in our own lives; we see his faithfulness over and over. In today's study, we looked at their fear and hesitation at the edge of the Red Sea. It was a moment when freedom was within reach, yet fear clouded their vision.

They had already witnessed God's power in Egypt via his protection from the plagues and their miraculous escape. But in the face of a new threat, they forgot what he had already done. In crisis, they questioned his presence and plan, allowing fear to speak louder than their memory of God's faithfulness. And while we may want to judge them for that, we often do the same. We panic in the moment and forget how God has carried us before.

One of the hardest parts of going through hardship is not knowing what God is doing while we're in it. We crave clarity and quick answers, but often, it's only in the rearview mirror that we can see how God was working all along. What seems chaotic or uncertain now can later turn out to be intentional or even redemptive. The Israelites missed seeing their situation from that perspective. The Israelites missed seeing their situation from God's perspective. They saw the sea blocking their path and feared the worst instead of trusting the God who had been with them all along.

I've had moments when my own doubts made me wonder if God was really going to show up. My circumstances felt impossible, and his silence felt like an absence. But looking back, I can see the fingerprints of God all over the situation. He had been working, guiding, and sustaining me even when I didn't recognize it in the moment.

Acknowledging our doubts doesn't disqualify us from faith; it positions us to grow. God doesn't always deliver us immediately or explain the path we are having to take, but he always walks with us through it. He uses our questions and doubts to draw us closer to him.

Let this story remind us how confusion today may make perfect sense tomorrow. And even if you can't see it now, God is already at work. His presence is constant. His purpose is unfolding. And his faithfulness often becomes most visible when we look in the rearview mirror.

CLOSING THOUGHT
When we admit our inability to trust and surrender our fear to God, our perspective shifts. Instead of fixating on our circumstances, we focus on God's faithfulness, both in Scripture and in our own lives. God welcomes our questions and doubts, assuring us he is present and tirelessly working on our behalf, even when we cannot see it.

CLOSING PRAYER
Dear Father,

Thank you for being patient with me, even during moments of doubt. Help me resist the temptation to question your ability to work all things in my life for good. As I continue this journey, grant me the strength and courage to take the next step and trust you are working in my life, even when I cannot see it. Help me look beyond my pain to find peace amidst my suffering, knowing you are orchestrating a greater plan for my life.

In Jesus' name,
Amen

Day Two
Trusting in God's Provision Through Transformation

Yesterday, we began exploring the story of the Israelites and their journey from slavery to freedom. Today, we'll continue walking alongside them as they navigate the wilderness. The wilderness was a place where their faith was tested and their trust in God's provision often wavered.

The wilderness was not just a physical journey for the Israelites; it was also a spiritual one. While they longed for immediate deliverance from their struggles, God had a greater plan. He was leading them through their wilderness experience, teaching them to trust in his faithfulness, and transforming them into his people.

This kind of transformation doesn't happen instantly. When the Israelites were delivered out of Egypt, their hearts were still tied to the familiarity of their old lives. They struggled to remember God's miraculous power and provision. But as they walked through the wilderness, God used their challenges to strengthen their faith and teach them to depend on him daily.

In our own lives, we may also long for immediate deliverance from pain or hardship. But God often chooses to walk with us through the journey, using it to transform us and teaching us to draw closer to him. Today, we will gain a deeper understanding of how to trust God despite doubt. We will learn how the Holy Spirit equips us to face life's challenges with faith.

SCRIPTURE REFLECTION 1
Exodus 16:2-4
"The whole community of Israel complained about Moses and Aaron. 'If only the Lord had killed us back in Egypt,' they moaned. 'There we sat around pots filled with meat and ate all the bread we wanted. But now you have brought us into this wilderness to starve us all to death.' Then the Lord said to Moses, 'Look, I am going to rain down food from heaven for you. Each day, the people can go out and pick up as much food as they need for that day. I will test them in this to see whether or not they will follow my instructions'."

UNDERSTANDING THE PASSAGE

The Israelites had barely begun their journey when their confidence in God started to unravel. Hunger set in, and fear followed. Instead of remembering how God had already performed miracle after miracle, they began to complain to Moses and Aaron. They were not convinced God would come through. Egypt, once a place of slavery and immense hardship, now seemed preferable to the Promised Land simply because it was familiar.

God didn't respond with punishment for the Israelites' lack of faith and complaining. Instead, he responded with provision. He promised to send bread from heaven called manna and gave clear instructions for them to gather only what they needed for that day. This provision wasn't just about food. It was a way to teach them how to trust him. Each morning, they would have to take a step of faith, believing his provision would be there again.

This passage highlights an important truth about human nature: we often return to what is familiar, even when it causes us pain. For the Israelites, the comfort of Egypt was tied to the predictability of their circumstances, even though it came with the cost of slavery. Even after all they had witnessed, they still struggled to trust God with what was ahead. Fear made their loss of freedom in Egypt seem more manageable than the uncertainty of the wilderness. Their hearts weren't yet ready to depend on God for each step forward, and instead of walking in freedom, they looked back with preference to what had once held them captive.

Returning to the familiar is a pattern we often see in our own lives. When faced with uncertainty or hardship, we sometimes allow fear and doubt to hold us back, convincing ourselves the familiarity of our current situation, even if it's painful, is better than the unknown of trusting God's plan. As a therapist, I often saw this pattern play out in the lives of women who were trying to leave an abusive relationship. They would leave, only to return to the same relationship or find themselves in another abusive one months later. Not because they wanted the pain, but because it was familiar. It was the territory they knew. As harmful as it was, the familiarity felt easier to navigate than the uncertainty of something different and unknown. It shows how easily we can stay stuck in patterns that feel known, even when God is calling us into something healthier and new.

Even so, God calls us to move forward, believing he will provide all we need. Just as the Israelites had to take steps to gather manna each day, we, too, must take steps of faith, trusting God's provision is sufficient for today, believing he is leading us toward transformation. I recommend reading Exodus 16:1-36 for the full narrative of how God miraculously provided for his people despite their complaints.

REFLECTION QUESTIONS

- What does the Israelites' grumbling reveal about their understanding of God's faithfulness and provision? How do you respond when you're tempted to grumble or doubt God's provision in your own life?

- Why do people sometimes choose the familiar, even when it is painful? How does fear keep us from stepping into the unknown with faith?

SCRIPTURE REFLECTION 2
Deuteronomy 8:2-3
"Remember how the Lord your God led you through the wilderness for these forty years, humbling you and testing you to prove your character and to find out whether or not you would obey his commands. Yes, he humbled you by letting you go hungry and then feeding you with manna, a food previously unknown to you and your ancestors. He did it to teach you that people do not live by bread alone; rather, we live by every word that comes from the mouth of the Lord."

UNDERSTANDING THE PASSAGE
As the Israelites stood at the edge of the Promised Land, Moses urged them to remember the journey behind them. He reminded them how God had led them through the wilderness, allowed them to experience hunger, and then fed them with manna. God didn't do that to punish them but to teach them. Each day, they received exactly what they needed. No more. No less. Through this season, they were learning to trust that God would be faithful, even when the path forward felt uncertain.

Their doubts had often taken center stage in the wilderness, but Moses urged them to look back and see what they had missed in real time as God faithfully showed up with his provision. This reflection was more than a call to remember; it was an invitation to carry those lessons forward.

In the New Testament, Jesus references this very moment in John when he says "I am the bread of life. Whoever comes to me will never be hungry again. Whoever believes in me will never be thirsty" (John 6:35, NLT). He explains to the crowd that the manna their ancestors received did not come from Moses but from God. And now in Christ, the Father offers us something far greater. Jesus identifies himself as the true bread from heaven, the one who fully satisfies the soul.

This passage in John beautifully ties together the Old and New Testaments, showing how the story of the Israelites in the wilderness foreshadows the greater work of Christ. The manna in the wilderness was a temporary solution for physical hunger, but Jesus offers himself as the ultimate and eternal solution for spiritual hunger. Jesus wants us to know God continues to provide today in the same way he provided for the Israelites in the wilderness.

When we think about the Israelites in the wilderness, we see how their fear of the unknown led them to doubt God's faithfulness. They longed for the familiarity of Egypt, even though it meant returning to slavery. In the same way, we can let fear and doubt cloud our vision. When clouded, we often turn to the familiar, even if it is not good, just like the Israelites did when they wanted to go back to Egypt. They knew it was not a good choice, but at least, for them, it was familiar and predictable. But Jesus wants us to shift our focus. He reminds us he is the true bread of life, not a temporary fix or a fallback plan, but the lasting provision that nourishes us in every way. When we're tempted to cling to what we know, he offers something greater. He invites us to trust him fully, to release our fears and doubts, and to believe he will provide what we truly need.

REFLECTION QUESTIONS

- How does the connection between manna in the wilderness and Jesus as the bread of life deepen your understanding of God's provision in your own life?

- When fear of the unknown tempts you to cling to what's familiar, how can you shift your focus to trust in God's lasting provision?

FAITH IN ACTION

1. **Trace God's Hand**

   Reflect on a season when you felt stuck, delayed, or unsure about what God was doing. Can you now see any moments when he was working in the background? Write out the key events and reflect on how God may have been arranging things behind the scenes, even when it didn't feel like it at the time.

2. **Practice Active Waiting**

   Waiting doesn't mean doing nothing. Choose one intentional action this week that reflects your trust in God's plan. It could be spending more time in prayer, offering encouragement to someone else, or taking one small step of obedience in a place where you've been hesitant.

3. **Shift the Focus**

   Instead of focusing on what hasn't happened yet, take time to notice what God is doing in you right now. List three things in this season that may be developing in your character. What qualities are being refined? How is your perspective shifting?

   1)

   2)

   3)

4. **Root Yourself in Romans 5:3–5**

   Use this passage as your anchor this week. Write it out and place it somewhere visible. Each day, reflect on how God is developing perseverance, building character, and deepening your hope not through the absence of trials but through walking with him in the middle of them.

SEEING THE BIGGER PICTURE

As we reflect on the Israelites' journey through the wilderness, it becomes clear their struggles with doubt and trust mirror our own. The wilderness was a place of transformation. God used hunger, fear, and the uncertainty of his plan to teach them dependence on him. He wanted his children to understand and know he was the only true God, and he loved them with an everlasting love.

We see this same truth in our own lives. When we face seasons of struggle or uncertainty, it's tempting to let fear and doubt take over, convincing us to turn back to what feels familiar, even if it isn't God's best for us. But as we've seen today, God's provision is always enough, and his presence is always with us. He doesn't only deliver us out of our circumstances; he walks with us through them, using the journey to refine us and strengthen our faith.

Jesus' declaration that he is the "bread of life" ties everything together. Just as God provided manna in the wilderness to sustain the Israelites, Jesus offers himself as the ultimate provision for our spiritual hunger. He encourages us to release our fears and doubts, to trust in his faithfulness, and to lean on him for strength and guidance. When we look back at our own journeys, we often see God's hand most clearly, recognizing that he has been guiding us and providing for us every step of the way.

CLOSING THOUGHT

The wilderness is not a place of abandonment; it is a place of transformation. God is using your journey to draw you closer to him, just as he did with the Israelites.

God's faithfulness remains steadfast whether you are being delivered out of a situation or walking through it. Trust he is working for your good, providing for your needs, and transforming your heart.

CLOSING PRAYER

Lord, thank you for your faithfulness and provision in every season of my life. Help me to release my fears and doubts and trust in your plan, even when the path ahead feels uncertain. Teach me to depend on you daily, knowing you are always with me, guiding me and providing for my needs. Strengthen my faith and transform my heart as I walk through life's challenges, trusting that you are working for my good.

In Jesus' name,
Amen.

Day Three
Patience Breeds Hope

Over the past two days, we have seen how the Israelites struggled with doubt and fear.

While different in context, Joseph's story shares a similar theme of waiting and trusting in God's plan. In the waiting, the Israelites became impatient and questioned God's faithfulness, but Joseph, on the other hand, trusted God in the waiting, believing he would eventually reveal his plan.

The Israelites and Joseph experienced seasons of uncertainty, but their responses highlight a crucial difference. The Israelites' lack of faith and impatience led them to despair and rebellion. However, Joseph remained secure in his faith as he patiently waited for God to deliver him.

Unlike the Israelites at the Red Sea, Joseph's story demonstrates the power of deep faith in a God who is sovereign over all things. Joseph never wavered in his understanding of who God is. Even during times of great suffering, he focused on what he knew to be true about God despite his circumstances. He was betrayed and sold as a slave by his brothers, falsely accused by his employer's wife, and then imprisoned. I don't know about you, but for me, that would shake my faith.

This journey, for Joseph, was about refinement and transformation. God was preparing him for something greater. His experiences remind us, despite our inability to see the complete picture, God is continually at work behind the scenes, orchestrating his plan for our lives.

Life often calls us to wait, sometimes in unbearable circumstances. The story of Joseph teaches us to be patient when we want to be delivered out of our circumstances. Joseph showed us it's in the waiting when we see the hand of God moving and working in ways we may not understand, but over time, God's plan unfolds in undeniable ways. Through all of Joseph's despair, he kept his eyes on God, and his unshakable faith and patience allowed him to see God's hand at work, even in the smallest details.

Over the next two days, we will take a deeper look into Joseph's life. We will learn from his example how to trust God during uncertain times. Today, we will focus on Joseph's patience, which helped him stay steady even when his situation looked hopeless. We will also think about how impatience can cause doubt and make us doubt God's timing. As we study Joseph's story, let's consider how we can see God's work in our own lives, even in small miracles, and remember to keep our eyes on the bigger picture.

SCRIPTURE REFLECTION 1

Genesis 37:23-28

"So, when Joseph arrived, his brothers ripped off the beautiful robe he was wearing. Then they grabbed him and threw him into the cistern. Now, the cistern was empty; there was no water in it. Then, just as they were sitting down to eat, they looked up and saw a caravan of camels in the distance coming toward them. It was a group of Ishmaelite traders taking a load of gum, balm, and aromatic resin from Gilead down to Egypt. Judah said to his brothers, 'What will we gain by killing our brother? We'd have to cover up the crime. Instead of hurting him, let's sell him to those Ishmaelite traders. After all, he is our brother—our own flesh and blood!' And his brothers agreed. So when the Ishmaelites, who were Midianite traders, came by, Joseph's brothers pulled him out of the cistern and sold him to them for twenty pieces of silver. And the traders took him to Egypt."

UNDERSTANDING THE PASSAGE

This passage marks the start of Joseph's long and difficult journey. Betrayed by his brothers and sold into slavery, Joseph's life seems to spiral out of control. Yet, God's hand was at work even during this moment of despair. Consider how Joseph might have felt sitting in that empty cistern, being thrown in and stripped of his precious robe. Then, being pulled out to be sold as a slave to the caravan's travelers. I honestly can't imagine what he thought. However, as we read his story now, we have the advantage of seeing the entire picture. We can clearly see how, despite this major betrayal and harsh treatment, God's providence is evident. We notice this particularly when Judah suggests his brothers sell Joseph instead of killing him. God ensured Joseph would survive. He was preparing the stage for what was to come.

Before Joseph reached this tragic moment, his life was full of promise. As the beloved son of Jacob, he was given a coat of many colors, which symbolized his favor, and he dreamed of a future where he would rule over his family.

His brothers, however, resented his coat and the prophetic dreams he so arrogantly shared. They reached a breaking point, and when they saw an opportunity to rid themselves of him, they took full advantage.

Imagine Joseph's confusion as he was thrown into that pit. One moment, he was sent by his father on an errand to check on his brothers, and the next, he was stripped of his robe and cast aside. Though we will never know what Joseph's exact thoughts and feelings were, it is easy to picture him crying out, wondering how his life had turned so quickly from privilege to peril. Perhaps you have experienced a moment like that when a sudden change in circumstances left you feeling abandoned and afraid. I know I have.

Though Joseph could not see it then, God was still writing his story. What seemed like the end of Joseph's dreams was actually the beginning of his journey toward fulfilling them. God even used his brothers' betrayal as a steppingstone to position Joseph where he needed to be.

I encourage you to read the full account of this portion of Joseph's story in Genesis 37-38. Seeing the entire picture helps us understand that despite the trials along the way, God's plans are always unfolding, even when we don't yet recognize them.

Joseph's story offers a powerful lens through which we can view our own seasons of uncertainty. Even in betrayal and loss, he remained steady in his belief that God was still moving. As we continue, we'll see how his patience became strength and how waiting with trust transforms us into the person God has created us to be.

REFLECTION QUESTIONS

- How does Joseph's betrayal by his brothers reflect moments in your life when you've felt abandoned or betrayed?

- What small details in this passage reveal God's hand at work, even in Joseph's darkest moments?

SCRIPTURE REFLECTION 2

Genesis 39:20-23

"So he took Joseph and threw him into the prison where the king's prisoners were held, and there he remained. But the Lord was with Joseph in the prison and showed him his faithful love. And the Lord made Joseph a favorite with the prison warden. Before long, the warden put Joseph in charge of all the other prisoners and over everything that happened in the prison. The warden had no more worries because Joseph took care of everything. The Lord was with him and caused everything he did to succeed."

UNDERSTANDING THE PASSAGE

Joseph's time in prison could have easily felt like a detour or even a dead end. He had been faithful, yet he found himself falsely accused and forgotten. His dreams, once so full of promise, seemed buried beneath disappointment. And still, God was with him. Not only was God present, but his favor remained evident. The warden trusted Joseph with a great deal of responsibility, and everything Joseph did was blessed. God had not abandoned him; rather, he was intentionally preparing Joseph for something greater.

At this moment, Joseph didn't have a roadmap or a timeline. He had no guarantee that freedom was coming soon, if ever. But he remained grounded in faith. His trust in God shaped how he lived and how he led, even behind prison walls. We don't see him lashing out in frustration or demanding answers. We see a man who stayed faithful in the waiting.

Waiting has a way of stretching us. When we want answers and relief, we often grow impatient. Impatience, if we're not careful, can make us doubt God's timing and question his goodness. Joseph shows us a different path. He teaches us how to wait well and remain steadfast when the outcome is unclear, and the silence is long.

Paul writes in Romans 5:3–5 that "We can rejoice, too, when we run into problems and trials, for we know that they help us develop endurance. And endurance develops strength of character, and character strengthens our confident hope of salvation." Joseph's story brings these words to life. His circumstances were not easy, but they produced something deep and lasting within him. Each trial shaped his character and strengthened his faith. He didn't allow bitterness to take root. He stayed anchored in his belief of who God was. He knew deep in his heart and mind that God was still writing his story, even if he couldn't see the ending.
This passage challenges us to recognize the same pattern in our own lives. Trials do not mean God has stepped away. More often, they are the very places where God is building

something within us that we will need later. Paul reminds us that the kind of hope built through endurance and character will not disappoint us. It's not a flimsy hope rooted in wishful thinking but a secure hope anchored in the love of God. That love, Paul says, has already been poured into our hearts through the Holy Spirit.

You may be in a season that feels heavy or unclear, where the outcome isn't visible, and the waiting feels long. If so, Joseph's story reminds us God is still working behind the scenes. In the same way he remained with Joseph in the prison, he stays with you now, preparing and strengthening you for what's ahead.

- How does Joseph's response to being falsely imprisoned challenge the way you respond during seasons of waiting or uncertainty?

- In what specific ways can you see God using your current trials to develop endurance, character, or hope in your life?

FAITH INTO ACTION

1. **Journal Your Journey:** Take some time to reflect on a difficult season in your life. What emotions did you feel? How did your patience (or impatience) affect your journey through it? Looking back, can you see ways that God was at work even when it felt like he was silent? Jot a few of those thoughts here.

2. **Write out Romans 5:3-8** and post on your bathroom mirror or someplace you can see it daily, You can even make a screenshot of it off the Bible App and make it your screensaver on your phone. Let these verses serve as a reminder that suffering is not the end of your story, rather it is part of your transformation.

3. **Challenge Your Thinking**: Identify a specific thought or doubt that arises when you go through trials. Write it down, then challenge it with biblical truth. What evidence do you have that God is still working? How can you replace that negative thought with a faith-based perspective?

4. **Reframe With Gratitude**: Write down one way a past trial has shaped you for the better. Even if you don't yet see the purpose of your current struggle, how has God used past difficulties to build your character and strengthen your hope?

SEEING THE BIGGER PICTURE

When we embrace the seasons of waiting and endure through difficulties with patience, we are transforming into the person God has called us to be.

Waiting is hard. Doubt can creep in, and it's easy to wonder if God sees what we're going through. Waiting is more than enduring time; it's a refining process where God strengthens our character and deepens our faith. Joseph's life reveals how transformation happens in the unseen moments. For Joseph, there were so many: in the well, in Potipher's house, in prison, in the nights of doubt, and in the times when nothing seemed to be going in a positive direction. God was working. He is never still. God is constantly refining our character, strengthening our faith, and preparing us for what's ahead.

When we look at Joseph's story, we clearly see God working behind the scenes even when everything seemed to be going wrong. Joseph's time in prison did not go to waste; it prepared him for his calling. The same is true for us. Even in seasons of uncertainty, God is developing perseverance within us, building our character, deepening our faith, and assuring us that hope in him will never lead to regret.

CLOSING THOUGHT

Today, we explored how Joseph remained steadfast, even when his circumstances seemed hopeless. We saw how impatience could have pulled him toward doubt, but instead, he trusted God's timing and stayed faithful in the process. As we reflect on

Joseph's story, we discover God's timing may feel delayed but it is never denied. Sometimes the detour is where real transformation happens.

CLOSING PRAYER
Father, I come before you, acknowledging how hard waiting is and how unbearable suffering can feel. But I trust you are working in my life, even when I cannot see it. Help me be patient in the process and trust my trials are not wasted. Give me endurance when I feel weak, shape my character through these challenges, and remind me of the hope that does not disappoint. Thank you for your unfailing love that has already been poured into my heart.

In Jesus' name,
Amen.

Day Four
Embracing Transformation

As we move into Day Four, we will continue Joseph's journey and further explore how transformation happens in the waiting. Hold onto this truth: The cup of doubt is not meant to break you, but to refine you.

Over the past few days, we've followed Joseph through some of the most painful and confusing moments of his life. His story has led us to reflect on what it means to trust God when answers don't come quickly and when suffering lasts longer than we expected. Today, we will focus on the power of transformation. We will discover how God uses seasons of hardship to refine us, trusting he is at work even when we can't see it, and recognizingthe miracles we seek are often already present in our lives.

Joseph's life teaches us God is working even when we can't see it. Instead of allowing doubt to take hold, we are called to trust him, even when his timing doesn't align with ours. Joseph continually looked to God to anchor his faith, refusing to let suffering define his purpose. His story reminds us we must look through the lens of God's truth to recognize his ways are not ours, and he always sees the bigger picture. He is working on a plan, even when all we see is the hardship and pain in front of us. True transformation happens *not* when we avoid suffering but when we trust God's timing is perfect, his sovereignty is unshakable, and his miracles are unfolding even in the waiting. It means allowing God to work in and through us rather than resisting the process.

SCRIPTURE REFLECTION 1

Genesis 41:14-16

"Pharaoh sent for Joseph at once, and he was quickly brought from the prison. After he shaved and changed his clothes, he went in and stood before Pharaoh. Then Pharaoh said to Joseph, 'I had a dream last night, and no one here can tell me what it means. But I have heard that when you hear about a dream, you can interpret it.' 'It is beyond my power to do this,' Joseph replied. 'But God can tell you what it means and set you at ease'."

UNDERSTANDING THE PASSAGE

Joseph had spent years in prison, falsely accused, waiting in uncertainty. Before this moment, he had interpreted the dreams of Pharaoh's cupbearer and baker, pleading with the cupbearer to remember him. Yet, two more years passed before Joseph was finally called upon. Troubled by mysterious dreams, Pharaoh sought an interpretation, and only then was Joseph remembered and summoned. Joseph was quickly brought from the dungeon. This moment did not occur by accident. It was divinely orchestrated. Joseph was being prepared for this moment through years of hardship. During this time, he had learned to carry himself with humility, and his faith continued to grow stronger. With each day that passed, he became more and more resilient. All of these qualities were necessary for him to step into the calling God had placed on his heart as a young immature teenage boy.

This passage marks a turning point in Joseph's life. It reveals his years of suffering were not in vain. Joseph did not allow bitterness to cloud his heart; instead, he embraced his role in God's bigger plan. His story makes it clear God's timing is always perfect, even when it seems delayed. Through faith, we can trust our seasons of waiting are not without purpose; they are used to shape us for something greater. After years of hardship and not knowing God's plan, Joseph's life took a dramatic turn. Despite the sudden shift in his circumstances, he stayed grounded in humility, recognizing his abilities came from God and not from himself. When Pharaoh credited him with the ability to interpret dreams, Joseph did not seize the moment for personal recognition. Instead, he immediately pointed to God, acknowledging wisdom and understanding come from God alone. His suffering shaped his heart, deepened his faith, and strengthened his character, revealing that true transformation isn't about personal gain but about embracing God's greater purpose.

Joseph had accepted his journey, not in resignation, but in trust. This kind of acceptance is important to note. Resignation means we give up, but trust means we believe in a sovereign God who is working behind the scenes to fulfill his purpose and plan for our lives. Joseph knew God's timing was perfect, even when it seemed unbearably slow. When he stood before Pharaoh, he was ready for his God-ordained purpose.

If you haven't already, I encourage you to take a few moments to read Genesis 41:1-40. Let the words sink in and picture yourself in Joseph's life. Imagine the suffering and the waiting and then stepping into a moment he never could have orchestrated on his own. See how God's plan was unfolding in ways he couldn't have imagined. He knew God's timing was perfect, even when it seemed the suffering would be endless. In this moment, standing before Pharaoh, he was ready for his God-ordained purpose.

REFLECTION QUESTIONS

1. What does Joseph's humility in this moment teach us about transformation?

2. How does trusting in God's timing challenge the way you respond to seasons of waiting?

SCRIPTURE REFLECTION 2
Genesis 45:4–8

"'Please, come closer,' he said to them. So they came closer. And he said again, 'I am Joseph, your brother, whom you sold into slavery in Egypt. But don't be upset, and don't be angry with yourselves for selling me to this place. It was God who sent me here ahead of you to preserve your lives. This famine that has ravaged the land for two years will last five more years, and there will be neither plowing nor harvesting. God has sent me ahead of you to keep you and your families alive and to preserve many survivors. So it was God who sent me here, not you! And he is the one who made me an adviser to Pharaoh—the manager of his entire palace and the governor of all Egypt'."

UNDERSTANDING THE PASSAGE

Joseph's words in this passage are some of the most deeply moving and powerful words in his entire story. After years of slavery and imprisonment, he stood face to face with the very people who caused his pain, and he chose mercy. His perspective had shifted. He didn't ignore what they had done, but he saw something greater, which was the hand of God at work.

Joseph came to a place of acceptance because he recognized there was purpose in his pain. He believed God was using even the worst parts of his story to accomplish something bigger than he could have imagined.

We get an even fuller picture of this in Psalm 105:16–19, where we read, "He called for a famine on the land of Canaan, cutting off its food supply. Then he sent someone to Egypt ahead of them—Joseph, who was sold as a slave. They bruised his feet with fetters and placed his neck in an iron collar. Until the time came to fulfill his dreams, the Lord tested Joseph's character."

This passage gives us insight into what was happening behind the scenes. What looked like tragedy from a human perspective was actually divine preparation. God was sending Joseph ahead. He did not abandon him. He actually did the opposite, he was orchestrating every detail and was with him through the entire journey. Even the shackles and iron collar had a purpose. Scripture tells us the Lord was testing and shaping Joseph's character until the time came to fulfill the dreams planted in him years before.

That phrase "until the time came" carries so much significance. It reminds us there is a process and a timeline. Joseph wasn't forgotten by God. No, God saw every moment and extended his hand through each trial, shaping him to bear the weight of the calling ahead.

Joseph's life teaches us something profound: some of the greatest miracles don't happen when we are delivered out of hardship but when we are delivered through it. The miracle is not always in the outcome. Sometimes it's in the perseverance. In the patience. In the transformation happening inside us when we choose to trust God, even when we don't understand his timing.

Maybe you're walking through something right now that feels endless. Maybe you're waiting for resolution or restoration, or relief. Like Joseph, you may not see the full picture yet. But that doesn't mean God isn't moving. Even in the silence, even in the struggle, God is working. He's shaping your heart and refining your faith. He is preparing you for what's ahead. You may not have asked for the journey you're on, but you can still trust in God. He is the one who's leading you through it.

FAITH INTO ACTION
1. **Reflection Exercise:**
   Consider a season you struggled to accept the circumstances you were having to walk through. Notice how you perceived it then, compared to how you see it now. Where has your understanding shifted, and what might that reveal about how God

was working beneath the surface? Write one or two sentences naming how God was working beyond what you could see at the time.

2. **Change your perspective:**
   Take a current challenge and shift your perspective. Instead of asking, *Why is this happening?* ask, *How might God be using this for my growth?*

3. **Gratitude Practice:**
   Write down one unexpected blessing or lesson from a past trial. Look for the miracles in the journey.

4. **Prayer:**
   Spend time in prayer, surrendering your current struggles to God. Ask him to help you see his timing and sovereignty at work.

SEEING THE BIGGER PICTURE

Joseph's story highlights God's ability to work out his plans even in the midst of hardship and despair. Joseph was not the same person when he stood before Pharaoh as he was when he first arrived in Egypt. God was shaping him through every trial, purifying his character, and preparing him for something far greater than he could have imagined.

When we lean into God and trust him as Joseph did, we find the strength and courage to face our pain rather than run from it. Transformation isn't about making it through suffering; it's about being changed in the process. As God delivers us through our circumstances, he is refining and molding us into the people he created us to be.

Waiting is never without purpose in God's hands. Every moment is an opportunity for growth, and every hardship is a lesson in faith. His timing is always perfect, and his presence is always constant.

The young man who once boasted about his dreams became the man who humbly served and fully trusted God with his life. His journey was not about surviving hardships; it was about becoming the person God intended him to become.

When we face challenges, we often want immediate relief, but genuine transformation occurs in the process. We grow in wisdom, humility, and faith when we trust God is working, even when we don't see the whole picture. Joseph's story gives us hope. Hope God is not only leading us somewhere, but changing us along the way so we can be ready for what he has prepared for us next. Over time, God transformed Joseph from a naive, arrogant teenager into a man of wisdom and humility. Through transformation, God prepared Joseph for his greater purpose.

CLOSING THOUGHT
The hardest thing about transformation is it happens in the waiting, and in the moments we don't understand. But God is never still. He is always working, and his plan is always unfolding, even now in the middle of what seems to be unanswered prayers. Instead of resisting the process, lean in and trust his timing. Open your eyes to the miracles already happening around you.

CLOSING PRAYER
Father, thank you for being near, even when I can't see what you're doing and I don't understand your ways, I trust you are working with purpose in every detail. I'm grateful you never let my pain or waiting be meaningless. Grow in me a heart that is patient and a faith that holds tightly to your promises. Let your peace settle over me, and open my eyes to the miracles unfolding around me. I surrender my struggles to you and ask that you transform me into the person you want me to be.

In Jesus' name,
Amen.

Day Five
Seeing God's Plan in the Journey

As we finish this week, take a moment to see the bigger picture. Joseph's life and the Israelites' journey were very different, yet God was equally present in both. He guided them through every challenge, met their needs, and stayed faithful to his promises. Our circumstances might be different, but the same unchanging God is at work in our lives today, just as he was then. The same God is still active in our lives now, fulfilling his plan. In every season, he leads us intentionally and reveals his glory through our story.

SCRIPTURE REFLECTION 1
2 Corinthians 1:8-10
"We think you ought to know, dear brothers and sisters, about the trouble we went through in the province of Asia. We were crushed and overwhelmed beyond our ability to endure, and we thought we would never live through it. In fact, we expected to die. But as a result, we stopped relying on ourselves and learned to rely only on God, who raises the dead. And he did rescue us from mortal danger, and he will rescue us again. We have placed our confidence in him, and he will continue to rescue us."

UNDERSTANDING THE PASSAGE
Paul speaks of suffering beyond what he could bear, yet he acknowledges trials teach us to depend fully on God. Like Joseph in prison and the Israelites in the wilderness, hardships often strip us of self-reliance and lead us to deeper trust in God.

Paul wrote this letter to the church in Corinth, a congregation he had founded during his missionary journeys. The Corinthians were struggling with division, false teachings, and external pressures from a culture that opposed their faith. In this passage, Paul is deeply personal, sharing the immense suffering he and his companions endured while spreading the gospel in Asia.

His words reflect both despair and complete trust in God. He had reached a point where he saw no way out, yet instead of losing faith, he learned a vital truth: our strength is limited, but God's power is infinite. This moment of suffering was not without meaning. It taught him and his companions to fully depend on God, the one who raises the dead.

Paul's testimony resonates with us because we, too, face trials that seem unbearable. There are seasons when we feel crushed, wondering how we will endure. I have been in a place where I wrestled with doubt, questioning how God could possibly bring good from my pain. But Paul's experience shows us God is not only a deliverer in the past but also in the present and future. Just as he was with Joseph in prison and as he provided for the Israelites in the wilderness, he is still faithful today. I have seen his faithfulness in my own life, in moments when I felt completely broken, and I know he is doing the same for you. Even when the road ahead feels uncertain, we can trust the same God who sustained his people then is the same God working in our lives today.

REFLECTION QUESTIONS

- In 2 Corinthians 1:8-10, Paul describes feeling "crushed and overwhelmed beyond our ability to endure." How does his response to suffering challenge the way you approach hardships in your own life?

- Paul states, "…we stopped relying on ourselves and learned to rely only on God." How does relying on God rather than ourselves transform the way we approach suffering and adversity?

SCRIPTURE REFLECTION 2
Hebrews 13:8
"Jesus Christ is the same yesterday, today, and forever."

UNDERSTANDING THE PASSAGE
This verse highlights the unchanging nature of God. The same God who delivered Joseph through his circumstances and led the Israelites out of the Red Sea is the same God who walks with us today. His faithfulness, provision, and sovereignty are unwavering, giving us confidence he will continue to fulfill his promises.

The author of Hebrews wrote to Jewish Christians struggling with uncertainty, persecution, and doubt. Much like Joseph in prison and the Israelites in the wilderness, these early Christians were facing hardships that made them question God's presence and plan. They were tempted to return to what was familiar, seeking safety in the Old Covenant, just as the Israelites longed for Egypt in the wilderness. But the writer of Hebrews reassured them God is the same God who has always been faithful, and he was still working, even when they could not see it.

Joseph's journey was filled with suffering, yet every betrayal and setback led him toward God's greater purpose. He could not have known, as he sat in a prison cell, he was being prepared for a position that would one day save many lives. Likewise, the Israelites could not have imagined, as they stood trapped between the Red Sea and Pharaoh's army, that God was about to part the waters before them. Their doubt blinded them to the faithfulness of God, but his unchanging nature remained steadfast. He was the same God who had made a covenant with Abraham, the same God who rescued them, and the same God who would lead them to the Promised Land.

And he is still that same God today. When we look at Philippians 1:6, we are told God doesn't leave things unfinished. "He who began a good work in you will carry it on to completion until the day of Christ Jesus." Whether we feel it or not, he's still working. He's still shaping us, still refining us, still walking with us through the hard places. The good work he started in Joseph wasn't obvious in the pit or the prison, but it was there. The good work he started in the Israelites wasn't always visible in the wilderness, but he was still leading them.

Maybe you're in a place where the future feels uncertain, and you're tempted to doubt God's timing or presence. I've been there. But the promise is this: Jesus Christ is the same yesterday, today, and forever. And the work he started in you he has not finished. His character doesn't shift with your circumstances. You can trust he is still leading, still providing, and still fulfilling his promises even when you can't yet see how it will all come together.

REFLECTION QUESTIONS

- What does it mean to you that God's character remains unchanging through every generation?

- How does knowing God was faithful to Joseph and the Israelites give you confidence in his plans for your own life?

FAITH INTO ACTION

1. **Compare Your Journey** – Write down a time when you felt like the Israelites: resisting, doubting, or longing for what was familiar. Now write about a time when you responded like Joseph and leaned into God's process. What made the difference?

2. **Surrender Your Timeline** – Reflect on an area of your life where you are struggling with God's timing. Pray specifically for the patience to trust Him.

3. **Recognize the Miracles** – What is one way, big or small, God is working in your life right now? What "miracles in the journey" have you overlooked?

SEEING THE BIGGER PICTURE

At the heart of both stories is God's ability to work through trials for his greater purpose. Joseph endured betrayal and imprisonment, but each moment was preparing him for the future. The Israelites faced a different struggle. They had to learn to let go of control and trust God was leading them somewhere good.

Like Joseph, we are being refined in the waiting. Like the Israelites, we sometimes resist what we don't understand. But the lesson remains: God is working, whether we see it or not. One of the biggest differences between these two journeys is how they experienced deliverance. The Israelites were delivered out of Egypt, while Joseph was delivered through his suffering. The Israelites longed for a quick escape, yet their doubt led to wandering. Joseph, on the other hand, embraced his journey and allowed God to shape him through every hardship. His suffering wasn't just something to endure; it was the very thing God used to position him for purpose.

When we face trials, we naturally want relief as quickly as possible. Yet, as we see in Joseph's story, God's greater work is often accomplished when he delivers us through difficulties rather than out of them. The waiting, the challenges, and even the pain are not without purpose but are shaping us in ways we may not yet understand. Doubt tempts us to seek the quickest escape, but faith calls us to trust God is moving, even when the road feels long and uncertain.

CLOSING THOUGHT
Both Joseph and the Israelites walked difficult paths, but their responses shaped their outcomes. Transformation happens when we stop resisting the process and start trusting God is working, even when we can't see it. I know how hard it can be to hold on when life feels uncertain, but I also know this: God has never failed, and he won't start now. Just like he was leading Joseph through every setback and guiding the Israelites even in their doubt, he is leading you, too. Trust his plans are greater than what you can see right now, and keep walking forward in faith. He is the same yesterday, today, and forever.

CLOSING PRAYER
Father, thank you for your perfect timing and for working in my life, even when I don't understand the path ahead. Help me trust your plan like Joseph did and surrender my doubts like the Israelites struggled to do. Give me eyes to see past my pain and a heart that is willing to be transformed in the process.

In Jesus' name,
Amen

Week Two
Group Discussion

Begin by watching the Week Two video together. Afterward, ask the group, "What stood out to you most from the video?"

After one or two participants have shared, take time to review last week's study. As a group, flip through each day's reading, briefly noting the Reflection Questions and Faith in Action prompts. Allow time for participants to share their responses to each prompt. If you finish early, use the Group Discussion Questions below to encourage deeper connection.

1. How does fear shape the way people interpret difficult situations, especially when they are trying to recognize God's presence?

2. What parallels do you notice between the Israelites' struggle to trust God and the broader human experience of wrestling with faith?

3. Why do individuals often cling to the familiar, even when it brings discomfort? How might fear influence that tendency?

4. Romans 8:28 says God works for the good of those who love him and are called according to his purpose. How does this verse illustrate the bigger theme of God's guidance and intention throughout Scripture?

5. What is the difference between acceptance and approval, and how might that distinction help us understand surrender from a biblical perspective?

Week Three

Perception

I hope you are beginning to understand how much God loves you and how he has a specific plan for your life. I'm glad we're on this journey together. This week, we will explore the power of perception through the story of Ruth and Naomi.

Perception, simply put, is how we view and interpret our circumstances; it influences our emotions and guides our actions. Both of these impact our faith. Our past experiences and core beliefs uniquely shape our individual perspectives, causing each person to see things differently. This difference is why two people can experience the same event but walk away with contrasting views on what they encountered.

Often, we are unaware of how our experiences and beliefs shape our perception of the world around us. What we see isn't always the whole picture. It is only part of the picture, and when we have past hurts, they can damage our ability to see things as they really are and distorting the truth of what God is doing in our lives.

The story of Ruth and Naomi perfectly illustrates this pattern of thought and behavior. Both Ruth and Naomi experienced devastating loss, but because of their past experiences, their perceptions of the future were completely different. Their story shows how deeply our beliefs influence how we see the future and influence the level of hope we carry for redemption.

This week, we will learn to recognize how false perceptions may shape our thoughts, feelings, and behaviors. We will begin to understand how our belief system may not align with God's truth. As we unpack concepts like mental filters and top-down processing, we will examine how these ideas connect with Scripture and help us respond differently to suffering. The goal isn't to erase the pain we have had to walk through, but to learn how to view life through a clearer lens shaped by God's promises instead of clouded by our wounds.

I know how easy it is to see life through the lens of past pain and disillusionment, but I've found real transformation begins when I allow God to renew my mind with his truth, not mine. As you move through this study, I pray you will begin to see your circumstances through the clarity of God's truth and grace, not through the weight of your past experiences.

I'm so honored to walk alongside you through this study. Let's dive in.

Day One

What We See vs. What Is True

Our perception of life is shaped by what we expect to see. When hardship strikes and we are faced with a cup we do not want to drink, we often filter that experience through past pain and deeply held beliefs. These beliefs are either handed to us or we have picked them up along the way. When our perspective has been shaped by hurt, it can greatly influence how we interpret what is happening around us and lead us to conclusions that may not be entirely true.

We see this clearly in Naomi's story. Naomi had worked hard to build a beautiful life serving God and caring for her family, but when life handed her an unexpected set of tragic circumstances, everything she once knew suddenly looked different. Grief setteled in, and she began to see her world differently.

It is easy to fall into that same pattern of seeing life through a tainted filter rather than through faith. Faith enables us to look beyond what is happening around us and recognize God is at work behind the scenes. In the midst of our crucible, it is easy to let our minds create a narrative that fits our feelings rather than aligning with the truth of God's word.

Today, we will continue exploring Naomi's story and how grief influenced her perception. We'll also look at Cognitive Restructuring, which involves identifying and transforming distorted thinking patterns. This practice aligns with God's desire to renew our minds. As we begin, my prayer is for us to gain deeper insight into Naomi and Ruth's story by seeing how their experiences mirror our own. Through their journey, we can recognize the many ways God works within ordinary circumstances by changing our perception, redirecting our steps, and revealing his faithfulness in the process of transformation. Naomi's story didn't end where her pain began. And neither does yours.

SCRIPTURE REFLECTION 1
Ruth 1:5, 16–18, 20–21

"Then both Mahlon and Kilion died. This left Naomi alone, without her two sons or her husband. But Ruth replied, 'Don't ask me to leave you and turn back. Wherever you go, I will go; wherever you live, I will live. Your people will be my people, and your God will be my God. Wherever you die, I will die, and there I will be buried. May the Lord punish me severely if I allow anything but death to separate us!' When Naomi saw that Ruth was determined to go with her, she said nothing more. 'Don't call me Naomi,' she responded. 'Instead, call me Mara, for the Almighty has made life very bitter for me. I went away full, but the Lord has brought me home empty. Why call me Naomi when the Lord has caused me to suffer and the Almighty has sent such tragedy upon me'?"

UNDERSTANDING THE PASSAGE
During a famine, Naomi left Bethlehem years ago with her husband to seek a better life. Everything changed when her husband and two sons died. After burying her family, she returned to Bethlehem feeling heavy-hearted and with what she thought was an empty future. Her sorrow was apparent to everyone. Her grief deeply affected her outlook on life moving forward.

Naomi viewed her suffering through a mental filter of compounding loss, assuming this succession of grief meant God had completely abandoned her. She believed her future was over because her expectations of what her life would look like had been shattered. Instead of seeing an opportunity for new beginnings, she could only see emptiness and feel heartache. She interpreted her present through the lens of her past pain. She assumed bitterness was her identity and deep sorrow was her fate. She failed to understand the depth of her pain was only a season she was having to walk through.

Naomi's response to the loss of her husband and sons was largely due to the cultural norms at the time. As a woman in ancient Israel, her well-being and security were directly tied to the men in her family. With their deaths, she lost more than her loved ones. She lost her financial stability and social standing. She had no sense of protection in a society where widows were among the most vulnerable. This context helps us understand the fear and despair that shaped her worldview.

In addition to all she had lost, Naomi also faced the unexpected devotion of Ruth. Ruth wanted to leave with Naomi and accompany her back to her hometown. But Naomi did not want Ruth to go, so she urged her to stay with her own people.

Naomi truly believed she had nothing to offer Ruth and thought she would have a better chance of rebuilding her life in her own homeland. Maybe, in her mind, Ruth's loyalty only added more stress to figuring out how to survive with no clear path ahead for either of them. But Ruth was committed to staying by her mother-in-law's side and serving her God. I think Naomi was, in some ways, glad Ruth wanted to go, but she was also overwhelmed with worries about how they would survive, so she emotionally withdrew from her.

Returning to Bethlehem with no husband, no sons, and no clear path forward, Naomi saw herself as completely empty. In her mind, God had turned against her. Her suffering reflected a broader reality for widows in her culture. She believed her circumstances left her with no future because that was simply how it was for widowed women with no family. But Naomi's perception was incomplete. She assumed her loss meant she had no means and no worth. She believed her suffering was the final word in her story because, in her mind, God had left her. What she couldn't see at the time was how God was already at work bringing restoration to her in ways she never expected.

In biblical times, names carried significant weight and meaning. Naomi believed her name, which meant "pleasant," no longer described how she felt, so she insisted on changing it. She declared her new name was Mara, which meant "bitter." In her mind, the suffering she had endured had permanently altered her identity and erased any hope of redemption. She believed bitterness was a better description of who she was.

We often interpret life through the lens of our past experiences. Without realizing it, our past shapes the way we see what's happening now. The brain is quick to draw skewed conclusions about our circumstances, especially when we've been hurt. We make sense of the moment by reaching for what we've already walked through. Sometimes that is helpful, but other times it can cloud what God may be doing right in front of us.

In my book, *Drinking the Cup You Are Served*, I share an example of a child looking out a dirty window and thinking they see a monster. In reality, it is just a tree. But because their brain and imagination draw from a previous fear, the child sees something that isn't real. This example illustrates top-down processing. This kind of processing happens when our minds use what we've previously experienced or feared to interpret what we're seeing now. It happens quickly, and most of the time it is not exactly accurate. That is how we end up responding to a threat that isn't really there.

Naomi believed God had forgotten her, and she couldn't yet see God was still at work. He had not forgotten her; on the contrary, he knew exactly what lay ahead. However, Naomi could not see the future, so she wove a narrative that aligned with her perception and feelings rather than what she knew to be true about the God she worshipped.

Like Naomi, we often view our circumstances through the lens of past pain, shaping our expectations for the future. When things don't unfold as we hope, we sometimes assume suffering means God has abandoned us. Our preconceived ideas about what life should look like can distort our ability to see what God is still doing.

Naomi's story shows us the power of perception. We see how she allowed her negative thoughts and false beliefs to precede her knowledge of who God was, leaving her feeling abandoned. Over the years, Naomi had told Ruth many stories of how God had delivered his children, but she was unable to acknowledge he could do the same for her. Her feelings of grief took over, leading her to draw conclusions about God that were not based on truth.

The same is true for us. Our suffering is not the end of the story, and our pain is not proof that God has turned away. However, if we allow our negative thoughts and feelings to distort our perception, we risk not seeing God move and work in our lives during our suffering. If we believe life doesn't unfold as we hoped, we often assign meaning to our suffering that isn't true. To read the full account of this part of the story, you can turn to Ruth 1:1–22.

REFLECTION QUESTIONS

- Naomi assumed her suffering was proof that God's hand was against her. Have you ever interpreted hardship in a similar way? Looking back, was your perception accurate?

- In what ways do preconceived ideas about your past influence how you process difficulties today?

SCRIPTURE REFLECTION 2

Ruth 2:8–12

"Boaz went over and said to Ruth, 'Listen, my daughter. Stay right here with us when you gather grain; don't go to any other fields. Stay right behind the young women working in my field. See which part of the field they are harvesting and then follow them. I have warned the young men not to treat you roughly. And when you are thirsty, help yourself to the water they have drawn from the well.' Ruth fell at his feet and thanked him warmly. 'What have I done to deserve such kindness?' she asked. 'I am only a foreigner.' 'Yes, I know,' Boaz replied. 'But I also know about everything you have done for your mother-in-law since the death of your husband. I have heard how you left your father and mother and your own land to live here among complete strangers. May the Lord, the God of Israel, under whose wings you have come to take refuge, reward you fully for what you have done'."

UNDERSTANDING THE PASSAGE

Ruth had every reason to expect rejection. After following Naomi to Bethlehem, she was now a foreigner in a new land with no wealth or status. And like Naomi, she was grieving the loss of her husband. She had stepped into the unfamiliar with no guarantee of provision and no clear plan for what would come next. She didn't know how their needs would be met, but she chose to move forward anyway. Her heart was heavy with grief, but her hope had not vanished.

Long before they lost their husbands, Ruth had repeatedly heard Naomi speak of the God of Israel. She likely recalled the stories of how he rescued his people out of the land of Egypt, parted the Red Sea, guided them with a pillar of cloud by day and a pillar of fire by night, and provided manna for them to eat while in the wilderness. These stories must have taken root in Ruth's heart. Even when Naomi struggled to believe those stories for herself, Ruth remembered them. Her decision to follow Naomi was rooted in her faith in God. She believed all the stories her mother-in-law had told her over the years and was convinced if God performed miracles for the children of Israel, then he would deliver them as well.

When Ruth arrived in Boaz's field to gather barley from his crops, his kindness was more than just a social gesture. His actions reflected God's provision. From the moment Ruth started working in the field, she received favor. This favor exemplifies how God shows up in the midst of sorrow and hardship. Boaz's kindness was unexpected, as seen in her question, "What have I done to deserve such kindness?" Because she refused to let fear or uncertainty stop her from stepping into the field, she positioned herself to receive God's provision. She moved forward without any guarantee of how she would survive. This choice is a beautiful testimony of faith in action.

Ruth, like Naomi, could have viewed her situation through the lens of her grief, but she chose not to. She entered Boaz's field with a different outlook. An outlook open to the unexpected. Her perspective wasn't clouded by despair; instead, it was guided by her faith in God. Her viewpoint was noticeably different from Naomi's.

Ruth's perspective helps us understand we don't need certainty to take the next step. Paul wrote to the Corinthians with this same kind of hope in mind. In 2 Corinthians 4:16–18, he encouraged believers not to give up, even when outward circumstances felt too hard or even hopeless. He wrote, "While our bodies are wasting away, our spirits are being renewed day by day." He urged the new believers not to focus on what is seen, because what is seen is temporary. He said to fix their eyes on what is unseen, because it lasts forever. His words point us to a higher reality and away from just what we see on earth, helping us view our life from an eternal perspective. If we focus only on what is visible, we might draw conclusions not based in truth. But if we keep our eyes on Jesus, everything we see begins to look different.

The tension between what we see and what we believe is where perception and faith meet. Naomi's perception had been damaged by loss after loss: first her home, then her husband, and finally her two sons. Each loss seemed to reinforce the story she feared most. She was afraid of being alone and destitute. Ruth also experienced loss, but her's was different. She lost her husband, and while that grief was very real and heartbreaking, it wasn't compounded in the same way. Her heart was broken, but she didn't let bitterness take over her perception. She held onto the stories Naomi had once shared about God's power and provision, and she believed they could still be true for her and Naomi. Their situations were similar, but their responses were not. Convinced her story was over, Naomi emotionally shut down. Ruth, however, kept an open mind and continued moving forward, trusting God would provide. Paul's words in 2 Corinthians 4:16–18 remind us of the same hope. He encourages us to focus not on what is seen, but on what is unseen. When we allow God's truth to reshape our view, we see through a different lens, which gives us the courage to keep going even when we don't know what lies ahead.

REFLECTION QUESTIONS

- What does Boaz's response reveal about how God uses others to show his faithfulness?

- Have you ever found yourself stuck in a negative perception, only to realize later God was providing in unexpected ways?

FAITH IN ACTION

Note to Reader: You may notice that some of the Faith in Action sections feel familiar in structure or approach. That's intentional. Growth takes repetition both in thought and practice. Each exercise builds on the last, helping you retrain your thinking, deepen your faith, and strengthen new patterns that align with God's Word. Though they share a similar rhythm, each one offers a new perspective and a fresh opportunity to apply what you're learning in a deeper way.

Ruth and Naomi both experienced devastating loss, but their thoughts about what would happen next led them in very different directions. Naomi's thoughts were shaped by hopelessness and seemed to confirm nothing good was coming. Ruth's thoughts, though rooted in grief, left space for the possibility of God's provision. Their differing perceptions shaped their feelings and ordered their next steps.

1. Identify one area in your life where your thoughts have been heavy or uncertain, and write down what you've been thinking about it. Be honest. Don't filter or edit them. Just put your thoughts on paper.

2. Circle any thoughts above that feel tainted by past pain. These may point to a distorted perception influenced by fear, disappointment, grief, or shame. Now name what might be at the root.

3. Read the following Scriptures and write down what you notice about God's character:

    Psalm 34:18

    Exodus 33:14

    Isaiah 41:10

    Deuteronomy 31:8

4. In prayer or journaling, ask God to help you interpret your circumstances through his faithfulness, not your fear.

SEEING THE BIGGER PICTURE

Two people can experience similar circumstances and draw completely different conclusions. Naomi believed her story was over. Ruth believed her story was still being written. That difference didn't come from what they lost; it came from how they perceived their loss. When our perception is clouded by pain and not filtered through truth, it can prevent us from seeing things as God sees them. What may seem impossible to us remains fully possible with God. Our perception doesn't limit his power, and his plans aren't confined to what we can see.

CLOSING THOUGHT

God is always working, even when we can't see it. When we recognize we are telling ourselves a false narrative and replace it with truth, our perception changes, and we begin to experience hope, healing, and renewal. What we see now is only part of the picture. Trust God is writing a greater story.

CLOSING PRAYER

Heavenly Father, thank you for being faithful even when we struggle to see it. Help me recognize when my perception is shaped by past pain rather than your truth. Teach me to fix my eyes on what is unseen. Help me trust in your faithfulness and believe you have a plan even if I can't see it. Renew my mind and guide me to walk by faith, not by sight.

In Jesus' name,
Amen.

Day Two
The Role of Expectation in Our Thinking

Today we continue our journey to understand how perception can either hinder or enhance our ability to see things as God does. I am excited because today's lesson will introduce us to Old Testament and New Testament scriptures that help us align our vision with God's.

Expectations play a significant role in how we perceive our circumstances. When we expect hardship and loss, we tend to notice things that confirm those beliefs. Naomi expected nothing but sorrow, so she filtered her reality through that lens, which left her feeling resentful and overcome by grief. Ruth, however, expected God to perform a miracle, which helped her see beyond her immediate loss, leaving her feeling hopeful.

We all have a mental filter that influences how we see our circumstances. This filter is the mechanism through which we process our thoughts and perceptions to form our core beliefs about God, ourselves, others, and the world we live in. These core beliefs don't develop all at once. They gradually take shape, often during times of pain or emotional struggle.

If our filter has been shaped by fear or shame, it can distort how we interpret what is happening in our lives and the role God is playing in it. This distortion of the truth can lead us to question whether anything good can still emerge from what we are going through. But when we allow God's Word to renew our minds, our thoughts begin to realign, and our perception starts to change. We begin to see our current reality through a different lens, one that is supernatural and rooted in truth and hope, while still allowing us to feel sorrow and grief.

Today, we will explore how our expectations influence what we think and feel. We will examine how we filter our perceptions of what's happening around us and recognize God's hand working on our behalf.

SCRIPTURE REFLECTION 1

Romans 12:2

"Don't copy the behavior and customs of this world, but let God transform you into a new person by changing the way you think. Then you will learn to know God's will for you, which is good and pleasing and perfect."

UNDERSTANDING THE PASSAGE

Paul wrote this letter to a group of believers in Rome, many of whom were new to their faith in Christ and trying to follow Jesus in a culture filled with idol worship and political pressure. Many of them were confused about their new faith. They believed following Christ only meant changing their actions, but Paul wanted these believers to understand that following Christ was more than just adjusting their behaviors; it was about allowing God to transform the way they think.

In this passage, Paul teaches us that transformation begins in the mind. We often try to fix what's on the outside, but Paul makes it clear that real change starts internally. Changing the way we think and what we believe to align with the Word of God helps us adjust our expectations and view our circumstances from a completely different perspective. That's why he tells the believers in Rome not to imitate the patterns around them but to let God rewire how they process what's happening in their immediate world.

This change in how we process and interpret events in our lives is where mental filters come into play. When our thoughts are shaped by past hurt, fear, disappointment, or shame, it alters the way we see what's right in front of us. Over time, these thought patterns become so familiar they start to feel like truth. This tendency to accept distorted thoughts as reality is what a mental filter does. It filters what we think is happening and adjusts our perception accordingly. In my book, I use another analogy to explain this process. I compare a mental filter to a coffee filter. A good coffee filter prevents the grounds from entering the brewed coffee, allowing only hot water to pass through. But if the filter is damaged or torn, the grounds slip in and distort the texture and flavor.

Similarly, a mental filter decides which thoughts we accept and which ones are blocked. If fear, lies, or past pain have shaped our filter, it will distort the truth, leaving us with a skewed perception.

When top-down processing relies on our past experiences to shape our perception of the present and our mental filter is damaged, we need to hear a different voice. We need to hear from God. When we study and read the Word of God, we become familiar with how he speaks to us. When we hear his voice, it has the power to cleanse our damaged mental filters and realign our thoughts with his.

Paul's words echo what we see in Ruth. Her past trauma didn't drive her decision to step into Boaz's field; rather, her decision was shaped by her trust in what she knew to be true about God and his character. Ruth expected God to change her current situation. Naomi, on the other hand, started seeing everything through a damaged mental filter, and her top-down processing caused her to interpret her present circumstances through the lens of everything she had lost. Consequently, she expected ongoing loss and hardship. This contrast in perception clearly shows we all have a choice: we can let pain influence how we see our circumstances, or we can allow God to renew our minds and reshape our thinking to align with his.

REFLECTION QUESTIONS

- What thoughts or expectations have been shaped by past experiences, and how might they be influencing the way you're interpreting your current circumstances?

- When you consider your own mental filter, are there beliefs about God or yourself that might be distorting how you see what's possible?

SCRIPTURE REFLECTION 2

Lamentations 3:19–24

"The thought of my suffering and homelessness is bitter beyond words. I will never forget this awful time, as I grieve over my loss. Yet I still dare to hope when I remember this: The faithful love of the Lord never ends! His mercies never cease. Great is his faithfulness; his mercies begin afresh each morning. I say to myself, 'The Lord is my inheritance; therefore, I will hope in him'!"

UNDERSTANDING THE PASSAGE

Lamentations was likely written by the prophet Jeremiah after the fall of Jerusalem. It was a time of devastation and national grief. The Israelites had lost their land and everything that defined them as a nation. Jeremiah had every reason to feel hopeless. Everything he had known was gone. And yet, right in the middle of his sorrow, he makes a significant shift.

He doesn't pretend the pain isn't real by pushing it aside; instead, he addresses his suffering face-on by calling it out truthfully and honestly: "I will never forget this awful time." But then he takes a breath and says, "Yet I still dare to hope." The turning point comes as he shifts his focus back to the character of God, even though nothing around him has changed. He remembers God's love hasn't ended. His mercies are still fresh each morning. I love how Jeremiah was able to turn his eyes toward the character of God and call out one of God's most precious attributes, mercy. What a beautiful example of trading his sorrow for the hope he found in knowing the true character of his Creator. Jeremiah's perspective wasn't shaped only by what he felt. He drew from what he knew to be true about God. This truth caused him to expect mercy to come to him every single day.

This kind of shift starts when we realize how pain and disappointment taint our mental filter. As we align our thoughts with God's voice and the truth of his Word, our perception begins to change. It might not make sense right now, but we need to remember what God says: "My ways are not like yours." When we trust his faithfulness, even without clear answers, our thinking begins to shift. That's what Jeremiah did. His circumstances hadn't changed, but his focus had. He saw devastation and, despite everything, declared, "Yet I still dare to hope."

Naomi's story shows us how easy it is to believe our pain proves that God does not care. But Jeremiah reminds us we can feel grief and still speak hope into it. Healing begins when we ask God to help us see our circumstances through the lens of his character, not through past hurts or current fears. It doesn't require us to ignore the pain, but it does require us to see it differently.

REFLECTION QUESTIONS

- What do Jeremiah's words reveal about how remembering God's character can change our perspective, even in the middle of pain?

- Describe a time when grief or disappointment shaped your expectations. How might focusing on God's faithfulness help reframe how you see that situation now?

FAITH IN ACTION
1. **Write down what you expect to happen** and what you hope from God. Reflect on the past few days. In conversations, decisions, or moments of stress, what were you anticipating? Is it disappointment, conflict, rejection, provision, peace? Write down a few specific expectations you carried without realizing it.

2. **Identify the root of those expectations.** Were they shaped by a past experience (top-down processing), a belief about yourself, or a fear of how others would respond (damaged mental filter)? Pinpointing the root helps you see the pattern of your thoughts.

3. **Challenge your interpretation.** Choose one moment or expectation and ask: What other interpretation is possible here? How might this situation appear if I filtered it through God's faithfulness instead of fear or disappointment?

4. **Speak what is true.** Use Scripture to speak truth into one expectation that has been distorted.

- John 8:32 – "Then you will know the truth, and the truth will set you free."

- Isaiah 26:3 – "You will keep in perfect peace those whose minds are steadfast, because they trust in you."

- Philippians 4:8 – "Fix your thoughts on what is true, and honorable, and right, and pure, and lovely, and admirable."

- Psalm 33:4 – "For the word of the Lord holds true, and we can trust everything he does."

SEEING THE BIGGER PICTURE

What we expect often reveals what we believe about God, ourselves, and others. When those expectations are shaped by past and present pain, it becomes easy to interpret our circumstances through drop-down processing and through a damaged filter. However, when we allow God's Word to reshape our thoughts, we can filter our experiences through the lens of truth, causing our perception to shift. Even when nothing around us has changed, we can still see signs of God's goodness.

I continue to experience moments when my thoughts drift back to old patterns. There are times I expect disappointment without even realizing it. But I'm learning that when I slow down and speak what I know to be true about God, I can reframe my thoughts. I remind myself that he sees me and he is with me. This truth is what keeps me anchored. I may not see everything clearly, but I can still trust he is already at work.

Romans 12:2 teaches us that transformation begins in the mind. Our perception will start to change when we focus on God and release the fears and wounds we have carried for far too long. What once looked like the end of the story begins to feel like the start of something new. Hope returns, even in places we thought were hopeless. When our perception is transformed by truth, we experience calm and peace in the middle of the storm. This kind of peace can only come from our heavenly Father, who loves us unconditionally.

CLOSING THOUGHT

Expectations influence everything. If we expect disappointment, we will only see disappointment. But if we expect God's goodness, we will begin to notice his hand at work in ways we never imagined. Like Ruth, let's trust in God's provision and take steps forward in faith.

CLOSING PRAYER

Father in heaven, I thank you for your goodness and mercy even during my suffering and heartache. Please renew my mind with the truth of your Word so I can see as you see. I surrender my past hurt and current fears into your healing hands. Help me trust in your goodness, even when my circumstances seem so uncertain. Like Ruth, give me faith to take the next step, knowing you will always provide for me.

In Jesus' name,
Amen

Day Three
When Faith Feels Fragile

Today, we will explore what it means to face a faith crisis resulting from a distorted view of God. Sometimes, we do everything correctly. We make plans, follow what we believe is right, and move forward with good intentions. But even then, things can fall apart. And when they do, it's difficult to understand what's happening and even harder to see where God is in the midst of it. These experiences often lead us into periods of doubt about the true nature of God. When this occurs, we may struggle to recognize God's presence in our circumstances.

A faith crisis often happens when life takes an unexpected turn, and everything feels completely out of our control, shaking the very foundation of our faith. When life doesn't go the way we hoped, it can leave us feeling broken, even shattered, and the path we find ourselves traveling feels unfamiliar. What once felt clear and predictable now starts to feel gray and unfamiliar. We wonder whether God is present in any of it. Fear creeps in, and doubt settles close behind. Before we know it, we're trying to hold together pieces of a story we don't understand.

I have experienced my own faith crises. It was during a season when life was not playing out as I had dreamed it would. I had done what I thought were all of the right things, only to see my hard work crumble in front of me. I felt as though everything was spinning in a direction I could no longer control. I desperately tried to hold everything together, but it all seemed to be slipping through my fingers. I cried and pleaded, even begged God to intervene. Yet nothing changed. If anything, things seemed to get worse.

In that season, I struggled with crushing disappointment and paralyzing fear. I wrestled with soul-searching questions about God and what I truly believed. I was desperate and overcome with despair, and my prayers felt unanswered.

Despite my hopelessness, I still continued to pray. I finally reached a breaking point where I had to let go of what I thought I understood about God and surrender my expectations of what I thought God should do in this circumstance.

I had to learn to trust him in a way I never had before. There were many days when I simply sat with God in my pain, not knowing if or when anything would change. Then, after some time had passed, something started to shift. Though my circumstances stayed the same, my heart began to change. As my heart changed, so did my perception. Even though I didn't have the answers to all my questions, I felt a peace that truly went beyond my understanding. God kept revealing himself to me in unexpected ways through friends, a prophetic word, and even answers to unrelated prayers. He was showing me that he saw my hurt and heard my cries. For the first time during that particular crisis, I experienced a profound love so present and personal it transcended every question I had. Though nothing around me changed, peace settled into my heart so deeply that it left me with no doubt God had everything under control and was working, even though I couldn't see it.

I felt deeply loved by God, not because my situation improved, but because his presence was undeniable. In the middle of my pain, I came to know him in a way I never had before, feeling his touch and sensing his presence deep within my soul. He became my anchor that steadied me when everything around me felt so uncertain and fragile.

Through this experience, I learned I was not responsible for fighting this battle; it was God who would fight it for me. Like Naomi, I discovered faith is not about waiting for everything to look like I thought it was supposed to, but about trusting that God is working in ways I cannot yet see.

Today, we will explore what it means to trust God when everything seems to be falling apart and life isn't unfolding as we expected. We will see how Naomi began to reconcile her faith crisis when she realized that faith isn't about having all the answers but about trusting God even when everything familiar feels lost and hope appears out of reach.

SCRIPTURE REFLECTION 1
Ruth 2:19–20
"'Where did you gather all this grain today?' Naomi asked. 'Where did you work? May the Lord bless the one who helped you!' So Ruth told her mother-in-law about the man in whose field she had worked. She said, 'The man I worked with today is named Boaz.' 'May the Lord bless him!' Naomi told her daughter-in-law. 'He is showing his kindness to us as well as to your dead husband. That man is one of our closest relatives, one of our family redeemers'!"

UNDERSTANDING THE PASSAGE

At the beginning of this story, Naomi went through a crisis of faith. She was a woman who strongly believed in God and served him faithfully. She often talked about her faith and shared stories she had grown up hearing, which influenced Ruth to turn away from her own family's beliefs and trust in Naomi's God.

But everything changed when Naomi lost her husband and her precious sons. The stories she told with such conviction were now a thing of the past. The God she once believed in and spoke so highly of had, in her mind, betrayed her. But in today's passage of Scripture, we see her heart change.

If you notice in this passage, Naomi's tone seems different. Although she is not speaking with certainty or full confidence in God's provision, her heart appears to be softening. Even though her sorrow has not lifted, she enthusiastically blesses Boaz and acknowledges his kindness, not only toward Ruth but also toward their family legacy. Receiving this provision may be the first moment Naomi entertains the idea that God hasn't abandoned her after all.

We often find our way back to faith through small, unexpected moments that help us push past our doubts and reconsider the thoughts that caused us to pull away. It can be a conversation or an act of kindness. It may be a glimpse of something we didn't expect. Naomi's losses caused her to question the goodness and faithfulness of God. As a result, she distanced herself from her faith and from the God she had once trusted. But something in this moment stirred Naomi's heart. Boaz's kindness doesn't fix everything, but it does offer her a glimpse of hope, and slowly, she returned to the bedrock of her faith.

This passage shows us how God continues to move, even in the middle of a crisis when our faith is fragile. His presence remains faithful and unwavering, despite our questions and doubts. God doesn't wait until we figure it out; instead, he meets us right where we are, even in the middle of our struggle. He gently nudges us to change our perception, one small moment at a time. Naomi doesn't recognize it at first, but God is already orchestrating their redemption.

REFLECTION QUESTIONS

- What does Naomi's shift in tone reveal about the beginning stages of returning to faith? How might you recognize a similar shift in your own life?

- Describe a moment when God was working behind the scenes before you could see it. How did that realization shape your perception of him?

SCRIPTURE REFLECTION 2
Ruth 3:1-5

"One day, Naomi said to Ruth, 'My daughter, it's time that I found a permanent home for you, so that you will be provided for. Boaz is a close relative of ours, and he's been very kind by letting you gather grain with his young women. Tonight, he will be winnowing barley at the threshing floor. Now do as I tell you—take a bath and put on perfume and dress in your nicest clothes. Then go to the threshing floor, but don't let Boaz see you until he has finished eating and drinking. Be sure to notice where he lies down; then go and uncover his feet and lie down there. He will tell you what to do.' 'I will do everything you say,' Ruth replied."

UNDERSTANDING THE PASSAGE

Naomi's response to Boaz's kindness in Ruth 2 marks a subtle yet meaningful turning point in her story. Although she is still mourning, her outlook begins to change.

She starts to recognize that God might not have abandoned her. That small moment opens the door for a renewed perspective, and now, in today's passage, we see her transition from gentle awareness to active faith.

What Naomi sees in Boaz isn't just provision; she sees the potential for redemption. The same woman who once called herself bitter now begins to make a plan. That alone reveals something powerful. Even if her faith is still vulnerable she begins to hope again. Her willingness to act shows she is no longer frozen by despair. Naomi starts to believe, albeit cautiously, that God may still be at work.

Ruth continued to walk in faith, trusting in Naomi's instructions on what to do and believing in God's provision and favor. Because Ruth could have easily been rejected or misunderstood, this plan was definitely risky. The whole experience had the potential to be incredibly humiliating. Given today's culture, I can hardly wrap my head around Ruth's willingness to follow this plan hatched by her mother-in-law. But she obeyed without hesitation, demonstrating faith that didn't need guarantees. Ruth's courage is compelling, but Naomi's reawakening to her faith might be even more so.

This moment reflects a pattern we see throughout Scripture, where God works in the supernatural, orchestrating his plan and inviting us to trust in his faithfulness. He challenges us to believe he is already at work, long before we recognize it. In Isaiah 43, God speaks to his people who had experienced loss and exile, urging them not to remain focused on what was behind them: "Forget all that—it is nothing compared to what I am going to do, for I am about to do something new. See, I have already begun! Do you not see it?" His message is clear. He wants them to know he is doing something new, even if they can't yet see it. That same truth shows up in Naomi's story. God is already working and already restoring, but she doesn't realize it until her perception of her circumstance begins to change.

God doesn't wait for Naomi to figure it all out. He meets her where she is in the midst of her grief and doubt. Her slow return to faith does not deter God from his plan. Naomi's story illustrates the depth of God's love and mercy towards his children. Even when we may experience a season like Naomi's, God remains faithful and continues to work on our behalf.

Naomi can't control the outcome, but the fact that she makes a plan shows hope is returning to her heart. This shift in perspective is the beginning of Naomi's transformation.

REFLECTION QUESTIONS

- Where in your life have you pulled back from faith because your perception was shaped by pain?

- What does Isaiah 43:18–19 reveal about how God works during seasons of loss or uncertainty?

FAITH IN ACTION

1. **What situation in your life** may be causing you to feel stuck in your faith or feel God is distant?

2. **Using Naomi's story as a guide**, write down what comes to mind when you ponder the goodness of God in your life. Be honest! It really is okay. Ask yourself: *What do I believe about God in the midst of my current situation, and what do I believe about myself?*

3. **If any negative thoughts** were written above, are they grounded in truth, or are they being shaped by fear, disappointment, past hurt, or shame?

4. **If you were to filter these same circumstances** through the truth of God's Word and his unconditional love and faithfulness, what would shift?

5. **As you identify distorted or incomplete thoughts**, take time to challenge them. What scriptures speak to that place of doubt? What has God already done that shows he is still present?

6. **Write out these Scriptures**

    Proverbs 3:5–6

Psalm 34:17–18

Psalm 121:1–2

James 1:5

- How do these verses help reframe your perception and strengthen your faith?

Replacing false or fear-based thoughts with truth is a process that starts with becoming aware of them and then paying attention to them. Write a simple statement grounded in truth that you can rely upon when old thoughts resurface.

SEEING THE BIGGER PICTURE
Naomi's story reveals how easily our pain, both past and present, can distort our perception of God and lead us into a faith crisis. One of the biggest challenges in managing our hardships and unwanted circumstances is our perspective on them. In the story of Ruth and Naomi, we gain a clear understanding of the profound impact our thoughts and beliefs have on our perceptions of what is happening around us. Naomi lost her ability to see things through the lens of what she knew to be true about God. Her pain took over, and when she took an account of all her losses, she concluded she must have been disqualified from the goodness of God. She failed to understand her grief, though warranted, was for only a season, and God had not abandoned her; he was with her the entire time, orchestrating an eternal plan not only for her life but for all of our lives, as you will see when you read the conclusion of her story!

CLOSING THOUGHT
I often tell my clients we can only control ourselves. When we have a circumstance where the outcome is beyond our control, we shouldn't lose hope because we do have some control. It may not be in how the situation will turn out, but we can control how we perceive the result. When we choose to view our suffering through the lens of Christ,

things look different. Life looks different. This difference lies within the power of perception. Naomi did not instantly feel whole again, but her perception realigned with what she knew to be true about God. That small shift created space for hope. Sometimes the work God is doing starts with a decisive change in how we choose to see and interpret what is happening. That choice, my friend, is something we can control!

CLOSING PRAYER

Father, thank you for loving me unconditionally! Thank you, Jesus, for the blood you shed on the cross for my redemption. Please forgive me for doubting you. I confess that waiting is hard and trusting you when I cannot see the outcome is difficult. Help me to step forward in faith, knowing you are leading me, even when the path is unclear. Show me the thoughts I have that do not align with your Word and help me to see things from your perspective. When doubt creeps in, remind me that your plans for me are good.

In Jesus' name,
Amen

Day Four
Seeing Clearly—Aligning Our Mental Filter with God's Truth

Have you looked back at something that had happened in your life and realized things were not exactly as they had seemed? Hindsight truly is 20/20. In the rearview mirror, the picture is much clearer, and that clarity reveals the incredible impact perception has on our outlook. We often draw conclusions that are not based on facts. The rearview mirror brings clarity we did not have in the moment.

We now have the benefit of seeing Ruth and Naomi's story in that rearview mirror. They did not know how their story would unfold, but we do.

Ruth and Naomi's story offers a deeper insight into how our perception of God can realign, even when our faith is uncertain. Today, we'll continue to follow Ruth's story and see what happens when we choose to view life through the lens of faith rather than fear.

SCRIPTURE REFLECTION 1
Ruth 3:6–11
"So Ruth went down to the threshing floor that night and followed the instructions of her mother-in-law. After Boaz had finished eating and drinking and was in good spirits, he lay down at the far end of the pile of grain and went to sleep. Then Ruth came quietly, uncovered his feet, and lay down. Around midnight, Boaz suddenly woke up and turned over. He was surprised to find a woman lying at his feet! 'Who are you?' he asked. 'I am your servant, Ruth,' she replied. 'Spread the corner of your covering over me, for you are my family redeemer'."

UNDERSTANDING THE PASSAGE
On Day Three, we observed Naomi's perspective change from feeling paralyzed by hopelessness to taking a step forward in faith, while Ruth responded by putting that plan into action. Naomi's move toward faith created an opportunity for Ruth to respond with bravery and trust. As we mentioned yesterday, Ruth's act of obedience required courage. Ruth was a widow and a foreigner. She was a woman in a vulnerable situation

with no guarantee of how Boaz would respond. Still, she chose to act in faith. Her obedience was not based on certainty. She trusted both Naomi's wisdom and God's provision.

This part of the story highlights the difference between Naomi's and Ruth's mental filters. Naomi saw her losses as a sign that nothing good would happen. Ruth, though grieving too, saw potential. Her filter wasn't clouded by fear or shame. Her strong faith cleared her perspective.

Boaz responded exactly as Naomi had hoped. He did not misunderstand Ruth's actions or look down on her situation. Instead, he respected her integrity and recognized her loyalty to Naomi and to God.

Ruth didn't let insecurity or doubt hold her back with fear; instead, she moved into the next chapter of her story trusting in God's provision. Ruth believed deep down that God was working, even though she couldn't see it.

When we begin to see as God sees, our perception pivots away from fear and moves toward faith. With this shift, we stop expecting rejection and start anticipating provision. We stop assuming defeat and start walking in the confidence of God.

REFLECTION QUESTIONS

- How does Ruth's faith challenge your view of what it means to take a bold step forward?

- In what areas might fear or insecurity be shaping your perception of what God is doing?

SCRIPTURE REFLECTION 2

Matthew 6:22–23

"Your eye is like a lamp that provides light for your body. When your eye is healthy, your whole body is filled with light. But when your eye is unhealthy, your whole body is filled with darkness. And if the light you think you have is actually darkness, how deep that darkness is!"

UNDERSTANDING THE PASSAGE

Jesus spoke these words during his Sermon on the Mount. He challenged the religious leaders' view of righteousness, which was deeply rooted in their legalistic beliefs and expressed through their highly controlled actions. In this passage, he uses the metaphor of our "eye" being like a lamp. Through this metaphor, Jesus directly addresses how perception influences our understanding of what is truly happening in our lives.

This is a clear example of the way mental filters influence our thinking. Jesus explains how a distorted mental filter can distort our view of the truth. When our perception is based on a false narrative about God's ability to intervene, we become disillusioned or, like Naomi, we grow bitter. Naomi's filter was warped by so much loss that her view of God became distorted, making her resentful and hopeless about what the future held.

Ruth's filter, on the other hand, remained unaffected by her grief, so she was able to see things more clearly. One could argue that Ruth had not experienced the same level of loss as Naomi, so it was easier for her to lean into her faith. While this is certainly plausible, it does not diminish the impact perception has on our lives. Regardless of what Ruth did or did not experience, she made the <u>choice</u> to surrender, and in time, so did Naomi. Naomi had to make a different kind of choice.

In the middle of her sorrow and crisis in faith, she chose to move forward in spite of her bitter outlook and complicated feelings of grief. This movement past her feelings is significant. When she stepped forward, her perception of God's provision changed to align with her faith.

Jesus knows how much our view of the world impacts how we live in it. When we take our eyes off the true nature of God and his promises to focus only on our pain, we are no longer able to see as God sees. Our vision becomes clouded by our filter that has been altered by heartache and suffering. If we expect pain, we'll miss his provision. If we expect rejection, we won't see redemption unfolding. But when we allow God to clear our vision and reshape how we see, even the darkest seasons start to look different.

REFLECTION QUESTIONS

- According to Jesus, what happens when our "eye" (spiritual perception) is clouded?

- Where in your life might your perspective need to be cleansed or reshaped by God's truth?

FAITH IN ACTION
1. **Spend a few minutes reflecting** on these questions in your journal:
- What situation in your life feels confusing or uncertain right now?

- Determine if your filter is lined with fear, shame, disappointment, or past hurts. Ask yourself if your faulty mental filter is distorting your perception of your current situation.

- What would it look like to view it through a filter of truth instead?

2. **Write out these verses:**

   Ruth 3:11

   Matthew 6:22

3. **Choose one distorted or fear-based thought** you've held and challenge it with the truth of these two Scriptures. Write a new statement of truth that is rooted in God's faithfulness. For example:

>   **Old belief:** "This will never get better."
>
>   **New truth:** "God is always working, even when I can't see it." (Ruth 3:11, Matthew 6:22).

>   Repeat this truth every time doubt creeps into your mind.

SEEING THE BIGGER PICTURE

Naomi's story illustrates how pain can cloud our perception, while Ruth's story shows us how faith can clear our vision. What seemed like a dead end was actually the start of something new. God was crafting a plan that wasn't obvious in their current situation. From all outward signs, it looked as if God had abandoned them. But we know He did not leave them alone. Instead, He was working behind the scenes for their benefit. His larger plan becomes clear to us now because we know the final outcome.

Ruth didn't know how things would end, but she trusted in God anyway. Because she stepped forward in faith, Naomi was able to gradually see God working, and as a result, she changed the narrative in her mind. When she believed a different story was being written, her perception of God and her circumstance transformed.

Ruth chose faith from the beginning, but many of us respond more like Naomi by letting our heartache and suffering take the lead. Yet even in a crisis of faith, God continues to work. When we pause long enough to notice him, especially in the small things, we, like Naomi, can change course and choose to move forward in faith, even when it's hard. Our perception will shift, our feelings will follow, and a new narrative will unfold.

CLOSING THOUGHT

God is always making a way even when we don't yet see it. When we allow him to reshape our perception, our thoughts will pivot, our feelings will change, and a different story will emerge.

CLOSING PRAYER

Father, thank you for not leaving me, especially when I have doubted your plan. Please help me see things as you do. Give me the courage to step forward in faith like Ruth and Naomi. Let your light fill the places that feel dark. Thank you, Lord, for your goodness and mercy, and for giving me the strength to keep moving forward despite my heartache.

In Jesus' name,
Amen.

Day Five
The Kinsman Redeemer—A Picture of Christ's Redemption

We have spent this week exploring how perception shapes our experiences. We have gained an understanding of the impact of top-down processing and learned how a damaged mental filter can alter our perspective on everything. We discussed how expectations influence our faith and how uncertainty can lead us into a faith crisis, challenging our trust in God. As we conclude this week, we will focus on Boaz, the kinsman redeemer. His role in Ruth's story reveals a much broader story. It reflects the greater redemption we receive through Christ.

Boaz doesn't just offer a temporary fix or a kind gesture. When everything seems lost, he steps into Ruth and Naomi's lives and secures a future they never could have imagined. Similarly, Jesus enters our brokenness. Like Boaz, he steps into our lives and secures our future. Jesus not only restores the broken and fractured pieces grief and hardships have stolen from us, but he also gives us hope and brings purpose to our pain.

This part of Ruth and Naomi's story foreshadows the redemption Christ brings to us through his death and resurrection. Understanding this kind of redemption changes how we see our circumstances, both past and present. Redemption gives us hope. It reminds us that God is working out a plan even when we don't see it or feel it.

SCRIPTURE REFLECTION 1
Ruth 4:9–10
"Then Boaz said to the elders and to the crowd standing around, 'You are witnesses that today I have bought from Naomi all the property of Elimelech, Kilion, and Mahlon. And with the land I have acquired, Ruth, the Moabite widow of Mahlon, to be my wife. This way she can have a son to carry on the family name of her dead husband and to inherit the family property here in his hometown. You are all witnesses today'."

UNDERSTANDING THE PASSAGE
To grasp the full weight of this moment, take time to read Ruth 4:1–10. These verses highlight Boaz's act of redemption, but the entire passage also reveals the legal, cultural,

and spiritual significance behind it. We see God's faithfulness woven through every detail.

In ancient Israel, a kinsman redeemer carried the responsibility of preserving a family's name and inheritance when a family faced loss, especially the loss of a husband. If a man died without children, the redeemer would marry the widow so she could bear a child, and that child would carry on the family name and keep the land within the family. This act was not only a legal responsibility, but it was a deeply personal act of loyalty. When Naomi's closest relative declined the role of kinsman redeemer, Boaz stepped into this role with integrity and pride by publicly claiming Ruth as his wife, thereby restoring her future and preserving the legacy of her late husband's family.

Boaz's actions give us a glimpse into the heart of Christ. Ruth could not change her circumstances on her own. Her future was uncertain, and her options were limited. She needed a redeemer, and Boaz came to her rescue, giving her what she could not obtain on her own, just as Christ rescues us and gives us what we cannot give ourselves.

Christ redeems our shame and restores everything that has been broken by calling us his own. Life may sometimes feel uncertain, but our future is already secure through the redemptive blood of Christ. The story of Ruth and Boaz didn't end with their marriage. Through their son Obed came Jesse, and through Jesse came David. From David's line, Jesus was born. God was creating a much bigger story than Ruth or Naomi could see. Their faith became part of a plan that would bring redemption to all of us.

REFLECTION QUESTIONS

- What does Boaz's willingness to redeem Ruth reveal about his character, and what does it teach us about Christ's love?

- In what areas of your life do you need to trust that Christ has already redeemed what feels broken or uncertain?

SCRIPTURE REFLECTION 2

Ephesians 1:7–8

"He is so rich in kindness and grace that he purchased our freedom with the blood of his Son and forgave our sins. He has showered his kindness on us, along with all wisdom and understanding."

UNDERSTANDING THE PASSAGE

Paul wrote these words to believers in Ephesus to help them understand their identity in Christ. Their worth no longer depended on their past or the values of the surrounding culture because their worth was in Christ.

Knowing we are fully redeemed, chosen, cleansed, and secured through Christ shapes how we navigate tough seasons. Redemption doesn't erase our pain, but it reframes it. Instead of focusing on what has been taken, we start to notice what has been given to us through Christ. He offers us unconditional love, grace, wisdom, strength, supernatural peace, and his faithfulness to always be by our side, working and interceding for us.

As we begin to see ourselves through the lens of redemption, shame loses its influence. Fear begins to fade. Circumstances may remain unresolved, but we carry them differently when we know who we belong to.

REFLECTION QUESTIONS

- How does knowing Christ has redeemed you change the way you see yourself? What is one practical way you can remind yourself daily that you are redeemed and treasured by God?

- How does understanding redemption deepen your trust in God during seasons of uncertainty?

FAITH IN ACTION

1. **Up until now,** how has your past shaped the way you perceive your value?

2. **Are there areas you struggle to believe** you are fully redeemed and treasured by God?

3. **Write out these Scriptures**:

    Ephesians 1:7

    2 Corinthians 5:17

    1 Peter 2:9

    Jeremiah 29:11

4. **Reflect on the truth of these four verses.** I am fully redeemed by Christ (Ephesians 1:7). My past does not define my future (2 Corinthians 5:17). I am valuable and chosen by God (1 Peter 2:9). I do not have to fear what is ahead because God has secured my future (Jeremiah 29:11). When fear rises or old thoughts return, pause and speak this phrase over yourself: "I am redeemed. My past does not define me. God is writing a bigger story."

- With those truths in mind, name one way you can shift your focus from your past mistakes to Christ's redemption.

- How might this shift bring peace and confidence? When you feel lost, unworthy, or abandoned, remind yourself of these truths:

SEEING THE BIGGER PICTURE

Naomi believed her story had ended in loss. But in the background, God was telling a new story. Ruth's faith and Boaz's obedience led to the birth of Obed, who became the grandfather of King David. Through David's line came the Savior of the world. God saw what they could not.

Throughout this week, we've seen how our perception can be shaped by pain, fear, or past disappointments. But we've also seen how one small step of faith can open the door to something new. Redemption isn't only about being rescued from our pain. It is also an invitation into a story much bigger than we ever imagined.

God continues working, even when all we see is the devastation and the pain of that cup we never wanted to drink. In the midst of our heartache, he is there, and his presence remains a steady force that keeps us anchored. He is both the author and the finisher. Every part of our lives, even the painful ones, is woven into a bigger story. When we begin to see his hand moving even in the smallest ways, our hope is renewed. And hope in him changes everything.

CLOSING THOUGHT

Redemption is not only about rescue. It is about restoration. It is about being seen, valued, and claimed by God. When we believe this, we stop striving and begin to rest. We stop questioning whether we are forgotten and start walking in the confidence that we are deeply known and fully loved.

CLOSING PRAYER

Thank you, Jesus, for the blood you shed on the cross for me. Thank you for redeeming me and making me whole. I need your strength to keep moving forward and resist the lies that try to tell me I am unworthy. Help me walk in faith and trust that you have a plan. I need your peace to lift me above the storm and give me strength when I feel weak. Thank you for your new mercies each morning and for always staying faithful to your promises.

In Jesus' name,
Amen.

WEEK THREE
GROUP DISCUSSION

Begin by watching the Week Three video together. Afterward, ask the group, "What stood out to you most from the video?"

After one or two participants have shared, take time to review last week's study. As a group, flip through each day's reading, briefly noting the Reflection Questions and Faith in Action prompts. Allow time for participants to share their responses to each prompt. If you finish early, use the Group Discussion Questions below to encourage deeper connection.

1. How does Ruth's story invite people to look at difficult circumstances through a different lens?

2. In what ways can challenging seasons cloud a person's thinking, and how might Naomi's experience offer a model for trusting God in those moments?

3. What does Ruth's example teach about taking steps of faith when outcomes aren't yet visible?

4. How do Isaiah 55:8–9 and God's "higher ways" shape the way we understand uncertainty or unanswered questions?

5. What is one practice or habit that helps you notice God's work in your life, especially when it's not obvious?

Week Four

Drinking The Cup Of Shame

I am so glad you're here as we continue this journey together. Grab a cup of coffee, get comfortable, and let's have an honest conversation about shame. Shame is something we don't talk about much, but it lurks in the shadows, influencing many of our thoughts, beliefs, choices, and actions.

Without us even realizing it, shame can have a huge impact on our lives. Shame is a powerful force that influences our identity, distorts our self-worth, and alters our perception of ourselves. Shame is not the same as guilt. Unlike shame, guilt points to something we've done wrong and can be resolved through repentance, but shame is much deeper. It goes beyond us making a mistake; it insists we are a mistake. It proclaims we are damaged and defective at our core. Shame can subtly whisper or overtly shout accusations, telling us we are unlovable and insignificant, trying to convince us we are beyond repair. If we don't confront these lies, they take root and establish a stronghold in our minds. Over time, they impact our decision-making, both in our faith and in our relationships.

Shame is a deeply held belief rooted in the idea we are broken, damaged, or not good enough. Feelings of shame often take hold early in life, perhaps through something spoken over us as children, an experience of rejection, betrayal, or loss of innocence. Over time, these seeds of shame grow as we subconsciously search for evidence to confirm the lie that tells us we are not good enough. When we believe these lies, the enemy uses feelings of shame to distort our perception of our identity, making it difficult to see ourselves through the lens of God's truth.

The stories of Leah and Rachel in the Book of Genesis provide a glimpse into the destructive power of shame. Leah longed for love and acceptance but was met with rejection by her husband, while Rachel, though loved, battled feelings of inadequacy due to her inability to bear children. Both sisters allowed their circumstances to define their worth. Neither of them could see their value as children of God.

Their pain is relatable. At some point, we all experience these feelings. Personally, there have been many occasions where I, like Leah, have felt unseen and unwanted. Like Rachel, I have had times when I felt inadequate or not good enough.

But God does not leave us in our shame. His truth tells us we are fearfully and wonderfully made; we are chosen; and we belong to him. This week, we will look at how the enemy's lies evoke feelings of shame. We will learn how to replace those lies with the truth of God's redeeming love. We will also learn how to embrace the identity God has given us. It's time to break free from the weight of shame and step into the healing and freedom found in Christ. I am honored to walk this journey with you.

Day One
When Shame Shapes Our Identity

Now that we understand how shame operates and the lies it tries to tell us, it's time to see how these dynamics unfold in the lives of two sisters, Rachel and Leah. Today, we're stepping into the story of Leah, a woman whose deepest longing was to be loved and chosen. I find her story so relatable because I think we've all felt what she felt at some point, overlooked, unwanted, and not quite enough.

Her story shows us what happens when we allow our circumstances and the opinions of others to define our worth. But it also reveals a powerful turning point, the moment when she stopped seeking validation from people and began to find her identity in God. As we walk through her journey together, I want you to ask yourself: *Where have I been looking for worth?* And what would it look like to anchor my identity in God's truth instead?

SCRIPTURE REFLECTION 1
Genesis 29:31-35
"When the Lord saw that Leah was unloved, he enabled her to have children, but Rachel could not conceive. So Leah became pregnant and gave birth to a son. She named him Reuben, for she said, 'The Lord has noticed my misery, and now my husband will love me.' She soon became pregnant again and gave birth to another son. She named him Simeon, for she said, 'The Lord heard that I was unloved and has given me another son.' Then she became pregnant a third time and gave birth to another son. She named him Levi, for she said, 'Surely this time my husband will feel affection for me, since I have given him three sons!' Once again, Leah became pregnant and gave birth to another son. She named him Judah, for she said, 'Now I will praise the Lord!' And then she stopped having children."

UNDERSTANDING THE PASSAGE
Leah's story is part of a larger narrative found in Genesis 29:15-35. If you would like to read the full story, take some time to explore the entire passage.

Laban was Jacob's uncle, the father of Leah and Rachel. When Jacob came to stay with Laban, Jacob fell in love with Rachel and agreed to work seven years to marry her. But on the wedding night, Laban deceived Jacob and gave him Leah instead of Rachel. A week later, Jacob also married Rachel, but it cost him another seven years of work. That moment set the stage for years of tension between the sisters. This deception created deep emotional wounds and lifelong rivalry between the two of them.

This family's story is marked by comparison. Leah was able to bear children, but she was not fully loved by Jacob. Leah knew Rachel was the one he truly loved, and she desperately wanted to experience the same affection. Rachel, though deeply loved by Jacob, could not give him any children. She wanted nothing more than to bear children like her sister. Her empty womb left her feeling broken. Both women experienced shame. Leah believed she had no real value because she felt unwanted, and Rachel believed she was damaged because she felt she was not enough. Their struggles highlight how shame can take over, distorting perception and keeping us trapped in cycles of striving and comparison.

Leah's story reveals the deep emotional wounds caused by shame. She believed that lacking the love and affection she desired from her husband meant she was worthless compared to her sister. Even though she didn't have her sister's beauty, she was able to bear children, and with each one, she sought validation from Jacob. She hoped that giving him children would turn into the love she so longed for from her husband. But with each birth, she did not receive the love she yearned for, so she kept believing she was not good enough. What Leah failed to see was her true value and identity were never based on Jacob's love and approval; instead, her worth was defined by God. This passage highlights the power of shame and how deeply it can root itself into our identity. Leah's belief that her husband did not love her dictated her feelings and caused her to resent her sister. She sought validation through her ability to have children rather than finding her worth in God. However, she did experience a change in her perception when Judah was born. Shortly after his birth, she proclaimed, "Now I will praise the Lord." We can infer from these words that Leah stopped striving for the affection of others and instead looked to God to fulfill her heart's desire for love.

The shift she made in her perception of what defined her changed everything. When she decided to be thankful for the blessing of her children, she seemed to finally embrace the joy of giving birth and raising her children. When we stop defining ourselves by human standards and start seeing ourselves through God's eyes, shame begins to lose its power. Leah's story shows our value isn't based on how others see us but on the unchanging love of our Creator and Redeemer.

REFLECTION QUESTIONS

- In what ways have you sought approval or acceptance from others rather than looking to God for your sense of value and worth?

- How does Leah's shift in perspective challenge you to trust God to meet your needs instead of focusing on your circumstances?

SCRIPTURE REFLECTION 2

Isaiah 54:4-5

"Do not be afraid; you will not be put to shame. Do not fear disgrace; you will not be humiliated. You will forget the shame of your youth and remember no more the reproach of your widowhood. For your Maker is your husband—the Lord Almighty is his name—the Holy One of Israel is your Redeemer; he is called the God of all the earth."

UNDERSTANDING THE PASSAGE

This passage was written to the Israelites during a time of exile, when they were in a state of despair. They had experienced significant loss and humiliation, which left many of them feeling discouraged and broken, but God spoke a word of restoration, assuring them shame would not have the final say in their lives. He promised renewal and redemption over their past failures and suffering. God wanted to confirm they were not defined by their past but by his redeeming love.

When Isaiah talks about widows in this passage, his intention is both literal and symbolic. He wants the reader to fully grasp the depth of the Israelites' feelings of loss, rejection, and especially disgrace. Last week, we talked about the devastation that fell upon women who suffered the loss of their husbands. We learned being a widow in their culture meant financial ruin and the loss of any kind of social status. They were unprotected and had to fend for themselves.

Drinking The Cup You Are Served

In this passage, God speaks to Israel as a forsaken people by using the imagery of a widow. He uses this picture to describe their feelings of abandonment and shame. He assures them they are neither worthless nor forgotten by their Redeemer. He is the one who will restore what was lost, and he will make them whole again. This promise extends beyond Israel's exile to all of us who carry the weight of shame. These words of God, spoken by Isaiah, make it clear God claims us as his own, and through him, we have purpose and value, no matter how rejected, forgotten, or unworthy we may feel.

Unlike human rejection, this declaration in Isaiah 54 roots our worth in God's unwavering love, not in how others see us or even how we see ourselves. God calls himself our Redeemer, the one who restores what was lost and who makes us whole again. He removes the shame and replaces it with honor and transforms our brokenness into beauty.

Just as Leah found her value in praising God rather than seeking human approval, we can do the same. When we anchor our beliefs in the truth of God's Word, we have a clear understanding of who we are in Christ.

Our past mistakes, the pain we have suffered, and the rejections we have experienced do not determine who we are. Our identity is in Christ alone. Through Christ's blood shed on the cross, he cleanses and redeems us from all sin, forever removing every blemish or stain we think we carry. When we receive his forgiveness and agree with God that the penalty for our sin is "paid in full," we can finally walk in truth and freedom from the shame that once kept us bound.

REFLECTION QUESTIONS

- How does knowing God as your Redeemer change the way you view your past mistakes and struggles?

- How does acknowledging the lies that cause you to feel shame change your relationship with Christ?

FAITH IN ACTION

To break free from shame-based thoughts and beliefs takes work on our part. Sadly, strongholds do not automatically disappear when we simply become aware of them. We must actively participate in challenging the lies the enemy tries to tell us.

Here are two steps to begin the process of breaking free from shame-based thinking:

1. **Identify and Challenge Shame-Based Thoughts.** Because shame lurks in the background, disguising itself as truth, it is vital you learn to recognize the beliefs and patterns of thought that promote your feelings of shame and drive your actions and behaviors. The first step in overcoming shame is to identify the thoughts produced by shame and challenge their validity:

- What does your shame tell you about yourself?

- Is this thought rooted in truth or based on past experiences/lies?

- Would God agree with this thought about you?

    For example:
    Shame's Lie: "I am unlovable."
    Truth from Scripture: "I have loved you with an everlasting love" (Jeremiah 31:3).

2. **Identify how Shame plays a role** in your actions and behaviors. Shame doesn't just stay in our minds; it affects how we interact with others. Like Leah and Rachel, it can fuel jealousy, comparison, and even perfectionism. Take a moment to reflect on your behaviors:

- Do you find yourself striving for approval to feel valuable?

- Do you withdraw from relationships to avoid rejection? Or do you blame others to avoid confronting feelings of inadequacy?

Recognizing how shame influences our responses allows us to break unhealthy patterns and replace them with truth-driven behaviors. Instead of striving for approval, we can rest in God's love. Instead of comparing, we can embrace our unique worth in Christ.

3. **Putting It into Practice:**
- Write down one shame-based thought you've believed about yourself.

- Find one Bible verse to challenge this thought and meditate on it this week.

    For example:
    Shame's Lie: "I am not worthy of love."
    Truth from Scripture: "But God demonstrates his own love for us in this: While we were still sinners, Christ died for us" (Romans 5:8).

    Shame's Lie: "My past mistakes will always define me."
    Truth from Scripture: "If anyone is in Christ, the new creation has come: The old has gone, the new is here!" (2 Corinthians 5:17)

    Shame's Lie: "I am all alone in my struggles."
    Truth from Scripture: "Never will I leave you; never will I forsake you" (Hebrews 13:5).

    Shame's Lie: "I am too broken to be used by God."
    Truth from Scripture: "My grace is sufficient for you, for my power is made perfect in weakness" (2 Corinthians 12:9).

    Shame's Lie: "I will never be enough."
    Truth from Scripture: "You are God's masterpiece, created in Christ Jesus for good works" (Ephesians 2:10).

This exercise will help you reshape your perspective and see yourself through God's eyes, rather than through the lens of shame.

SEEING THE BIGGER PICTURE

Shame tells us we are unworthy, but as believers in Christ, we can refuse to listen to its voice. Because Christ shed his redeeming blood on the cross for us, we are called "redeemed." The stain of our sin is gone forever. Out of God's deep love for us, he has forgotten our sin as "far as the east is from the west" (Psalm 103:12).

But because of what we have done or what has been done to us, shame would have us believe otherwise. When we fail to challenge false beliefs steeped in shame, it roots itself deep into our belief system, shaping how we think, feel, and behave, influencing the choices we make and how we interact with others.

So at its core, shame is built on lies and these lies taint our mental filter, distorting our thoughts and beliefs about who we are. Due to this skewed self-perception, we develop behaviors that attempt to conceal or compensate for it. We may shift blame to avoid exposure, overcompensate by striving for perfection, or completely withdraw in fear, believing we are inherently flawed. These behaviors create dysfunction in our relationships.

We see this dysfunction in the relationship between Leah and her sister Rachel. Both were consumed with what the other had, so they failed to recognize their own worth and value. Jealousy and comparison robbed them of a relationship they could have shared. Neither of them was able to fully embrace their God-given gifts. Although they were different, each was given something with its own unique beauty.

When we view ourselves and our circumstances through a filter damaged by shame, we struggle to accept God's love and redemption. A distorted perception can lead us to mask our true selves. We cover up what we think needs to be hidden. We hide behind things like perfectionism or blame, which often lead to insecurity and comparison, reinforcing false beliefs about our worth.

However, there is good news! God promises us freedom from shame. When we realign our perception with his Word, we begin to see ourselves through the lens of redemption and grace, not through the lies of shame. Through the power of the Holy Spirit living within us, the lies that have shaped our identity can be uprooted and replaced with the promises of God.

CLOSING THOUGHT

Shame uses our past experiences, hurts, failures, and the lies we've believed about ourselves to convince us we are damaged goods, unworthy, unloved, and beyond redemption. But God's truth speaks louder. He does not define us by what we've done or what has been done to us. He doesn't listen to what others say about us. Instead, he defines us by who he is. He irreversibly states that our redemption comes through the shed blood of Jesus on the cross.

You are not the sum of your mistakes. You are forgiven and redeemed. You are not unlovable. You are deeply cherished. You are not broken beyond repair. You are made whole in Christ.

God sees you through the lens of restoration, not shame. He calls you chosen, loved, and his own. When shame tries to tell you lies, stand firm in the truth: You are not what shame says you are. You are who God says you are.

CLOSING PRAYER

Dear Lord, today I lay my shame at the foot of your cross. I surrender my thoughts that do not align with the truth of your Word. I want to see myself as you see me. I pray your Word becomes sealed in my mind, giving me the wisdom and courage to rebuke the thoughts that are not from you. Your Word says I have been made new. Help me to walk in this truth every single day. I love you, Father, and I am so thankful to be called worthy and a daughter of the King, forever redeemed and made new by what you accomplished for me on the Cross!

In Jesus' name,
Amen

Day Two
Breaking the Cycle of Shame

Today, we are going to talk about the cycle of shame, and we will discover how to break the cycle. Many of us have been caught in this cycle without realizing it. It begins with painful experiences and subtle thoughts that make us question our worth. Over time, these moments accumulate, gaining momentum to solidify a false core belief about our worth. These unsolicited lies are what initiate the cycle. When we believe we are not enough, it can lead us to feel inadequate and unlovable. When we feel this way, it has a direct impact on the choices we make and the actions we take. The cycle begins with a lie, which is then reinforced by our feelings and confirmed through our actions. Before we recognize what is happening, shame becomes the filter through which we interpret life. It affects how we make decisions, and it interferes with our relationships.

I know this struggle well. After experiencing the pain of childhood trauma, I carried the weight of shame for years. I thought I was bad, dirty, and unworthy of love. I believed I was damaged at my core and wore my shame like a heavy blanket, trying to cover myself, but it didn't work because I never felt clean. No matter what I did, I couldn't shake or hide the feeling of being damaged beyond repair.

Maybe you've experienced this too. You believe your worth is tied to what you've done or what has been done to you. Perhaps shame has influenced how you interact with others, leading you to seek validation, withdraw in fear, or compare yourself to those around you. That mindset is how shame works: it creates patterns of thought, emotion, and behavior that keep you stuck in feelings of inadequacy.

But here's the truth: Shame does not define you. God does.

Today, we will talk about how comparison often fuels these feelings, making us feel inadequate as we measure our worth against others. We will identify the lies comparison tells us and replace them with the truth of who we are in Christ. You are not meant to live in the shadow of comparison or under the weight of shame. It's time to step into the freedom and identity God has already given you.

SCRIPTURE REFLECTION 1

Genesis 30:1-3

"When Rachel saw that she wasn't having any children for Jacob, she became jealous of her sister. She pleaded with Jacob, 'Give me children, or I'll die!' Then Jacob became furious with Rachel. 'Am I God?' he asked. 'He's the one who has kept you from having children!' Then Rachel told him, 'Take my maid, Bilhah, and sleep with her. She will bear children for me, and through her, I can have a family too'."

UNDERSTANDING THE PASSAGE

Although she was beautiful and deeply loved by Jacob, Rachel struggled with feelings of inadequacy. In ancient culture, a woman's worth and social status were often linked to her ability to bear children. Watching her sister Leah give Jacob multiple sons while she remained barren filled Rachel with jealousy and despair. Instead of trusting God's timing, she tried to take control of her situation by offering her servant, Bilhah, to Jacob as a surrogate.

To fully understand Rachel's struggle, read the entire account in Genesis 29-30. These chapters offer deeper insight into the rivalry between Rachel and Leah, as well as how shame and comparison shaped their lives.

Comparison is a tool the enemy loves to use to make us feel as if we do not measure up. It is one of shame's greatest weapons. It causes us to focus on what we lack instead of recognizing what God has given us. Rachel fell prey to comparison. Her pain over her infertility was valid given the culture of that time, but her response shows how shame distorted her thinking. Instead of mourning her inability to have children and redirecting her thoughts to the gifts she had, she shifted her focus to her sister. This gave way for comparison and jealousy to take root in her heart, leaving her feeling inadequate and bitter. These feelings interfered with her ability to love her sister and her sister's children. Ironically, both Rachel and Leah wanted what the other had, but if the roles were reversed, I bet the outcome would have been the same. The familiar phrases, "we want what we can't have" and "the grass is always greener on the other side," lead us to destructive thoughts and cause us to feel shortchanged.

Like Rachel, we often believe we are not enough. There are many ways shame sets us up to feel this way. We become oversensitive about how we look or what we are capable of doing. There always seems to be someone who can do it better. As Christians, we are notorious for comparing our "spiritual walk" with others, saying to ourselves, *"So-and-so is so much closer to God than I am."* Shame leads us to compare ourselves in ways that only reinforce our feelings of inadequacy. Genesis 30:1-3 reveals the emptiness of comparison. Comparing ourselves to others does not bring peace; it only leads to more striving. Our worth is not defined by what we achieve, what we lack, or how we compare. We will always feel like we fall short when we measure ourselves by these things. True worth comes from being fully known and unconditionally loved by God.

REFLECTION QUESTIONS

- In what areas do you struggle with comparing yourself to others?

- How can you shift your focus from what you lack to the truth of who God says you are?

SCRIPTURE REFLECTION 2
Romans 8:1-2
"So now there is no condemnation for those who belong to Christ Jesus. And because you belong to him, the power of the life-giving Spirit has freed you from the power of sin that leads to death."

UNDERSTANDING THE PASSAGE
Paul wrote these words to new believers in Rome, a group of Jewish and Gentile Christians who were navigating the tension between law and grace. Like us, many of them struggled with guilt and the weight of their past. They were unsure how to fully embrace the freedom Christ had given them. In this passage, Paul assures them they are free from condemnation. He wants them to understand, as believers in Christ, sin no longer has a hold on them, and their past mistakes do not define them.

To fully grasp the power of this passage, it is essential to understand the difference between guilt and shame. Guilt is a conviction of having done something wrong. Guilt is often viewed as a negative thing, but on the contrary, guilt actually leads us to repentance and restoration. Shame is different from guilt. It is not an indicator of making a mistake; it is a warped belief that directly distorts our identity based on who we are, not what we have done. Shame convinces us we are not just guilty of sin, but we are fundamentally unworthy and beyond redemption from our sin. (We will explore the difference between guilt and shame more in-depth on Day 4.) Paul's words in

Romans 8:1-2 directly confront shame by reminding us we are not condemned. In Christ, we are no longer identified by our past, failures, or struggles.

Shame tells us we must try harder to be enough, but Romans 8:1-2 offers us the truth. In Christ, we don't have to earn our worth or prove our value because we have been redeemed and made new in him! Just as Leah and Rachel struggled to see themselves through God's eyes, we, too, can forget our identity is secure in Christ, not in our failures or shortcomings. This passage calls us to stop looking at ourselves through the lens of shame and instead see ourselves through the truth of our redemption.

REFLECTION QUESTIONS

- In what ways have you struggled to embrace the freedom that comes with knowing there is no condemnation in Christ?

- What are some ways you have sought validation outside of God's truth?

FAITH IN ACTION

Below is the first strategy you can use to break free from the cycle of shame:

Strategy One: Recognize the Lie and Replace It with Truth

Set two or three check-ins during the day. Ask yourself, *What have I been thinking about most?* If you notice a shame-filled thought, use a technique called cognitive restructuring to challenge it. This technique involves examining the thought, looking for evidence for and against it, and then creating a more balanced statement rooted in God's Word. For example, if you think, "*I always fail,*" ask yourself, "*Is that true every time?*" Then replace it with, "*I have faced challenges before, but God has helped me grow and persevere.*" Or "*There have been times when I have failed, but that does not make me a failure.*" You can then back this up with Scripture:

Philippians 1:6
"I am sure that God, who began the good work in you, will keep on working in you until the day Jesus Christ comes again."

2 Corinthians 12:9–10
"And He said to me, "My loving-favor is enough for you. When you are weak, My power is strong." So I am very happy to talk about my weaknesses and the many ways I suffer. Then Christ's power can rest on me. For this reason, I am happy in weaknesses, in insults, in hard times, in troubles and in all kinds of suffering for Christ. For when I am weak, then I am strong."

As we consistently practice this cognitive restructuring technique, we begin to dismantle the neural pathways shame has carved in our minds. Each time we replace a lie with God's truth, we weaken shame's grip and create new patterns of thinking rooted in our true identity in Christ. This is not merely positive thinking; rather, it is spiritual warfare fought with the weapon of God's Word. The Holy Spirit empowers us to take every thought captive, and as we rehearse Scripture over the lies of shame, we experience the freedom Christ promised. The transformation may not happen overnight, but with each intentional choice to speak truth over our lives, shame's voice grows quieter and God's voice becomes louder and more clear.

SEEING THE BIGGER PICTURE

Shame is more than a feeling. It is a deep-seated set of beliefs that takes root in our core and distorts how we perceive ourselves. When we are unaware of the grip shame has on us, we often mask it by comparing ourselves to others by looking outward for validation rather than inward to Christ.

Comparison makes us believe our worth is relative, measured against others' success, beauty, or spiritual maturity. But God created us with a unique purpose and value, and no comparison can take that away. In Christ, he accepts us exactly as we are. When we embrace this truth, we stop looking for validation through comparison and instead accept that our true identity is in Christ. We are his, and that is enough.

Yet comparison is just one way shame tries to distort our identity. In the days ahead, we'll explore other strongholds shame builds and discover how Christ's grace breaks every chain.

CLOSING THOUGHT

Rachel and Leah both chased what they thought would make them whole, but neither found lasting peace in what they gained. We can fall into the same pattern, trying to prove our worth or earn the love God has already given to us. True freedom comes when we stop comparing ourselves to others and chasing their approval. It comes when we learn to embrace Christ's unconditional love for us and rest in the beauty we have in Christ.

Tomorrow, we'll discover how shame not only drives us to compare ourselves to others but also tempts us to control our circumstances, and how God's power can demolish even the deepest strongholds in our minds.

CLOSING PRAYER

Dear Lord, thank you for loving me just as I am. Help me to challenge each lie that tries to tell me I am not good enough and unworthy of your love. From your Word, I know I am fearfully and wonderfully made, and the blood you shed for me on the cross has made me new. I need your help to resist thoughts that tempt me to believe otherwise. Please forgive me for allowing myself to believe the lies of the enemy. I trust your Word is true when you said you have made me whole through your redemptive blood, and I am enough! Thank you, Father, for your goodness and mercy in my life, and I praise your Holy name!

In Jesus' name,
Amen

Day Three
Breaking Strongholds

As we move into day three, we will examine how shame further distorts our identity by creating strongholds in our minds. We will also discover why submitting every thought to the authority of Christ is essential.

As we have already discussed, shame is a powerful tool the enemy uses to trap us in self-doubt and feelings of unworthiness. He wants us to believe we are defined by our past, including both our mistakes and how we've been wronged. He tries to convince us that our past hurts and failures disqualify us from redemption. He accomplishes this by spreading many different kinds of lies. Ultimately, his goal is to make us believe we are flawed, broken, not good enough, or even unlovable.

When these lies go unchecked, they build a fortress of false beliefs, called strongholds, in our minds. A stronghold keeps us stuck in unhealthy thought patterns. This kind of thinking gives the enemy a bigger foothold in our minds. A foothold means Satan gains access that allows him to have more control over our thoughts and actions. But Scripture tells us we are not powerless against the enemy or any stronghold within our minds because God has given us divine weapons to tear down strongholds and replace lies with truth.

Today, we will explore what it means to take every thought captive and make it obedient to Christ. We will gain insight into this process and learn how to demolish these false beliefs and unwanted thoughts.

SCRIPTURE REFLECTION 1
2 Corinthians 10:3-5
"We are human, but we don't wage war as humans do. We use God's mighty weapons, not worldly weapons, to knock down the strongholds of human reasoning and to destroy false arguments. We destroy every proud obstacle that keeps people from knowing God. We capture their rebellious thoughts and teach them to obey Christ."

UNDERSTANDING THE PASSAGE

Paul wrote this letter to the Corinthian church to address Spiritual battles in the mind. He introduces the concept of strongholds, which are deeply ingrained patterns of thought that keep people bound in lies from the enemy. At the time, Corinth was a city full of competing worldviews and intellectual pride. It was a culture that celebrated status and promoted the idea of personal freedom. (Sound familiar?) The people of the church were struggling to stay grounded in their faith because they were surrounded by ideas that lacked spiritual truth. Some had even begun to question Paul's authority and started looking to leaders who spoke with confidence but didn't reflect the heart of Christ.

In that environment, Paul aimed to anchor them in a different kind of power, one not based on human wisdom or clever arguments, but on the kind of power that destroys lies and restores the mind. His words speak directly to us today because we also face many of the same challenges the people of Corinth faced. Like them, we are trying to hold onto God's truth in a world that constantly presents us with counterfeit versions. Paul recognized how easily we can become entangled in thought patterns that seem true but are actually strongholds, the mental footholds the enemy uses to keep us trapped.

Strongholds are fortresses of lies that keep us stuck in beliefs inconsistent with God's truth. These lies can take many forms. Sometimes they're about ourselves—*I'm worthless, I'm too broken, I'm beyond forgiveness.* Sometimes they're about others—*People can't be trusted, everyone will hurt me, I have to protect myself at all costs.* And sometimes, they're even about God himself—*he doesn't really care about me, he's holding out on me, he's punishing me for my past.* Regardless of where they land, strongholds keep us from experiencing the freedom and truth God offers. Paul shows us a way to break free from these lies and provides a path that can lead us out of shame, fear, bitterness, and doubt.

He explains we have been given supernatural power to break down strongholds and demolish the lies the enemy uses to deceive us. What Paul makes clear is this: we are not powerless. We have been equipped to fight with different weapons. Through the power of the Holy Spirit living within us, we have been given supernatural weapons to fight against the lies of the enemy and to set our minds free. We have the ability to cleanse our mental filter and reshape the distorted thoughts we have believed about ourselves, about others, and about God to correctly align them with his truth. In the

Bible, we are told our worth and value come directly from God. We're reminded God is good, he is for us, and his love never fails.

Taking every thought captive means identifying the thoughts and false beliefs that contradict God's Word. Once identified, these thoughts and beliefs can be measured against Scripture and replaced with God's unchanging truth. Instead of accepting shame's narrative, we replace it with God's promises, declaring we are deeply loved and have been redeemed by the cleansing blood of Christ and through him we have been made new. Instead of believing God is distant, we anchor ourselves in the truth that he is near and he is good. Instead of living in fear of others, we remember we are held and protected by a God who goes before us.

Breaking free from destructive thought patterns means showing up and doing the work. We must be intentional in replacing the lies the enemy tells us with the reality of who God is and who we are in Christ. This process requires action. It involves actively recognizing false beliefs, confronting them, and ultimately replacing them with truth. This process does not happen without effort because strongholds have a tight grip on us and do not want to easily let go.

> What makes strongholds so challenging to break, however, is how deeply they take root in our beliefs. Strongholds do not form overnight, nor do they typically break overnight. Because these beliefs are deep-seated, they require time, prayer, and persistence to dismantle.

> Breaking free requires effort and patience. Mastering our thoughts is a lifelong journey. Satan always tries his old tricks with lies, but with persistence, we can gradually overcome the hold these patterns have on us and step into the freedom God offers.

> Though it may take time, don't be discouraged because freedom is within reach, and every step forward makes a difference. We must stay committed and persistent, diligently taking every thought captive. As we do so, strongholds will begin to crumble, paving the way for us to step into the fullness of who God created us to be.

The good news is, as believers, we are not alone; we have the help of the Holy Spirit. The Holy Spirit reveals the root of these lies and gives us the courage and wisdom to replace them with the unshakable foundation of who God says we are, who we truly are, and how he sees those around us.

REFLECTION QUESTIONS

- In what ways does the awareness of God's supernatural power change how you will face the strongholds in your life going forward?

- Paul tells us the weapons we fight with have the divine power to demolish strongholds. What are some spiritual weapons God has given us to combat destructive thought patterns, and how can you begin using them in your daily life?

SCRIPTURE REFLECTION 2
Genesis 30:14–16, 22

"One day during the wheat harvest, Reuben found some mandrakes growing in a field and brought them to his mother, Leah. Rachel begged Leah, 'Please give me some of your son's mandrakes.' But Leah angrily replied, 'Wasn't it enough that you stole my husband? Now will you steal my son's mandrakes, too?' Rachel answered, 'I will let Jacob sleep with you tonight if you give me some of the mandrakes.' So that evening, as Jacob was coming home from the fields, Leah went out to meet him. 'You must come and sleep with me tonight!' she said. 'I have paid for you with some mandrakes that my son found.'....Then God remembered Rachel's plight and answered her prayers by enabling her to have children."

For the full account, read Genesis 30:14–24.

UNDERSTANDING THE PASSAGE
This passage reveals how deeply rooted the strongholds of comparison and insecurity were in Leah and Rachel's lives. Their faulty beliefs not only influenced how they felt about themselves but also shaped their choices. Their rivalry kept increasing. Rachel desperately wanted what Leah had, and Leah longed for Jacob to love her as he loved her sister. Their argument over the mandrakes clearly shows how comparison and jealousy distorted their self-worth and disrupted their ability to have a loving relationship. Rachel, who was unable to have children, believed the mandrakes could help her conceive. Leah, craving Jacob's love, used them as leverage to draw his attention. Both women thought their worth and happiness depended on something they couldn't control. They failed to trust God's plan, and instead, they took matters into their own hands.

Mandrakes were a type of plant found in the Middle East, often associated with fertility and love in ancient cultures. Their roots sometimes resembled human figures, leading people to believe they possessed mystical properties, particularly in aiding with conception. In Rachel's time, infertility was seen as a mark of disgrace, and a woman's worth was primarily measured by her ability to bear children. Given this cultural pressure, it's no surprise Rachel, desperate to conceive, placed her hope in mandrakes. But it was deeply disappointing that she did not trust in God.

We do this, don't we? When life feels out of control and we feel exposed in our inadequacy, we reach for something, anything, that promises to fix what feels broken inside us.

Have you ever tried to fix something on your own because waiting on God felt too uncertain? Have you ever manipulated a situation because you feared surrendering it to him wouldn't produce the results you wanted? The lies shame tells convince us we are nothing without those desired results. For example, some of us might push a relationship forward despite seeing red flags. We ignore them because we believe being alone would mean we are unworthy of love. Or some of us may compare ourselves to someone else's success and overextend ourselves because we fear falling behind will prove we don't measure up.

When God asks us to trust him to work things out, shame often stands in the way of our surrender. When we are focused on specific results, we are tempted to step out of God's plan and take control. We are essentially saying God will not intervene in the way we think he should, meaning we do not trust that he has our best interests at heart.

This kind of thinking is what led Leah and Rachel to step outside of God's plan. Often, when we believe, in our core, we are unseen, forgotten, or unworthy, we allow shame to stand in the way of God's grace and redemption. Can you see how this line of thinking does not align with God's Word?

We may not be chasing mandrakes, but the chase is still the same. We fight to prove our worth, strive to fix what feels broken, and silence the shame that tells us we'll never be enough. We often tell ourselves, *"I'll be okay if I can just fix this. Then no one will have to see how broken I really am."*

In this story, mandrakes symbolize more than just an ancient fertility remedy. They expose how shame fuels our need for control. When circumstances don't change, we take matters into our own hands, convinced we must make something happen. If we don't fix a situation ourselves, we confirm our deepest fear of being unworthy and not enough. Yet, no matter how hard we strive, our actions never truly heal the wounds we carry.

Despite Leah and Rachel's efforts, it was God, not mandrakes, who eventually opened Rachel's womb (Genesis 30:22). This moment in their story reminds us of a powerful truth: Our self-worth cannot be found in what we achieve or control. It is found through complete surrender and acceptance of God's unconditional love. When we fully surrender, we can see our value through his eyes rather than through the lens of a desired outcome. In other words, our value isn't determined by whether our prayers are answered in the way or in the timing we had hoped. It is determined by God's perspective, which is anchored in his love for us, not in our performance or results.

Like Ruth and Naomi's story, when we step back and look at Leah and Rachel's entire journey, we can see God's plan was at work all along. God always saw Rachel, understood her pain, and never forgot about her. He had a plan to give her a child, but more than that he wanted her to find her worth in him and trust that he heard her heart's cries. The same is true for us: we may not understand what's unfolding, but we must let go of control and trust God is sovereign over all our circumstances. Our worth doesn't come from what we do or can fix; it comes from Jesus taking our brokenness and making us new. He declares us worthy and calls us his beloved children.

REFLECTION QUESTIONS

- Have you ever believed having something, whether success, approval, or relationships, would make you feel complete? How does this passage challenge that belief?

- Rachel and Leah wanted something the other had, yet neither felt fully satisfied. What does this teach us about where we should find true fulfillment?

FAITH IN ACTION

Here are two more strategies to help you break free from strongholds. Practice them daily and record your progress in your journal.

Strategy Two: Use A Thought-Stopping Technique

Each time you notice a thought rooted in shame, fear, or hopelessness, mentally say "stop" or picture a red stop sign to interrupt the thought. Then search a Bible app or website for verses tied to that thought (for example, "Bible verses about fear" or "God's love") and choose one that speaks to your situation. Replace the lie with a word of affirmation that aligns with Scripture.

Strategy Three: Use The Rehearsal Technique

When you have aligned yourself with a passage of Scripture, repeat and memorize the verse until it becomes your default way of thinking.

Examples:

- **Thought/Lie:** "I am not good enough." → **Affirmation/Truth:** "I am God's workmanship, created in Christ Jesus to do good works" (Ephesians 2:10).
- **Thought/Lie:** "I will never get through this.: → **Affirmation/Truth:** "I can do all things through Christ who strengthens me" (Philippians 4:13).
- **Thought/Lie:** "I am worthless." → **Affirmation/Truth:** "I praise you because I am fearfully and wonderfully made" (Psalm 139:14).
- **Thought/Lie:** "I will always be stuck in fear." → **Affirmation/Truth:** "For God has not given us a spirit of fear, but of power, love, and a sound mind" (2 Timothy 1:7).

SEEING THE BIGGER PICTURE

As we reflect on the story of Leah and Rachel, we see how they both struggled with self-worth, control, and shame. Their journey highlights how often we place our value in external things, whether success, relationships, or achievements, hoping they will make us feel whole. But in doing so, we are often left feeling empty because these things can never truly define us. God's plan is different. He doesn't call us to earn our worth or heal our brokenness on our own. Instead, he wants us to trust in his perfect timing and sovereignty, knowing he is in control of every situation.

The story of Leah and Rachel ultimately points us to hope. Despite Rachel's longing and Leah's search for validation, God was orchestrating a plan beyond their understanding. His perfect timing was at work, showing his deep care for them throughout their journey. The same is true for us. When we face moments of doubt or feel like our efforts are insufficient, we can remember God is at work behind the scenes. Like Rachel and Leah, we may not see the entire picture now, but we can rest assured God's plan for us is unfolding exactly as it should.

CLOSING THOUGHT

Shame fueled Leah and Rachel's rivalry, which robbed them of a relationship that could have brought them joy and fulfillment. In spite of their poor choices, God's plan was still at work. When we let shame drive our choices, we can rob ourselves of the joy and fulfillment God desires for us. Choose instead to release control, lean into his love, and trust that he is working for your good even when you cannot see it.

CLOSING PRAYER

Dear Lord,

Thank you again for your goodness and mercy. Help me to take every negative and shameful thought captive. Give me discernment to recognize when my thoughts are not from you. Let your Word come alive in my heart and mind, transforming my thoughts to reflect your truth. When I am tempted to give up, empower me with strength and courage through the Holy Spirit to stand firm and fight for what is true.

In Jesus' name,
Amen

Day Four
The Difference Between Guilt and Shame

Today, we'll explore a critical distinction to help us better understand how God works in our lives. It is the difference between guilt and shame. While both are feelings we have all likely experienced, they serve very different purposes.

Guilt, when it's experienced in the right way, can lead us to repentance and healing. It's the feeling that arises when we recognize we've done something wrong, and it calls us to make things right. Shame is much deeper. It not only makes us feel bad about our actions, but it also leads us to believe something is inherently wrong with us. It makes us feel unworthy or unlovable. Shame seeks to define us, while guilt is an opportunity for change.

In today's study, we'll explore how Jesus' grace separates conviction from condemnation. Understanding the difference between the two can help us experience freedom from shame.

SCRIPTURE REFLECTION 1
John 8:10-11
"Then Jesus stood up again and said to the woman, 'Where are your accusers? Didn't even one of them condemn you?' 'No, Lord,' she said. And Jesus said, 'Neither do I. Go and sin no more'."

UNDERSTANDING THE PASSAGE
This passage is deeply meaningful because of both the message Jesus gives the woman and the situation in which it occurs. In John 8:1-11, we learn about a woman caught in adultery, an act punishable by stoning according to Jewish law (Leviticus 20:10). The Pharisees bring the woman before Jesus, hoping to trap him into either enforcing the law or demonstrating mercy. They ask Jesus, *What should we do with her?*

Jesus doesn't answer immediately. Instead, he bends down and writes on the ground. When the Pharisees press him for an answer, he responds, "Let anyone who is without sin cast the first stone." One by one, her accusers leave, and Jesus remains alone with the woman. He then tells her, "Neither do I condemn you; go and sin no more."

It is important to understand the historical context here. The Pharisees are using the woman to test Jesus. Under Mosaic Law, adultery was a serious offense, punishable by stoning. The Pharisees hoped to trap Jesus by forcing him into a decision that would either violate Roman law, which did not allow Jews to carry out capital punishment, or the Law of Moses, which demanded justice.

Instead of answering directly, Jesus wisely separates guilt from shame. He shows us that guilt is the awareness of our wrongdoing, which leads us to repentance, while shame is a falsehood that tells us we're unworthy and beyond redemption. Jesus recognizes the woman's sin but doesn't let it define her. He offers grace, inviting her to turn away from sin without judging her. Jesus doesn't condemn us; instead, he extends grace, guiding us on how to move forward even after we've made mistakes.

Knowing and recognizing the difference between guilt and shame is crucial. Satan wants to keep us trapped in shame so we can't see guilt for what it really is. When guilt becomes entangled with shame, it feels like condemnation. But Christ tells us we are not condemned, so when we feel shame, we know it is not from Christ. In this story, we learn guilt leads us to repentance, not condemnation. To receive healing and forgiveness, it is vital to separate guilt from shame.

REFLECTION QUESTIONS

- How does Jesus' response to the woman differ from the accusations of others?

- Have you ever felt defined by your mistakes? How might this passage shift your perspective?

SCRIPTURE REFLECTION 2
Psalm 103:12
"He has removed our sins as far from us as the east is from the west."

UNDERSTANDING THE PASSAGE

This verse from Psalm 103 beautifully illustrates God's mercy and forgiveness. The psalmist speaks of how God removes our sins completely, as far as the east is from the west, an impossible distance to measure. This image highlights how God not only forgives but also forgets our sins, choosing to no longer hold them against us. When we repent and seek God's forgiveness, He removes our sins from us, never to bring them up again. God's forgetting our sins is essential to understanding the nature of guilt and shame.

The purpose of guilt is to guide us toward repentance and help us recognize our mistakes. When we repent, God washes us clean, meaning our sins are completely erased. Shame, however, tries to make us believe we are forever defined by what we've done. It tells us that we are unworthy, even after we've been forgiven. But God's Word makes it clear: once we are forgiven, our sins are as far from us as possible, and they do not define us.

This verse highlights how bringing our guilt to God in repentance means he no longer holds our sins against us. Instead, he offers grace, and it is this grace that helps us dismantle the lies of shame. We are not who our past mistakes say we are; we are who God says we are: forgiven, loved, and made new.

REFLECTION QUESTIONS

- How does the phrase "as far as the east is from the west" emphasize the permanence of God's forgiveness and the removal of sin?

- How do you personally feel when you read this phrase: "He has removed our sins as far as the east is from the west?"

FAITH IN ACTION

1. **Identify areas where you feel shame:** Take some time to reflect on areas in your life where you have allowed shame to define you. Are there past mistakes or struggles that still feel like they control your thoughts or actions? Write them down and acknowledge how they've shaped your view of yourself.

2. **Bring your guilt to God:** If you're carrying guilt over a specific mistake or sin, bring it to God in prayer. Ask for forgiveness and thank him for his grace. Let go of the weight of guilt, knowing God offers you freedom and healing.

3. **Embrace grace and extend it to others:** As you accept God's grace, allow it to transform how you interact with others. Show grace to those who may be struggling with guilt or shame. Extend forgiveness and compassion, just as Jesus does for us.

SEEING THE BIGGER PICTURE

Understanding the distinction between guilt and shame is crucial for our spiritual growth. When understood properly, guilt serves as a healthy response to wrongdoing, directing us toward repentance and change. It brings us face-to-face with our actions and invites us to make things right. Shame, however, goes beyond guilt. It attempts to define us by our failures, telling us we are unworthy of grace or love. While guilt helps us acknowledge our mistakes and move forward, shame binds us to the past, making it feel impossible to move beyond it.

The passage from Psalm 103:12 beautifully reveals the completeness of God's forgiveness. When God removes our sins, he doesn't simply set them aside or lessen their impact; instead, he completely removes them, never to be remembered again. This passage reflects the ultimate freedom we have in Christ, where sin no longer defines our identity. Jesus' response to the woman caught in adultery echoes this same truth. Grace replaces condemnation, offering us a path to repentance without allowing our past mistakes to shape our future.

In our own lives, we can become entangled in guilt and shame, allowing them to dictate our actions and self-worth. But when we fully understand and willingly receive God's forgiveness, it releases us from the burden of guilt and sets us free from shame. It allows us to see ourselves as he sees us. He sees us as his forgiven children who have been redeemed by his blood. He loves us so much that he gave his life for us. Embracing this truth contradicts the lies of Satan and challenges us to leave behind the weight of shame and to move forward in the freedom God's grace offers.

CLOSING THOUGHT

Understanding the difference between guilt and shame frees us from the weight of self-condemnation. Guilt leads us to repentance, while shame keeps us trapped in a false identity. In God's grace, we find freedom from both, allowing us to walk in the truth of who we are in his eyes.

CLOSING PRAYER

Dear Heavenly Father,
Thank you for your forgiveness of my sins. I am so grateful you shed your blood to cast all of my sin into the sea of forgetfulness, never to be remembered again. Please help me release the lies that tell me I am unworthy of your love and forgiveness. Guide me in embracing your grace and truth, knowing my worth is found in you alone. Thank you for redeeming me and reminding me of your unconditional love. I surrender my shame and self-doubt to you, trusting in your perfect love to heal and restore me. You are holy and worthy to be praised.

In Jesus' name,
Amen.

Day Five
Freedom from Shame — Walking in Redemption

As we conclude this week's study, we will continue to focus on finding freedom from shame and learn to walk in the redemption of Christ by taking every thought captive that does not align with the truth of God's Word. Throughout this week, we have discussed how shame lies about our worth and traps us in the past. We can demolish those lies through the power of the Holy Spirit.

Today, we'll explore how God's grace transforms us by replacing ashes with beauty. We will learn how to walk in the freedom of redemption. Just as Rachel and Leah's lives were marked by shame and comparison, we, too, can fall into the trap of letting shame define us. But in Christ, we have the opportunity to move forward with our God-given identity, free from shame and restored by grace.

SCRIPTURE REFLECTION 1
Isaiah 61:1-3
"The Spirit of the Sovereign Lord is upon me, for the Lord has anointed me to bring good news to the poor. He has sent me to comfort the brokenhearted and to proclaim that captives will be released and prisoners will be freed. He has sent me to tell those who mourn that the time of the Lord's favor has come, and with it, the day of God's anger against their enemies. To all who mourn in Israel, he will give a crown of beauty for ashes, a joyous blessing instead of mourning, festive praise instead of despair. In their righteousness, they will be like great oaks that the Lord has planted for his own glory."

UNDERSTANDING THE PASSAGE
Isaiah 61:1-3 is a prophetic passage that speaks directly about God's redemptive plan for his people. Written during Israel's exile, when they were suffering the consequences of their sin and brokenness, this passage brought hope for the restoration of all they had lost. It promises the coming of a Savior who will bind the brokenhearted, set the captives free, and comfort those who mourn. This Savior, Jesus Christ, fulfills this

prophecy in his life, crucifixion, and resurrection. It is a type and shadow of the story of Christ's redemption, both then and now.

The imagery of beauty replacing ashes makes this passage even more significant. In ancient Israel, ashes symbolized mourning and repentance, a mark of sorrow and shame. Jesus' death and resurrection are the ultimate acts of this transformation, where the ashes of our shame, sin, and death are replaced with the beauty of new life. Jesus took on the weight of our shame at the cross, paying the price so we could walk in freedom. Through his resurrection, he established a way for us to have a personal relationship with him. In that relationship, we can live in joy and peace, regardless of our circumstances. The ashes of our sin are no longer our identity. Christ offers us beauty in its place.

When we think about Rachel and Leah, we see how their lives were marked by comparison and jealousy. Their circumstances were filled with unmet expectations and bitterness. This story reveals how we experience shame and suffer disappointment, even bitterness, when our life is not playing out the way we think it should. However, we learn in this passage God promises to exchange ashes for beauty, and Christ offers us release from shame, allowing us to step into the fullness of who we are in him, despite our shortcomings and disappointments. He doesn't just forgive us; he transforms us. Our mistakes and pain no longer define us because he has made us new.

It is my prayer this passage brings renewed hope. No matter how deep our shame or guilt is, Christ's crucifixion and resurrection are the foundation of our transformation. His victory over death means we are no longer bound by shame and the lies the enemy tells. We are redeemed and made whole. Christ loves us with an everlasting love. As we reflect on the difference between guilt and shame this week, remember: Jesus has already removed our ashes and replaced them with beauty, giving us value and purpose. Our identity is rooted in Christ, not in the shame of our sin.

REFLECTION QUESTIONS

- When you read the description "a crown of beauty instead of ashes" in Isaiah 61:3, how do you think that applies to you?

- What do you think the phrase "they will be called oaks of righteousness" in Isaiah 61:3 means, and how do you think that applies to your life?

SCRIPTURE REFLECTION 2
Genesis 30:22-24

"Then God remembered Rachel. He listened to her and enabled her to conceive. She became pregnant and gave birth to a son and said, 'God has taken away my disgrace.' She named him Joseph, and said, 'May the Lord add to me another son'."

UNDERSTANDING THE PASSAGE

Rachel had waited and waited. After years of infertility and disappointment, her prayers were answered, and she conceived. This marked a turning point in her life. God finally met her in her deepest need. For so long, Rachel's worth and sense of fulfillment were tied to having children. She felt invisible compared to Leah, a blessed mother of many children. But when God answered Rachel's prayer and allowed her to conceive, she began to see herself differently. The lie she believed about her infertility was silenced. Without the lie, she was able to see God's faithfulness at work in her life.

When she named her son Joseph, which means "may the Lord add to me another son," we gain insight into what she was feeling. She was filled with hope. Her son was the same Joseph we studied in Week Two. We witness again how God orchestrates our lives to fulfill a larger plan. At just the right time, he brought Joseph into the world to fulfill his plan to preserve the entire nation of Israel during a devastating time of famine. What began with Rachel's desire to have a child would one day be part of God's greater plan. God always has a plan, but often we can only see in the rearview mirror.

Leah's story follows a different path. She wanted Jacob to love her as much as he loved Rachel, and for years, she placed her worth in what she could give him. But when her fourth son was born, she declared, "This time I will praise the Lord" (Genesis 29:35). With the birth of Judah, Leah made a different choice. Rather than continuing to seek what she could not have, she decided to surrender. And with that surrender came a change in perspective. Her new perspective did not happen because she got what she wanted; it changed because she made a different choice. She decided to anchor her identity in the goodness of God, not in what her husband thought of her.

Together, these stories remind us that true freedom doesn't come from getting what we want or think we need. It comes from learning to see ourselves through God's grace. Rachel experienced God's grace through the birth of Joseph, and Leah received God's grace by choosing to praise him despite her circumstances. Both stories point us to God's greater redemption. He is always working, even when we can't see or understand it. His grace is what cleanses us, makes us whole, and gives us a specific purpose. Our worth and calling are defined by Christ alone.

REFLECTION QUESTIONS

- When you think about the name "Joseph," meaning "may the Lord add," how does it encourage you to shift from dwelling on past disappointments to trusting God with what lies ahead?

- In what ways does Rachel's recognition of God's faithfulness through Joseph's birth help you see God's timing and provision in your own life?

FAITH IN ACTION

Breaking free from shame is a process that does not happen all at once. We must make a choice every day to silence the voice of the enemy in our minds. Leah and Rachel spent years striving for what only God could provide. We don't have to repeat their story. Through the power of the Holy Spirit, we have the power to stop striving for perfection or looking for the approval of others. Here's how to put your faith in action this week:

1. **Recognize the Trigger:** Pay attention to moments when shame tries to surface. It might be after a social interaction, a comment from someone, or when you notice yourself comparing your life to someone else's. Catch it early.

2. **Replace the Reaction:** Instead of responding from a place of striving or self-protection, pause and ask, *If I fully believed I am loved, chosen, and secure in Christ, how would I respond right now?* Then choose that response.

3. **Rely on the Holy Spirit:** Each morning, invite the Spirit to guard your thoughts and guide your responses. At the end of the day, thank him for the ways he has helped you stand in truth and ask him to strengthen you where you feel weak.

SEEING THE BIGGER PICTURE

Leah and Rachel's jealousy and rivalry were not just about personal struggles. There is more to their story. Their jealousy most likely originated from a generational curse in their family. A generational curse is a toxic or destructive pattern of behavior that is passed down from one generation to the next. Unless the generational curse has been surrendered to God, it will continue to pass on to the next generation. When a generational curse is not surrendered, we, along with our children and their children, will suffer the consequences.

Leah and Rachel's family was marked by deep jealousy, so deep it became generational. Their husband Jacob carried that same struggle. He longed for the birthright so intensely that he deceived his father, Isaac, and stole it from his twin brother, Esau. Leah and Rachel lived in constant comparison, each aching for what the other had. What began in one generation did not stay contained. It carried into the next. The same jealousy showed up in their sons, growing stronger and more destructive. When Joseph was favored by his father, his brothers could not tolerate it. Their jealousy consumed them, and they threw him into a pit, setting into motion years of pain and separation.

This is how these patterns take hold. What is left unaddressed does not disappear. It moves through a family, shaping perceptions, influencing responses, and repeating itself until someone within the family chooses to surrender it to God and allows him to break the pattern.

Scripture warns us of this reality in Exodus 20:5, where God speaks of sin carried into future generations, called a generational curse. Unless it's broken, it repeats itself over and over throughout the family line. But the good news is this: God's redemption can break any cycle. His grace replaces sin and shame with freedom, knowing our identity is in him. Through Christ, we don't have to carry the weight of the past. We can step out of old cycles and walk into the newness of Christ.

CLOSING THOUGHT

Leah and Rachel's story is a great illustration of how shame can drive us to strive for worth we already have in Christ. When we allow the enemy's lies to take root in our minds, our ability to view ourselves through the lens of truth becomes distorted, so we look outward to find our value and worth.

We have learned the stronghold of shame does not define us because the Holy Spirit has equipped us to demolish shame, step by step, thought by thought. In Christ, we can walk forward in confidence, knowing we are loved, chosen, and empowered to live in freedom.

CLOSING PRAYER

Dear Lord, thank You that I am not alone in this fight. Thank You for giving me the Holy Spirit, who lives in me and grants me strength and wisdom. Thank you for reminding me of who I am in you. I reject the lies shame has spoken over my life and receive your truth. Help me stand firm when shame tries to return and give me courage to walk daily in the freedom you have already given me. I trust you to finish the work you have begun in me.

In Jesus' name,
Amen.

WEEK FOUR
GROUP DISCUSSION

Begin by watching the Week Four video together. Afterward, ask the group, "What stood out to you most from the video?"

After one or two participants have shared, take time to review last week's study. As a group, flip through each day's reading, briefly noting the Reflection Questions and Faith in Action prompts. Allow time for participants to share their responses to each prompt. If you finish early, use the Group Discussion Questions below to encourage deeper connection.

1. How does Leah's longing for acceptance help us understand the human tendency to feel overlooked or undervalued?

2. What truths from Isaiah 54:4–5 speak to how God views us when shame tries to influence our identity?

3. In what ways does comparing ourselves to others shape the way people view their worth, as seen in Leah and Rachel's story?

4. How can recognizing the difference between guilt and shame change the way someone approaches a difficult situation?

5. How does God's promise of true fulfillment shift the way we think about seeking approval from others?

Week Five

Drinking the Cup of Fear

I am so glad you are back and ready to dive into Week Five. Before we begin, I want you to pause for a moment. Set aside your to-do list and any thoughts that are pulling you in multiple directions. Allow the noise of the day to quieten as you create the space to lean in and reflect on this week's study. This moment is your time for God's Word to speak directly to you in a new way.

In the past few weeks, we've confronted shame, doubt, and despair, along with lies that persuade us to doubt God's ability to intervene in our lives. Confronting these struggles has given us insight into how truth can bring freedom.

This week, we will explore how Peter responded to fear and found redemption. We will also face our own fears and learn how to walk in redemption as well.

Peter, one of Jesus' closest disciples, experienced moments of profound fear and doubt, particularly when faced with persecution and circumstances he did not fully understand. Peter's shortcomings often stood in the way of his faith, but through it all, Jesus extended grace and restored Peter. Peter was able to walk in his calling with freedom and confidence, understanding deep within his heart and mind that Jesus was indeed the Messiah.

As we turn our attention to fear, we will discover how this emotion becomes a force that often dictates the decisions we make. Fear can be obvious, like the overwhelming feeling of panic when stepping into the unknown, or it can be subtle, quietly nudging our thoughts in the background, telling us to stay where it feels safe.

Fear can keep us stuck in unhealthy patterns of behavior, such as avoidance or impulsive reactions. It may also involve a habitual belief in worst-case scenarios or trying to control outcomes or things that don't truly matter. Fear often convinces us that the worst will happen, that we are not in control, that we are not capable, or that we are not safe. Our responsibility is to recognize when these fears are based on lies instead of God's truth.

Peter knew this struggle well. His life was full of moments of faith and moments of fear. One minute he was walking on water, and the next he was sinking beneath the waves. One minute he was declaring Jesus as the Son of God, and the next he was denying he even knew him. Peter's journey shows how fear can take hold and influence our beliefs and actions. In the end, his story teaches us how we can conquer fear.

As we move through each day, we will explore how fear takes hold and how we can break free from its grip.

Together, we will learn how to recognize the lies fear tells us and replace them with truth, thereby changing our perspective from fear to faith. I hope by the end of our study, you will feel equipped to move from reacting in fear to responding with the assurance that God is in control.

Day One
Peter's Fear and the Call to Courage

Today, we're stepping into one of Peter's most dramatic encounters with Jesus, the moment when faith and fear collided in the middle of a storm. It's a story many of us have heard before, but I want us to look at it with fresh eyes because it reveals something crucial about how we navigate our own storms: what we choose to focus on determines whether we stand or sink.

Peter's experience teaches us that fear doesn't just make us feel afraid; it distorts our perception of reality and causes us to doubt what we know to be true about God. I've been there—haven't you? Knowing the truth but feeling overwhelmed by circumstances. As we walk through this passage together, I want you to think about your own life. What circumstances are demanding your attention right now? And where is Jesus in the middle of them? Let's discover what Peter's story reveals about our own.

SCRIPTURE REFLECTION 1
Matthew 14:28-31
"Then Peter called to him, 'Lord, if it's really you, tell me to come to you, walking on the water.' 'Yes, come,' Jesus said. So Peter went over the side of the boat and walked on the water toward Jesus. But when he saw the strong wind and the waves, he was terrified and began to sink. 'Save me, Lord!' he shouted. Jesus immediately reached out and grabbed him. 'You have so little faith,' Jesus said. 'Why did you doubt me'?"

UNDERSTANDING THE PASSAGE
In this passage, Peter's moment of walking on water vividly illustrates how fear and faith intersect. Peter takes a remarkable step of faith when he responds to Jesus' call and steps out of the boat. But as soon as he shifts his focus from Jesus to the storm around him, fear takes over. The storm was forceful. The wind was fierce, and the waves were high, but despite the storm's aggression, Peter trusted Jesus to protect him; however, fear overtook him when he looked away, causing him to overestimate the storm's power and underestimate Jesus' presence and authority. It is in this part of the story where fear distorts his understanding of what is real.

We can begin to see how Peter's perception started to shift. Fear did not change the reality of the storm; however, it did change how he perceived it. The moment Peter took his eyes off Jesus, he suddenly stopped trusting him as his Savior. Peter had already witnessed Jesus' power through countless miracles. He knew Jesus had the authority to sustain and deliver him. However, despite this knowledge, fear took hold and dictated his reaction. The storm did not immediately grow stronger, but in Peter's mind, it became greater than Jesus. The lie Peter believed about his Savior's ability to intervene caused him to doubt God's power, and with that doubt, he began sinking into the depths of the water.

We can take Peter's reaction of fear a step further. I believe Peter's core belief about Jesus' deity was being questioned. On the surface, Peter thought Jesus was, in fact, the Messiah, but deep down, I believe he was not completely convinced Jesus was God in the flesh.

Now, let's pause and think about this for a moment. The storm was real, but Peter's belief that the storm was stronger than God's ability to step in and perform a miracle was not. The lie Peter believed told him Christ could not save him, and he was going to sink. We know this thought is a lie because it does not align with God's promise as our protector and provider. I believe this lie stemmed from a damaged filter in Peter's mind, causing him to feel afraid. His filter was unable to see the truth of God's promises at that moment because of an unconscious, deep-seated belief about the deity of Christ. I think Peter's doubt caused his thoughts to become distorted versions of the truth. His doubts about Christ being the Messiah changed his perception of Jesus as the true Son of God. He suddenly doubted Christ's supernatural power to defy nature and rescue him from sinking, making the storm in his mind more powerful than Jesus.

Fear tries to convince us our circumstances have more control over us than God's supernatural ability to act on our behalf. But the truth, according to the Word of God, is our circumstances are never greater than God's ability to deliver us. As Christians, our faith is meant to anchor us in times of struggle. The storms of life will come, and they will feel overwhelming. It's natural to feel the weight of them.

When I was in graduate school, I remember my professor telling us, eager soon-to-be therapists, to allow space for warranted feelings when working with a client reeling from a crisis. When a storm hits, initial feelings of fear are justified. I am sure Peter initially felt fear, but he stepped out of the boat in faith. Then, when he took his eyes off Jesus, his fear took over, and he forgot who Jesus was, his Savior and Lord.

Do you see yourself in Peter? I know I do. How often have we taken our eyes off Jesus and only focused on our circumstances? Because of that, we doubted God's ability to intervene, even though we've seen him show up in our lives time and time again. Even though fear may be a warranted emotion, we must step out in faith, trusting God will carry us through. However, if we, like Peter, take our eyes off Jesus and his truth, we will sink.

It is essential to understand faith is not the absence of fear; rather, it is the choice we make to trust in God despite the fear. Just as Jesus called Peter to walk on the water, he calls us to trust him, especially when the waves of our circumstances rise. Our faith, not our fear, should be the force behind our reaction to the relentless waves crashing in on us. Although fear may increase, we are called to step forward in faith, knowing God is with us and sustaining us through every challenge.

As we face life's storms, we can shift our focus from the overwhelming winds and waves of uncertainty to the reality of God's faithfulness and promise to never leave us. Jesus is with us in the storm, offering us the same grace he gave to Peter. Fear might cause us to stumble, but it doesn't have to define our journey. God's grace always meets us where we are, and his power is greater than any storm we encounter.

REFLECTION QUESTIONS

- What does Peter's reaction to the storm teach you about your relationship between faith and fear?

- When have you felt like Peter, sinking under the weight of fear, and what did you come to understand about God in that experience?

SCRIPTURE REFLECTION 2

Mark 9:23-24

"What do you mean, 'If I can'?" Jesus asked. "Anything is possible if a person believes." The father instantly cried out, "I do believe, but help me overcome my unbelief!"

UNDERSTANDING THE PASSAGE

This story takes place in the Gospel of Mark after Jesus, Peter, James, and John descend from the mountain where Jesus was transfigured. As they return, they find a large crowd gathered around the other disciples, who are caught in a dispute with the religious teachers. A desperate father brings his son, who has been tormented by an evil spirit since childhood, to Jesus. The disciples had tried to cast out the spirit but failed. When Jesus arrives, the father turns to him and pleads for help, saying, "Have mercy on us and help us, if you can" (Mark 9:22). Jesus' response, "What do you mean, 'If I can'?" is a reminder his power is not limited, and our faith is essential for experiencing God's miraculous work.

In this passage, I believe the father is also battling fear alongside his disbelief. After years of watching his son suffer, he is afraid to believe and hope his son can be delivered. This father, I imagine, has struggled with so much disappointment and grief that he does not want to be disappointed again. He saw the disciples fail to heal his son, which reinforced his fear that nothing would change. Now, standing before Jesus, he wants to believe, but the fear of unmet expectations still lingers. His cry, "I do believe, but help me overcome my unbelief!" demonstrates the dilemma he faces at this moment. He must balance his faith with his fear of disappointment, which begins by being honest about it.

This struggle between faith and fear is similar to what Peter faced when he stepped onto the water. In Matthew 14:28-31, Peter initially walks in faith, but the moment he shifts his focus from Jesus to the wind and waves, fear takes hold. The storm doesn't die down, but his perception of the storm changes. Instead of seeing Jesus' power, he feels threatened by his circumstances, and in that moment, fear deceives him into thinking he will sink. Fear distorts reality, making obstacles seem bigger than they are and God's power seem smaller than it is.

Psychologically, we see this pattern unfold in our lives. False beliefs create faulty perceptions, which lead to fear-driven thoughts and behaviors. The father in this passage had seen failure, so he feared failure. Peter saw the storm, so he feared the storm. Satan uses these lies to weaken our faith, reinforcing the belief God is distant, incapable, or unwilling to help. This cycle of fear and unbelief continues until we begin to identify the false beliefs we have accepted as truth and replace them with the real truth that comes from the Word of God.

Jesus does not condemn our fear. He loves us exactly as we are, so he responds to us with mercy and grace. Just as Jesus reaches out to rescue Peter as he begins to sink, he also meets this father in the midst of his fear. Rather than rejecting him for his struggle with belief, Jesus invites him to trust. The father doesn't have to overcome his fear alone. No, all he has to do is to surrender it to Jesus.

This passage shows how fear stands in the way of fully trusting God. Fear clouds our vision, making our circumstances appear bigger than God, thereby keeping us trapped in doubt and uncertainty. When we recognize the lies fear tells us, we can break free from the cycle that keeps us stuck and step into a faith that is no longer dictated by our circumstances but anchored in truth.

If you would like to read the full account of this father's encounter with Jesus, you can find it in Mark 9:14-29, where Jesus not only heals the boy but also explains why the disciples could not cast out the demon.

REFLECTION QUESTIONS

- What does the father's plea, "Help me overcome my unbelief!" teach you about the relationship between faith and doubt?

- How does the father's request for help with his unbelief show you how to ask God to strengthen your faith in moments of doubt?

FAITH IN ACTION

Fear doesn't appear out of nowhere; it grows through a pattern of thoughts and beliefs that feed each other until they feel impossible to escape. Understanding this cycle helps us recognize where to interrupt it and invite God's truth to reshape how we think, feel, and respond. So let's identify the lies that fuel false beliefs.

1. **Understand How False Beliefs Take Root**:

False Belief:
It begins with a false belief formed from a lie we've accepted about ourselves, God, of our circumstances.

Distorted Perception:
That false belief distorts how we see reality, shaping what we focus on and how we interpret what happens around us.

Irrational Thoughts:
From that distorted perception comes irrational or negative thoughts that reinforce fear and doubt.

Fear-Based Feelings:
Those thoughts stir fear-based feelings such as anxiety, insecurity, or hopelessness.

Reactive Behaviors:
These feelings drive behaviors like avoidance, control, or impulsive reactions.

Reinforcement of the Lie:
Acting on those fear-driving impulses strengthens the original false belief, keeping the cycle alive.

And so the pattern continues: belief, perception, thought, feeling, behavior which loops back again and again until we recogniez it and break the cycle by renewing our minds with God's Word.

2. **Identify Your False Beliefs:**

- Write down a fear you are currently facing.

- Ask yourself: *What belief is fueling this fear? Is it rooted in truth or a distorted perception?*

- Trace it back through the cycle: What thoughts, feelings, and behaviors have stemmed from this belief?

3. **Challenge the False Belief with Truth:**

- Look at the list of Scriptures at the end of this week's lesson and find a verse that directly disputes the false belief you have written down.

- Write this verse next to the false belief as a declaration of truth to replace the lie.

SEEING THE BIGGER PICTURE

It's easy to focus on the moment Peter begins to sink, but the greater miracle is his willingness to step out of the boat in the first place. Peter had faith to believe. Even if Peter's faith was brief, Jesus could hold him up in the middle of the impossible. That single step, even though he collapses for a brief moment in fear, positioned him to experience God's power in a deeply personal way. It shows us we are not perfect, nor does God expect us to be perfect, when our faith wavers as a result of fear. Jesus will always reach out his hand to help us when we feel taken under. Jesus will also help us with our unbelief, just as he did with the hurting father who sought healing for his son.

These two stories remind us how faith will give us the courage to move forward despite our fears. God never expected Peter to be fearless, but he did want him to trust him fully.

God wants the same for us. He doesn't expect us to never be afraid, but he does want us to surrender our fear to him and trust he will protect us from the storm and always provide a way through to the other side.

Fear tries to convince us the storm will overpower us, but God sees the bigger picture and knows the way the storm will go. When we surrender our fears to him, he reveals himself to us in the middle of the storm. The storm can uncover something deeper about how we view ourselves and how we see God.

Fear isn't always the enemy we assume it is. Sometimes it becomes the very ground where faith begins to grow. God isn't waiting for us to show up as the "perfect" Christian with massive amounts of faith before he moves. No, just as we are, he calls us to look at him, not our circumstances. He wants us to stop measuring the size of the storm and start trusting in his strength, regardless of what is happening around us. Remember, God is greater than any storm we may face.

CLOSING THOUGHT

Fear is often loud, immediate, and overwhelming, but it is not the final voice in our circumstances. Like Peter and the desperate father, we may waver, but we are never without hope. God doesn't ask us to be fearless; he wants us to trust him in the middle of our fears. His hand is always reaching for us, offering strength when we feel weak and grace when we feel unworthy. When we move our focus from the storm to the Savior, we will see things differently, and as a result, we will feel differently. Rather than feeling afraid, we will feel safe in the arms of our Savior.

CLOSING PRAYER

Father, thank you for your steady presence in the middle of the storm. When fear rises and doubt creeps in, help me to fix my eyes on You. I confess there have been times when I have allowed fear to shape my thoughts and distort my perception of who you are. I surrender my fear and the false beliefs associated with it at your feet and ask you to replace them with truth. Strengthen my faith, even when it feels small, and remind me your grace is always enough. Teach me to trust you in all things.

In Jesus' name,
Amen

Day Two
When Fear Controls Our Reactions

Peter often reacted out of fear. His impulsiveness in cutting off the servant's ear during Jesus' arrest reveals how fear can trigger immediate and instinctual reactions rather than thoughtful, faith-driven responses. Today, we will look at the difference between reaction and response. We will discover how fear-driven reactions often bypass wisdom, leading us to act in ways that contradict what we believe.

We have already discussed how false beliefs shape our perceptions and fuel fear. Now, we will explore how these beliefs not only influence our thoughts but also drive our actions.

SCRIPTURE REFLECTION 1
Luke 22:47-51
"But even as Jesus said this, a crowd approached, led by Judas, one of the twelve disciples. Judas walked over to Jesus to greet him with a kiss. But Jesus said, 'Judas, would you betray the Son of Man with a kiss?' When the other disciples saw what was about to happen, they exclaimed, 'Lord, should we fight? We brought the swords!' And one of them struck at the high priest's slave, slashing off his right ear. But Jesus said, 'No more of this.' And he touched the man's ear and healed him."

UNDERSTANDING THE PASSAGE
In this passage, Peter reacts impulsively when Jesus is about to be arrested. When Peter sees the crowd approaching, he immediately draws his sword and cuts off the servant's ear. This action, driven by fear and desperation, shows how strong emotions can lead to impulsive behaviors shaped by false beliefs. Much like a reflex, our responses to fear are often automatic, driven by deep-seated beliefs we may not even recognize. In Peter's case, he instinctively tried to protect Jesus, believing God's plan depended on his acting on Jesus' behalf. Peter believed he needed to take matters into his own hands by drawing his sword and cutting off the servant's ear. In that moment, Peter failed to trust God was in control, not him. His reaction also reveals a deeply held belief that God's kingdom on this earth would come through force, not through sacrifice.

Like many Jews of his time, Peter likely believed the Messiah would establish his kingdom by overthrowing the Roman empire and restoring Israel's independence. The Jewish people had been oppressed for hundreds of years, and many expected when the Messiah came, he would lead a military uprising to defeat their enemies. Peter had witnessed Jesus' power firsthand. He had healed the sick, fed multitudes, and even controlled the forces of nature. With this in mind, Peter probably assumed Jesus would use that same power to defeat Rome and establish his rule. This belief shaped Peter's perception of what should happen, and when Jesus spoke of his coming suffering and death, Peter refused to accept it (Matthew 16:21-23). In Peter's mind, a suffering and crucified Messiah did not fit what he believed to be true.

When the soldiers came to arrest Jesus, Peter's actions reflected his belief that the new kingdom would come only through force, which was not aligned with God's plan. He was afraid for Christ and for what would happen if he did not take control of the situation. So Peter reacted by reaching for his sword. He thought this was his moment to fight, prove his loyalty, and protect Jesus from what should not happen. His reaction, though well-intended, was based on a misunderstanding of God's plan. These beliefs clouded his perception, causing fear and impulsivity to become his first response rather than trusting Jesus to lead him.

This moment reveals how deeply held beliefs shape our reactions. When we believe something false about God, ourselves, or the world, we interpret situations through that lens, leading us to react in ways that are out of alignment with God's will. Peter was not intentionally resisting God's plan; he simply could not see past his own perception of how things should be. When we are unaware of our false beliefs, we react in fear rather than respond in faith. We react so quickly that we often fail to evaluate whether our actions align with our faith. Reactions are impulsive, emotion-driven, and often destructive, whereas a response is deliberate and measured. When emotions run high and dictate our actions, we struggle to trust God's plan and align our steps with his.

Peter's reaction in this moment highlights the consequences of fear-driven actions. Jesus intervened at once and put a stop to the attack. He healed the servant's ear and made him whole. In doing so, he teaches a crucial lesson: emotion-driven actions are often impulsive and destructive, and they do not typically align with the will of God.

Fear-based reactions, like Peter's, often reveal our deep-seated false beliefs. These beliefs influence how we see and understand our circumstances. When our perception is distorted by fear based on a false belief, our thoughts drift away from God's sovereignty, leading us to doubt he has a better plan. When uncertainty takes over our minds, it clouds our judgment and causes us to react impulsively.

Just as Peter instinctively reached for his sword, we often react based on false narratives that shape our understanding of ourselves and God. These reactions happen so quickly that we fail to pause and reflect on what God would have us do in that moment.

Whether we want to control a situation, prevent a particular outcome, or protect ourselves from harm, fear prompts us to act immediately. This impulse to react out of fear is exactly what happened to Peter. His instinct was to fight, take control, and react without thinking about the consequences. But Jesus immediately corrected him, showing fear-driven reactions are not part of his plan.

REFLECTION QUESTIONS

- When you consider Peter's impulsive action in Luke 22:47–50, how does it help you reflect on times when your own reactions may have been driven by fear rather than trust?

- How does Jesus' response in Luke 22:51 encourage you when you think about the way he addresses your own fear-driven actions?

SCRIPTURE REFLECTION 2
2 Timothy 1:7
"For God has not given us a spirit of fear and timidity, but of power, love, and self-discipline."

UNDERSTANDING THE PASSAGE
In this verse, Paul addresses Timothy, a young leader and pastor of the church in Ephesus. Timothy, a trusted companion of Paul, was likely facing significant opposition and intense pressure as a leader. He may have felt insecure and hesitant amid persecution, conflicts within the church, and his youthfulness compared to more experienced leaders around him. Paul's letter to Timothy acts as a source of

encouragement, reminding him to be bold and confident in his calling despite the challenges he faces.

Paul tells Timothy God has not given us a spirit of fear but one of courage, confidence, and strength, all qualities that are essential when facing adversity or the unknown. This spirit of fear does not come from God and can prevent us from taking action or making decisions that align with God's will. The enemy uses fear to keep us stuck, distorting our view of our circumstances and clouding our judgment. Instead of acting in faith, we often react in panic or doubt.

Paul highlights how God's spirit of power, love, and self-discipline equips us to stand firm when fear arises. This supernatural assistance is the Holy Spirit working within us, providing the strength, love, and clear mind needed to overcome fear. Power, love, and self-discipline each represent a different aspect of God's provision. Power gives us strength and courage, love fills us with compassion and a willingness to sacrifice, and self-discipline helps us stay focused and grounded in truth, even amid our emotions. These gifts from God enable us to face life's challenges with faith instead of reacting out of fear.

Paul knew Timothy was likely dealing with fear and uncertainty in his ministry, and Timothy needed this reminder to walk in God's strength and grace rather than be paralyzed by the spirit of fear. This passage speaks to all of us: fear may rise, but it doesn't have to control us. God has equipped us to face challenges with boldness, love, and a disciplined mind, enabling us to confidently live out his calling.

FAITH IN ACTION

Fear often makes us react before we think, but we can learn to take a short time out to think before acting. Today, you can use this exercise to help you break the cycle of fear-driven reactions:

1. **Recognize the Trigger:** Write down a recent moment when you reacted out of fear. What set it off?

2. **Name the Belief:** What belief was fueling your reaction? Was it control, doubt, insecurity, fear of failure, or anything else that you think caused you to react in that way?

3. **Reframe the Response:** How could you have taken a moment to reassess? What would a faith-filled response have looked like?

4. **Replace with Scripture:** Choose a verse from the list at the end of this week's study that speaks directly to the fear or false belief. Write it beside your situation as a declaration of truth.

Example:

Trigger: I snapped when I felt things slipping out of control.

False Belief: "If I don't hold everything together, it will all fall apart."

Faith Response: If I had taken a brief time out to reassess my thoughts and feelings and say a quick prayer, I could have spoken calmly instead of reacting.

Scripture: 1 Peter 5:7 "Cast all your anxiety on him because he cares for you."

SEEING THE BIGGER PICTURE

Peter's impulsive reaction in the garden highlights how easily we can fall into fear-driven behaviors, especially when we feel overwhelmed. In that moment, Peter faced a threat he couldn't predict, which shook him. His immediate action, thrusting his sword at the soldier, was driven by fear, doubt, and uncertainty about the future. Peter walked beside Jesus for three years, watching miracles and hearing his teaching. Yet, when faced with Jesus' arrest, Peter's beliefs about God's sovereignty were tested.

Peter's fear wasn't only about protecting Jesus; it also stemmed from his fear of the unknown. He was afraid of potentially losing Jesus, the soldiers harming the Son of God, and the uncertainty of what would happen next. The thought of everything ending in horror and violence made him react rashly. Peter feared his own future and what this moment meant for him personally. His deeply rooted false beliefs about God and God's ability to fulfill his ultimate plan illustrate how fear clouds our perception, leading us to act in ways that contradict what we know to be true about God and his sovereignty.

False beliefs, left unchecked, will continue to grow deeper roots. Deeper roots lead to more intense reactions. When fear operates beneath the surface, it subtly begins to impact how we interpret our circumstances and influences our responses. Instead of pausing to seek wisdom, we instinctively react, often reinforcing the very fears we want to overcome. Like Peter, we may feel the need to take control, believing action is the only way to bring security or resolution. But Jesus shows us another way. He shows us how to surrender to his Father and let go of our need to take matters into our own hands. With practice, we can refine our ability to confront false beliefs and allow our faith to shape our responses rather than our fear.

CLOSING THOUGHT

By identifying and challenging our false beliefs, we shift from reaction to response, grounding our actions in faith and trust in God's sovereignty. Aligning our actions with God's truth enables us to face life's challenges with confidence and clarity, just as Jesus demonstrated during his time on earth.

CLOSING PRAYER

Lord, help me recognize the false beliefs that cause me to react in ways that are not aligned with you and your plans for my life. Give me the courage to replace them with your truth. Teach me to respond in faith, not fear, and to trust your sovereignty even when life feels uncertain. Align my thoughts with yours so I can walk in confidence and peace. Jesus, thank you again for the blood you shed on the cross for my sins. You are a loving God and a good Father. I am blessed to be a child in your Kingdom. Help me reflect your love today!

In Jesus' name,
Amen

Day Three
The Cycle of the Lie

Today, we will explore how fear-based beliefs can trap us in a continuous cycle of lies, making us feel stuck by the fear of looming disaster. Now that we understand how beliefs rooted in fear can shape our perceptions and responses, we will look at how these false beliefs and the lies we've internalized can keep us stuck in a vicious loop, as we discussed on Day One.

I have personally struggled with this pattern of thinking, especially when my daughter became ill. The fear I experienced was not fleeting; instead, it was the kind of fear that embedded itself deep within me. Fear dominated my thoughts and distorted my perception of God's goodness. The more the lies lingered and the more I entertained them, the deeper they rooted themselves into my core beliefs. For example, I thought, *"She will never get better, she will never have a normal life."* Then I started to believe God was not in control and he wouldn't intervene. When I embraced these lies by refusing to dispute them, I sunk into depression and hopelessness.

Thoughts like these are how lies take root. Our beliefs influence our perception of what is happening around us, and these perceptions imprint us in such a way that they shape how we think, feel, and behave. When our beliefs are grounded in truth, such as knowing God is sovereign, good, and always present, we may still face fear. As we discussed in yesterday's study, there are many circumstances where feelings of fear are warranted, even when we know God is in control. Rather than trying to dismiss these feelings altogether, which doesn't work, we should embrace them, turn our hearts toward God, and surrender them to him.

As we study today, we'll uncover how false beliefs driven by fear shape our thoughts, feelings, and responses to life's challenges, and we will learn how we fall prey to this repeating pattern. Ruminating on these fears and the lies that fuel them keeps us trapped in a spiral of uncertainty, even hopelessness, preventing us from recognizing God's hand at work in our lives. Together, we will examine what Scripture says about the liar and the lies he tells and discover how God's truth can break this loop of deception. As you move through today's study, you will learn how to identify and confront these lies, replacing them with the empowering truth of who God says you are. By the end of the week, we will be equipped to break free from the lies fueling our fears, and we will know how to step into the hope and confidence found in God's truth.

SCRIPTURE REFLECTION 1
John 8:44

"For you are the children of your father the devil, and you love to do the evil things he does. He was a murderer from the beginning. He has always hated the truth. There is no truth in him. When he lies, it is consistent with his character; for he is a liar and the father of lies."

UNDERSTANDING THE PASSAGE

In John 8:44, Jesus addresses a group of Jews who challenge him about his authority and identity as the Messiah. The conversation takes place during a tense discussion in which Jesus confronts the religious leaders about their unbelief and failure to recognize him as the Son of God. In this moment, Jesus refers to Satan as the "father of lies," drawing a stark contrast between himself and the enemy.

Jesus is specifically addressing the Pharisees, a group known for their hypocrisy and for holding onto traditions and laws that blind them to the truth he embodies. He tells them they are children of the devil because, like the devil, they have rejected the truth and embraced lies. This statement goes beyond an accusation as it reveals the profound impact of the false beliefs we carry and their ability to influence our perceptions and actions. The deeply ingrained lies of Satan, so evident in our fallen world, distort our perception of ourselves, others, and God.

Satan, who Jesus called the "father of lies," uses deception to separate us from God's truth. Satan wants to drive a wedge between us and God, causing us to live in fear and insecurity. The distortions of truth, which he constantly taunts us with, fuel the cycle of the lie, affecting how we interpret our circumstances and preventing us from fully trusting God's promises.

The deceitfulness of Satan is relentless, and he wants to trap us into a perpetual cycle of believing and reacting to his lies. As believers in Christ, it is so important we recognize how this cycle works. You've already seen how it takes shape on Day One, but let's look at it again so the pattern is clear:

1. First, our core beliefs shape our perception of the world around us.

2. Then, these perceptions influence our thoughts, which in turn trigger our feelings.

3. Finally, those feelings drive our behavior. Our behaviors then confirm our core beliefs, which affect our perceptions, and subsequently dictate our thoughts and feelings, creating a cycle that repeats itself.

This thought process is the insidious nature of fear; it begins with our beliefs, then distorts our reality, and ultimately takes hold of our thoughts, feelings, and behaviors, strengthening the lies that keep us stuck in feelings of despair and hopelessness.

The bottom line is this: when our core beliefs are rooted in lies, our perception is distorted, leading us to think, feel, and act in ways that are inconsistent with God's Word. So, for me, when I started to adopt the belief of God's inability to step into my daughter's life, it left me feeling hopeless, which caused me to stop praying and trusting in God, which then confirmed my belief in God being distant and inactive, and the cycle continued. It wasn't until I was willing to surrender my overwhelming feelings of fear that I was able to challenge the lies and cause my beliefs and perception about God to change.

Understanding this cycle is crucial because unchallenged lies not only distort our thoughts, beliefs, and perception, but they also affect how we engage with God. If we fail to recognize these deceptions for what they are, we will continue to react out of fear rather than respond in faith. This reaction is why Jesus' words are not just a rebuke but a powerful reminder of the destructive nature of lies.

REFLECTION QUESTIONS

- How does John 8:44 help you understand the connection between false beliefs and your perception of truth?

- Jesus calls Satan the "father of lies." How does that title shape the way you think about the lies you've struggled to believe and the effect they've had on your thoughts, feelings, and actions

SCRIPTURE REFLECTION 2

Romans 12:2

"Don't copy the behavior and customs of this world, but let God transform you into a new person by changing the way you think. Then you will learn to know God's will for you, which is good and pleasing and perfect."

UNDERSTANDING THE PASSAGE

In Romans 12:2, Paul writes to a group of believers in Rome who are learning how to live out their faith in a culture that doesn't reflect the values of Christ. After spending the first part of his letter explaining the depth of God's mercy and the gift of salvation, Paul changes his focus from God's mercy to God's strength. Paul wants everyone to understand how the Living Word of Christ has the power to renew our minds and transform our lives. This transformation doesn't come through willpower; instead, it comes through the power of the Holy Spirit living within us. Transformation occurs when there is a shift in our way of thinking; Paul calls this the renewing of the mind. When we surrender our thoughts to Christ, he changes our perceptions and aligns our thoughts with truth.

Paul's words are both a command and an encouragement. He tells everyone not to conform to the ways of the world because he knows the culture can easily dictate our thoughts and beliefs, causing us to stray. So, he urges us to let God reshape our minds to be more like Christ, knowing this change will free us from the bondage of Satan's lies.

For the believers in Rome, and for us today, renewing our minds can be a daily battle between the truth of the gospel and the pull of the world around us. We cannot "renew our minds" on our own. We need the power of the Holy Spirit to help us navigate our thought patterns. Through his power, we can learn to replace the lies our culture leads us to believe with the truth of God's Word. When we saturate our minds with the promises of God, faith will always override fear, and that kind of faith, my friends, is how we transform into a new person.

Renewing our minds is central to breaking the strongholds of fear, disputing false beliefs, and re-routing toxic thoughts. This transformation is ongoing but deeply empowering. We are not victims of our thoughts. Through Christ, we can and must reject lies and receive truth. When our minds are renewed, a faithful response, instead of an emotional reaction, will follow. We no longer have to live at the mercy of fear, because the Holy Spirit empowers us to see as Christ sees.

REFLECTION QUESTIONS

- According to 2 Corinthians 10:5, what role do your thoughts play in shaping your faith and actions? How can capturing and surrendering rebellious thoughts to Christ transform the way you respond to fear?

- In 2 Corinthians 10:5, Paul speaks about demolishing strongholds and making thoughts obedient to Christ. What does this passage reveal about the nature of spiritual strongholds, and how does Scripture equip you to break free from them?

FAITH IN ACTION

Fear grows stronger when we believe the lies it plants. But when we name the lie, confront it with God's Word, and choose to see it differently, the cycle begins to break.

1: **Identify the Lie:** Write down one false belief you've carried about yourself, God, or your circumstances. Notice how it has shaped your thoughts, feelings, or actions.

2: **Dispute the Lie:** Ask: *Is this belief based on fear or truth?* Use a verse from the list of Scriptures at the end of this week's study that speaks directly against it.

3: **Reframe with Truth:** Reframing simply means looking at your situation through a new lens. Instead of seeing it through fear, choose to see it through God's truth.

- Recognize how the lie distorted your perception.

- Replace it with what Scripture says.

- Rewrite the way you see the situation in light of God's promises.

Example:
   Lie: "I will always fail."

   Truth: "My grace is sufficient for you, for my power is made perfect in weakness" (2 Corinthians 12:9).

   Reframed: Failure is not final. God can use it to grow me and strengthen my faith.

When we practic this, our thoughts and feelings begin to align with God's truth, and fear loses its grip.

SEEING THE BIGGER PICTURE

Satan is the father of lies, but through the Holy Spirit living within us, we have the power to break free from believing the liar. Paul helps us see the importance of renewing our minds with the Living Word of God. When we meditate on his Word, we experience supernatural transformation. Our minds influence our feelings and actions, so if you want to feel differently and take control over your behavior, Paul tells us not to follow the ways of the world but to follow God's way instead. As we continue this journey together, even in our weakest moments, God's truth remains strong enough to overcome feelings of fear caused by a false belief system. Remember, the lies we have been tricked into believing don't have to keep us stuck in a cycle. Through faith, we can challenge those lies and replace them with the truth of who God is and who he says we are.

CLOSING THOUGHT

This process of breaking free from the cycle of lies is not a one-time event but a journey. Every day, we can confront the lies of the enemy and embrace the truth, written in Scripture. By aligning our beliefs with God's Word, we can move away from fear and toward transformational faith in Christ.

CLOSING PRAYER

God, I'm tired of carrying the weight of lies that were never meant for me. Today, I choose to let go of what isn't true and make room for what is. Teach my heart to recognize your voice above all others and give me the strength to live from a place of freedom. Shape my mind with your truth and lead me forward with clarity and courage.

In Jesus' name,
Amen

Day Four
Confronting Irrational Fear –
Peter's Denial and the Power of Truth

As we continue to explore Peter's journey, we will now focus on irrational fear. Irrational fear is the kind of fear that clearly distorts reality and leads us to act impulsively. Peter's denial of Christ in the face of fear is a powerful example of how this intense emotion can drive us to behave in ways that contradict our core beliefs.

Peter, like many of us, struggled with irrational fear. This kind of fear is based not on reality, but on exaggerated thoughts that distort our perception of what is really happening. Today, we'll examine the difference between irrational fear and warranted fear and learn what to do when we are overcome with thoughts that exacerbate this emotion and lead us down a path that shakes the core of our faith.

SCRIPTURE REFLECTION 1
Matthew 26:69-75
"Peter was sitting outside in the courtyard. A servant girl came over and said to him, 'You were one of those with Jesus the Galilean.' But Peter denied it in front of everyone. 'I don't know what you're talking about,' he said. Later, out by the gate, another servant girl noticed him and said to those standing around, 'This man was with Jesus of Nazareth.' Again Peter denied it, this time with an oath. 'I don't even know the man,' he said. A little later some of the other bystanders came over to Peter and said, 'You must be one of them; we can tell by your Galilean accent.' Peter swore, 'A curse on me if I'm lying—I don't know the man!' And immediately the rooster crowed. Suddenly, Jesus' words flashed through Peter's mind: 'Before the rooster crows, you will deny three times that you even know me.' And he went away, weeping bitterly."

UNDERSTANDING THE PASSAGE
This passage, recorded in the Gospel of Matthew, was written by Matthew, one of Jesus' twelve disciples. As a former tax collector, Matthew had a unique perspective, writing mainly to a Jewish audience to show that Jesus was the long-awaited Messiah. His

Gospel is filled with Old Testament references to help the Jewish people see Jesus as the fulfillment of prophecy.

At this point in the narrative, Jesus had been arrested and taken before the Sanhedrin, the Jewish ruling council. Peter now found himself in a precarious situation. He was in the courtyard of the high priest's residence, surrounded by people who could easily link him to Jesus. The religious leaders were actively trying to find a reason to condemn the man who called himself the Son of God, so they were eager to question Peter. His Galilean accent gave him away, marking him as one of Jesus' followers.

When Peter was confronted just outside the courtyard, fear overwhelmed him, despite what he knew to be true in his heart. Peter had fully acknowledged that Jesus was indeed the Messiah. He had seen him perform miracle after miracle, again and again. Peter believed Christ was who he claimed to be, and without fear, he boldly expressed his love and loyalty to him in front of all the disciples. However, the moment fear crept in, his thoughts took over and distorted his perception of what might happen if he clung to the truth.

At this point in the story, it's easy to focus on Peter's failure, but it's also important to consider the real danger he faced. He thought identifying with Jesus could have led to his arrest or even death. And he wasn't wrong to think that; however, Peter saw Jesus defy the principles and laws of nature many times. But in this case, Peter became so caught up in earthly logic that he failed to recognize and accept the miraculous power of Jesus. Let's go back for a moment to Peter walking on water. It was a miracle that defied everything we understand about the natural world. By all logic, Peter should have sunk, but he didn't because Jesus isn't bound by natural law. His authority over creation made it possible for Peter to do the impossible. But here we are: Peter, once again, allowed fear to take over his actions.

In this passage, irrational fears distorted Peter's perception of who Christ was and what God could do. He reacted by denying Jesus. This reaction wasn't based on truth, but on a distorted belief about what would happen if he was identified as a follower of Jesus. Irrational fear doesn't deny real risk, yet it twists it out of proportion and removes God from the picture.

Peter's fear wasn't just about rejection or failure; it was much deeper. Having walked with Jesus, seen his power, and even called him the Messiah, he still faced moments of doubt. In his moment of distress, his thoughts spiraled into worst-case scenarios. Like us, he probably ruminated on the what-ifs. He might have thought, "What if they arrest me, what if they kill me, what if this is the end?" His anxiety stemmed from uncertainty, revealing a deeper issue: doubt. In his panic, he questioned everything, including whether Jesus was truly who he claimed to be. He might have wondered, if Jesus really is the Messiah, then why would he allow all this to happen? Instead of holding onto what he knew to be true, Peter let fear take over, distorting his view of God's plan. His faulty thinking, driven by worry, led him to act impulsively, resulting in his denial of Jesus. That moment of weakness clouded his judgment and made him act irrationally, directly contradicting what he knew about his relationship with Jesus.

This moment reveals how irrational fear can cause us to forget the truth of God's promises. Fear that is not based on real facts or discounts God's ability to intervene will inflate the risks of a situation and lead us to make decisions based on the enemy's lies rather than on God's timeless truths.

Just as Peter reacted out of fear and shame, we too can fall into the trap of irrational thoughts when we face challenges. The truth, however, is that our circumstances never compromise, negate, or override God's promises.

REFLECTION QUESTIONS

- What does Peter's response in Matthew 26:69-75 reveal about how irrational fear can distort perception and influence behavior? How do you envision this pattern unfolding in your own life when fear takes over?

- Despite knowing Jesus personally and witnessing his power, Peter still allowed fear to dictate his actions. According to this passage, what led Peter to deny Jesus? What can you learn from him about recognizing and overcoming the lies that fear tells us?

SCRIPTURE REFLECTION 2
Isaiah 41:10
"Don't be afraid, for I am with you. Don't be discouraged, for I am your God. I will strengthen you and help you. I will hold you up with my victorious right hand."

UNDERSTANDING THE PASSAGE

The Book of Isaiah was written by the prophet Isaiah, who ministered in Judah during a time of political upheaval and uncertainty. Isaiah's prophetic messages were directed to the Israelites, who faced the looming threat of exile and destruction due to their rebellion against God. Isaiah 41 is part of a broader section where God reassures his people of his faithfulness, even in the face of overwhelming fear. Powerful nations surrounded the Israelites, and their future seemed uncertain; yet God reminded them that he was in control.

This verse isn't just a general encouragement; rather, it is a direct call to trust in God's sovereignty. The phrase "I am with you" echoes throughout Scripture, declaring God's presence as greater than any opposition or fear we face. In this context, God is speaking to a nation on the brink of hardship, yet his promise of strength and divine help reassures them they have not been abandoned. Today, this verse reminds us of God's steady and unwavering power in every moment of fear and uncertainty we face.

The reassurance God gives to Israel extended beyond their situation, offering the same hope to us today. Isaiah 41:10 directly speaks to our fear and anxiety, offering God's promises of strength and help. This passage makes it clear that false beliefs and distorted perceptions lose their power when measured against the unchanging truth of God's Word and the knowledge of who he is. When we are overwhelmed by thoughts of rejection, failure, doubt, insecurity, or even a threat, God calls us to change our perspective and focus our thoughts on him and away from our circumstances. When we focus on God's provision and authority, we gain a new mindset that overrides what we know in the natural. We learn to see as he sees.

Recognizing this truth allows us to see fear for what it is. Fear is an unreliable guide that warps our perception of our reality as followers of Christ. The irrational thoughts we have often magnify the worst-case scenario, convincing us that danger is imminent, failure is certain, or we are powerless to change our situation. But God's power is limitless, and his presence is unshakable. There is never a moment when he is not fully in control, fully aware, and fully able to help us. He has equipped us with everything we need to face our fears and walk confidently in his strength. Instead of reacting impulsively, like Peter did, we can choose to lean into our faith by meditating on the promises of God and not ruminating on the what-ifs.

REFLECTION QUESTIONS

- When you think about the words "I am with you," how does that promise speak to the fears that feel overwhelming in your own life?

- Isaiah 41:10 tells us God will strengthen, help, and uphold us. As you think about your current circumstances, which of these promises do you need to hold onto most today?

FAITH IN ACTION

Irrational fear often begins with a thought that exaggerates what might happen and blinds us to God's presence. Today, take time to pause and practice sorting your thoughts.

1. **Name the Fear:** Write down one fear that has been replaying in your mind. Be specific about the "what if" that keeps surfacing.

2. **Test the Thought:** Ask yourself: *Is this fear based on fact, or is it an exaggerated thought that distorts reality? What evidence do I have that this outcome will happen?*

3. **Reframe with Truth**: Choose one verse from the list of Scriptures at the end of this week's study (you might start with Isaiah 41:10) and write it beside your fear. Rewrite your thought through the lens of this promise.

   Example:

   Fear: "If I fail, everything will fall apart."

   Truth: "God upholds me with his righteous right hand" (Isaiah 41:10).

Reframed: "Even if I fall short, God's strength sustains me, and he won't let go."

When you practice naming, testing, and reframing your thoughts, you are teaching your mind to shift from distorted fear to faith. Over time, this new way of thinking will shape how you feel and respond, allowing you to walk in the strength God has already promised you.

SEEING THE BIGGER PICTURE

Peter's denial serves as a reminder of how irrational fears can distort our perception of reality. Fear exaggerates the threat, making us believe the worst possible outcome is inevitable. But as we see in Peter's story, fear does not have to control us. Jesus extended grace to Peter, and he extends that same grace to us. When we recognize irrational fears for what they are, we can begin to replace them with faith in God's promises.

As we continue to face challenges, remember fear does not define us. We have been given the tools to confront irrational fears, and with God's help, we can walk forward in faith, trusting his plan. Like Peter, we may stumble, but God will always give us grace and help us redirect our steps, enabling us to stand firm in his truth.

CLOSING THOUGHT

Breaking free from irrational fear requires us to confront the lies we've been believing and replace them with the promises of God. As we break free from the lies that make us afraid, we move from fear-driven reactions to faith-filled responses, walking in the confidence that God is in control and his truth is far greater than any fear we face.

CLOSING PRAYER

Lord, like Peter, I have faltered in moments of doubt and fear, but I know my story doesn't end there. You are the God who restores, upholds, and calls me forward in faith. Today, I surrender my fears to you. Replace them with bold confidence in your presence, power, and perfect plan. I trust you to sustain me.

In Jesus' name,
Amen.

Day Five
From Fear to Faith – Breaking Free

I am so happy you have made it to the end of the week. This deep dive into fear has been a powerful study! Being equipped to dismantle the choking grip fear can have on our minds is a major step to walking in freedom from the lies the enemy likes to tell us.

As we conclude our study, let's reflect on the journey we've shared. We've faced our fears and learned to identify false beliefs, replacing them with the truth of God's Word. We've seen how Peter's fear and moments of failure reflect our own struggles with irrational fears, self-doubt, and insecurity. Like Peter, we can move forward from fear to faith, from failure to redemption.

We've explored how fear can distort our perceptions, leading us to react impulsively in ways that go against God's truth. We've also discovered how Peter's redemption shows us that grace and forgiveness are always available, no matter how many times we stumble. Today, we will conclude by reflecting on the steps we've taken this week and how we can continue walking in faith, instead of being held captive by fear.

As we look at the bigger picture, remember: God is not disappointed in you because of your fears. He sees your potential and is ready to guide you towards the faith-filled responses that reflect his truth. We are all on a journey where we can break free from the grip of fear and embrace the power of God's promises.

SCRIPTURE REFLECTION 1
2 Corinthians 12:9
"Each time he said, 'My grace is all you need. My power works best in weakness.' So now I am glad to boast about my weaknesses, so that the power of Christ can work through me."

UNDERSTANDING THE PASSAGE
Paul wrote 2 Corinthians to the church in Corinth, a city known for its wealth, culture, and rampant immorality. This letter was written after a period of tension between Paul and the Corinthians, as some false teachers had questioned his authority as an apostle.

In response, Paul defended his ministry. Rather than bragging about his accomplishments, he chose to highlight his sufferings and weaknesses.

In this specific passage, Paul describes a personal struggle which is often referred to as his "thorn in the flesh." While the exact nature of this thorn is unknown, scholars believe it could have been a physical ailment, persecution, or some other kind of hardship. Paul had prayed for relief, but instead of removing the struggle, God assured him his grace was enough, and his divine power is best displayed through human weakness.

This truth connects directly to Peter's story. In the midst of fear and failure, he was not rejected by Jesus but restored by him. His weaknesses and denial of Christ were not the end of his story, but the turning point that refined his faith. Just as Peter's failure became the place where his faith grew stronger, Paul discovered that weakness does not hinder God's power; rather, it is where his power is most clearly revealed.

Similarly, Peter's faith was refined and strengthened through his failures. This passage shows that God's grace is completely sufficient for us. God operates through our weaknesses rather than in spite of them. God's ability to work through our weakness is good news because God is not looking for perfection, not even near perfection; instead, he seeks surrender. When we turn our shortcomings over to him, he can strengthen us in them. Like Peter, we often feel defeated when we fall short. But when we surrender our limitations to God, his power takes over. Instead of letting fear control us, we can rely on his strength and grace to break free from the stronghold of fear and step into the freedom of our faith.

REFLECTION QUESTIONS

- How have you experienced God's strength working through a weakness or limitation in your own life?

- When fear makes you feel like your shortcomings disqualify you, how can this verse remind you of God's grace and power at work in you?

SCRIPTURE REFLECTION 2
Romans 8:37

"No, despite all these things, overwhelming victory is ours through Christ, who loved us."

UNDERSTANDING THE PASSAGE

Paul wrote the Book of Romans to believers in Rome during a time when Christians faced growing opposition. Although large-scale persecution under Emperor Nero had not yet begun, many early Christians were already experiencing hostility, social rejection, and pressure to conform to Roman culture and pagan practices. The Roman Empire was a place of immense power and corruption, and being a follower of Jesus often meant exclusion from society, economic hardship, and even threats to personal safety.

Paul's words in Romans 8 were a bold declaration to these believers. He proclaimed they were more than conquerors through Christ, regardless of the trials they endured. He wanted Christ-followers to know they were more than just survivors. They were children of God who were filled with the Holy Spirit and equipped to overcome the enemy and anything the world threw at them.

The phrase "more than conquerors" (hypernikōmen in Greek) implies overwhelming victory. In context to this passage, being more than a conqueror means we overcome adversity through God's love and power rather than through our own efforts. This kind of victory does not imply that we escape hardship, but rather we overcome it through faith and perseverance. Paul is proclaiming God has the power to do more than fight the enemy; instead, he has the power to overcome the enemy!

This truth directly applies to Peter's life. His denial was not the end of his story. Even though fear and failure seemed to have the final say, Jesus restored Peter, and he became a bold witness for the gospel. The blood of Jesus on the Cross transformed Peter's life. He was no longer a man ruled by fear and impulse. Peter, who denied Christ in front of a few, became an apostle who boldly proclaimed that Christ was the Messiah in front of thousands at Pentecost. Peter not only conquered his fear but also became one of the loudest voices to declare Christ as Lord and Savior.

Like the believers in Rome, Peter faced trials that tested his faith, yet his story shows God's love is greater than fear and powerful enough to redeem even our worst moments.

This passage speaks to the freedom we have in Christ. Fear and past failures do not define us. Jesus has already secured the victory, and through him, we can walk forward in faith, confident that nothing can separate us from his love.

FAITH IN ACTION

1. **Recognize A Fear That Holds You Back**

- What fear has kept you from stepping into God's plan?

- Identify the false belief connected to it.

2. **Use Thought-Stopping To Break The Cycle**

   Thought-stopping is a technique used to interrupt negative thought patterns before they take root. When fear-based or irrational thoughts arise, this method helps halt the mental spiral and redirect focus to God's truth.

- Recognize the Fear-Based Thought – Pay attention to the moment fear enters your mind.

- Physically or Mentally Stop the Thought – Some people say "Stop!" aloud or visualize a stop sign to break the pattern.

- Replace the Thought with Truth – Immediately counter the lie with a scripture from the list at the end of this study or a personal declaration of faith.

- Refocus on God's Promises – Shift your attention to prayer, worship, or an action that reinforces faith over fear.

3. **Declare Victory Over Fear**

- Write a personal declaration using Scripture to replace fear with faith.
  Example:
  "I am not controlled by fear, for God has given me a spirit of power, love, and a sound mind" (2 Timothy 1:7).

4. Take A Bold Step Of Faith

- Choose one way to act in faith despite fear.

- Trust God's strength to sustain you.

SEEING THE BIGGER PICTURE

Fear is more than an emotion; it can become a stronghold that shapes our thoughts, feelings, and behaviors, keeping us stuck in patterns of avoidance and impulsivity. Like Peter, we may react in ways that contradict our faith, whether by succumbing to fear, acting impulsively to regain control, or distancing ourselves from truth when the pressure feels overwhelming. Peter's story shows us how fear may cause us to stumble, but through Christ we can defeat its tight hold in our minds.

Breaking free from fear requires us to uncover any deeply rooted false beliefs we may have. Once we discover a false belief, we can then understand how it has influenced our perceptions, thoughts, feelings, and behaviors. When we have a complete understanding of this process, we can then refute the lies and dismantle any stronghold the enemy has established in our minds.

Every time we confront fear with faith, we weaken the stronghold and step into the freedom Christ has already won for us. The grip of fear loses its power when we replace Satan's lies with truth. With God's strength and grace, we can begin to respond to fear instead of reacting to it. As we turn to him, fear loses its power, and trust takes its place. Fear will always try to hold us back, but in Christ we find the freedom to move forward with confidence, knowing his grace is greater than whatever we face.

CLOSING THOUGHT

Fear may feel overwhelming, but it is not unshakable. Strongholds built on false beliefs lose their power when we confront them with truth, respond in faith, and trust in God's unwavering faithfulness. Like Peter, we may falter, but God's grace meets us where we are, restoring and strengthening us. With each step of faith, we walk deeper into the freedom of Christ.

CLOSING PAYER

Father, I confess that fear has distorted my perception and kept me from fully trusting you. I don't want to be ruled by false beliefs or anxious thoughts. Help me measure my fears against the truth of your Word. When doubt creeps in, remind me you are constant, sovereign, and always working on my behalf. Strengthen me to see fear for what it is; powerless compared to you.

In Jesus' name,
Amen

SCRIPTURES TO OVERCOME FEAR AND LIES THE ENEMY TELLS

These scriptures serve as truths to replace the lies that keep us trapped in fear. Use them to challenge false beliefs, meditate on God's promises, and strengthen your faith.

GOD'S PRESENCE AND STRENGTH IN FEAR

Isaiah 41:10
"Don't be afraid, for I am with you. Don't be discouraged, for I am your God. I will strengthen you and help you. I will hold you up with my victorious right hand."

Truth: You are never alone. God is with you, strengthening and sustaining you through every fear.

Psalm 34:4
"I prayed to the Lord, and he answered me. He freed me from all my fears."

Truth: When you seek God, He delivers you from fear. His response is protection and peace.

John 14:27
"I am leaving you with a gift—peace of mind and heart. And the peace I give is a gift the world cannot give. So don't be troubled or afraid."

Truth: Jesus offers a peace that the world cannot provide. Fear and worry do not have to dominate your thoughts.

FEAR IS NOT FROM GOD

2 Timothy 1:7 (NLT)
"For God has not given us a spirit of fear and timidity, but of power, love, and self-discipline."

Truth: Fear does not come from God. He has given you power, love, and a sound mind to overcome fear.

1 John 4:18
"Such love has no fear, because perfect love expels all fear. If we are afraid, it is for fear of punishment, and this shows that we have not fully experienced his perfect love."

Truth: God's perfect love removes fear. You are completely loved, and love overcomes fear.

YOUR IDENTITY IN CHRIST OVERCOMES LIES

Romans 8:1
"So now there is no condemnation for those who belong to Christ Jesus."

Truth: Your past does not define you. In Christ, you are free from guilt and shame.

2 Corinthians 5:17
"This means that anyone who belongs to Christ has become a new person. The old life is gone; a new life has begun!"

Truth: You are a new creation in Christ. The lies that once held you no longer define you.

Ephesians 2:8-9
"God saved you by his grace when you believed. And you can't take credit for this; it is a gift from God. Salvation is not a reward for the good things we have done, so none of us can boast about it."

Truth: Your worth is not based on your performance but on God's grace.

VICTORY OVER FEAR AND INSECURITY

Romans 8:31
"What shall we say about such wonderful things as these? If God is for us, who can ever be against us?"

Truth: Nothing can stand against you when you walk in God's purpose.

Romans 8:37
"No, despite all these things, overwhelming victory is ours through Christ, who loved us."

Truth: You are more than a conqueror through Christ. Fear does not have the final say.

Philippians 4:13
"For I can do everything through Christ, who gives me strength."

Truth: Fear does not limit you—God empowers you to do all things through Him.

FAITH OVER FEAR

Philippians 4:6-7

"Don't worry about anything; instead, pray about everything. Tell God what you need, and thank him for all he has done. Then you will experience God's peace, which exceeds anything we can understand. His peace will guard your hearts and minds as you live in Christ Jesus."

Truth: Prayer and gratitude shift your focus from fear to trust. God's peace will guard your heart and mind.

Matthew 17:20

"You don't have enough faith," Jesus told them. "I tell you the truth, if you had faith even as small as a mustard seed, you could say to this mountain, 'Move from here to there,' and it would move. Nothing would be impossible."

Truth: Even a small amount of faith has the power to overcome obstacles and fear.

How to Use These Scriptures:

1. Write them down – Choose a verse that speaks to your specific fear; keep it where you can see it.

2. Speak them aloud – Declare God's truth over your life, replacing fearful thoughts with Scripture.

3. Meditate on them – Reflect on these verses daily, allowing them to reshape your perspective.

4. Pray them over your life – Ask God to help you believe and walk in the truth of His Word.

WEEK FIVE
GROUP DISCUSSION

Begin by watching the Week Five video together. Afterward, ask the group, "What stood out to you most from the video?"

After one or two participants have shared, take time to review last week's study. As a group, flip through each day's reading, briefly noting the Reflection Questions and Faith in Action prompts. Allow time for participants to share their responses to each prompt. If you finish early, use the Group Discussion Questions below to encourage deeper connection.

1. How does Peter's experience show the impact fear can have on decision-making, and what can his journey teach us about responding with faith?

2. How do false beliefs contribute to fear, and how might passages like Isaiah 41:10 or 2 Timothy 1:7 help challenge those patterns?

3. What's one moment this week where you reacted out of fear, and how might pausing to respond in faith change your approach?

4. What does Jesus' grace toward Peter reveal about how God responds to our moments of fear or hesitation?

5. How can Peter's story encourage someone to take a small step of faith when navigating a difficult or uncertain situation?

Week Six

A Cup of Sorrow

I am excited to begin our study on feelings and emotions and the impact they have on our beliefs, perceptions, thoughts, and behaviors. As a reminder, this study is your time to be present with yourself and God. Let the pace of the day fade into the background so you can create space in your heart for what lies ahead.

If you are feeling weary from the emotional work of the past few weeks, I want to encourage you to keep pressing forward. While the journey may feel long, each step brings you closer to a place of freedom, and the tools you have gained will equip you to continue walking ahead. Over the past several weeks, we have been naming lies, confronting fears, and peeling back layers of shame, doubt, and despair. This week, we will slow down and deliberately explore something deeper and more personal, focusing on our feelings, particularly those of sorrow, but not exclusively, as all our feelings have an impact on our behavior.

Sorrow is often misunderstood. We tend to view it as something negative to escape rather than something meaningful to engage. It can often feel hard to carry, so we try to set it aside because the heaviness feels easier to ignore than to embrace. But sorrow doesn't just go away. It lingers, waiting in the background to express itself. It can feel like a weight on our chest, a quiet ache smoldering in silence. Unlike the demand of despair that feels like water boiling over the top, sorrow sits and simmers just below the surface.

In the biblical sense, sorrow isn't something only to endure. It can be a sacred space where we encounter God in our rawest moments; a space where lament meets faith. It is where we begin to understand the depths of our compassion and start moving toward healing. As we will see, through the life of David, sorrow isn't the enemy of faith. On the contrary, sorrow is an emotion that can function as a doorway to deepen and strengthen our walk with Christ.

This week, we will learn from David's experience of his deeply felt feelings and the intense emotions he encountered. David dared to express his immense sorrow to God personally and intimately. We, like David, will learn how to sit with what hurts, to speak it out loud, and allow God to meet us in the middle of our pain. We'll uncover what it means to feel our feelings honestly and without judgment. We will understand the value of processing our feelings with God and learn to move forward with peace.

Sorrow is not something to fear. Sorrow is something we bring to the Father to experience a deeper intimacy with him. This particular study on feelings is not about spiraling into sadness or getting lost in grief; it is about learning to sit with our feelings long enough to feel God's presence with us and hearing him say he will help us get through to the other side of our grief.

Before we begin, I want to discuss something essential to framing our entire week: the distinction between emotions and feelings. Though we often use the words interchangeably, they're not the same. Emotions are automatic. They are our body's biological response to something in our environment. They happen quickly and without our permission. Feelings, on the other hand, come a little later. They are the conscious interpretation of those emotions, shaped by our perception of what is happening. Our perception of our emotions is where things can get messy. When we experience a surge of emotion, such as despair, fear, or anger, our minds immediately try to make sense of it, assigning meaning that may or may not accurately reflect the truth of what is happening.

Understanding this distinction gives us room to reflect. Instead of labeling what we feel as wrong or trying to shut it down, we can begin to explore it by asking ourselves a few key questions: *What emotion am I experiencing? What am I feeling as a result of that emotion? And what belief might be shaping my interpretation?*

For example, I might notice the emotion of sadness and realize I'm feeling unimportant because a friend didn't return my message. As I sit with that, I might uncover a belief that says, *"If I were truly valued, I wouldn't be ignored."*

This moment of awareness opens the door for healing. David did this again and again in the Psalms. He honestly acknowledged what was stirring inside him, and then he let God meet him in his moment of despair.

Day One
When Sorrow Becomes a Stranger

We have all experienced moments when sorrow felt distant, like something we've pushed aside or buried for so long it becomes hard to recognize when it finally emerges. When sorrow unexpectedly surfaces, we may find ourselves unsure of how to sit with it, having avoided the depth of our emotions for so long.

Today, we'll reflect on two types of sorrow. One that comes from loss, and the other that comes from sin. Both can be overwhelming when left unacknowledged, yet as David shows us, when we bring them before God, they can become the very doorway to healing. We will look at how David experienced both: the devastating loss when his wives and community were taken captive by raiders as well as the crushing sorrow following his sin with Bathsheba. Both moments in David's life reveal how acknowledging emotion isn't a weakness but an essential step toward healing. The emotions and feelings we experience, whether from loss, betrayal, disappointment, or sin, are valid and need to be acknowledged.

David's story invites us to embrace our emotional world instead of running from it. Before he was a king, he was a shepherd and a musician. He felt deeply and never shied away from expressing himself. He wasn't afraid to cry out to God and name what was hurting inside him. His psalms reflect the full range of human feelings and emotion: grief, loneliness, betrayal, and regret. Yet, in the midst of experiencing these feelings and emotions, he never stopped pursuing God.

SCRIPTURE REFLECTION 1
1 Samuel 30:1–6
"Three days later, when David and his men arrived home at their town of Ziklag, they found that the Amalekites had made a raid into the Negev and Ziklag; they had crushed Ziklag and burned it to the ground. They had carried off the women and children and everyone else but without killing anyone. When David and his men saw the ruins and realized what had happened to their families, they wept until they could weep no more. David's two wives, Ahinoam from Jezreel and Abigail, the widow of Nabal from Carmel, were among those captured. David was now in great danger because all

his men were very bitter about losing their sons and daughters, and they began to talk of stoning him. But David found strength in the Lord his God."

For the full story of how God led David to pursue the Amalekites and recover everything that had been taken, you may want to read 1 Samuel 30:1-20 in its entirety.

UNDERSTANDING THE PASSAGE
Before David became king, he spent years on the run from King Saul, the man who held the throne of Israel at the time. Although David had once served Saul faithfully, Saul became increasingly jealous and threatened by David's success and popularity. His jealousy turned to hatred, and David was forced into hiding to escape Saul's attempts to kill him. During this time, David lived in the wilderness with a band of loyal men and eventually settled in a Philistine town called Ziklag. While away on a three-day journey, David and his men returned to find Ziklag burned to the ground and their wives and children taken captive by the Amalekites. The devastation was immediate and personal. These men were not just soldiers; they were husbands and fathers, and their home had been destroyed. Overwhelmed by grief, these men who followed David turned on him and threatened to stone him.

It's in this emotionally intense moment that David demonstrates something deeply meaningful. He turns to God for strength instead of giving in to pressure. In the midst of deep loss, David wrestles with feelings of betrayal and fear while carrying the heavy burden of leadership. The emotions swirling around him are intense and confusing. The grief his men feel has turned into rage, and amid David's own sorrow, he finds himself becoming their target. All the chaos, grief, anger, and betrayal bear down on him. Yet, in the midst of it all, David finds strength in the Lord his God.

This moment offers a compelling example of how to hold space for intense emotions without letting them take control. Emotional intensity often hijacks our ability to think clearly, making it harder to access logic, reason, and, above all, our spiritual grounding. When emotions like grief, fear, or anger reach a certain level, they can override our usual coping skills, leading to impulsive reactions, withdrawal, or emotional shutdown, often called "fight or flight." But learning to take a moment to regulate that intensity allows us to access a supernatural strength that only comes through the power of the Holy Spirit living within us.

David models this beautifully. He doesn't react impulsively to his sorrow or the anger directed at him. He pauses. And in that pause, he strengthens himself in the Lord. That is the shift from emotion-driven reaction to faith-centered response. David didn't run from his feelings or let them take control either; he faced the depth of what he was experiencing and chose to ground himself in God. This practice of slowing down to make space for our emotions and seeking God in the middle of them is essential in emotionally intense moments. It's not about minimizing the pain; rather, it is about facing the pain with courage and honesty, trusting that God is with us in it.

Let's break this down. When David returned to Ziklag to find the city burned and his family taken captive, he was flooded with the **emotion** of sorrow. That sorrow triggered **feelings** of devastation, fear, and even isolation as the men who had followed him turned against him, ready to stone him in their grief. Beneath those feelings was a **belief** he had failed as their leader and lost everything that gave his life meaning. But instead of reacting from that place of despair, David took a moment to lean in and let himself grieve. Scripture says he wept until he had no strength left, and then he strengthened himself in the Lord. Because he took time to fully allow himself to feel and then lean into the supernatural strength that comes from God, his perspective began to change. He moved from seeing only loss to trusting God could still lead him forward. When he sought God's direction, God gave him a plan that led to provision and restoration.

Today, we can use David's example in our own lives. When faced with loss, betrayal, or overwhelming sorrow, we can choose to acknowledge the depth of our emotions instead of letting them dictate our actions. We can find strength in God, trusting he is not only with us in our grief, but he can also provide strength to move forward one step at a time. Because David chose to surrender and seek God's direction rather than react in despair, God not only gave him a plan but restored to him everything that had been taken. God not only restored everything that had been stolen from David, but he also gave them more, allowing David and his men to carry off the plunder from their enemies as their own. When we, like David, turn to God in our sorrow, we, too, find the path to healing and restoration.

REFLECTION QUESTIONS

- According to 1 Samuel 30:1–6, how did David respond differently from his men in the face of shared grief and devastation? What does this contrast show you about managing the intensity of your emotions?

- Describe how David's response in verse 6 reflects the shift from emotional reaction to spiritual grounding. What does this teach you about how you can respond when your emotions feel overwhelming?

SCRIPTURE REFLECTION 2
Psalm 32:3–5
"When I refused to confess my sin, my body wasted away, and I groaned all day long. Day and night, your hand of discipline was heavy on me. My strength evaporated like water in the summer heat. Finally, I confessed all my sins to you and stopped trying to hide my guilt. I said to myself, 'I will confess my rebellion to the Lord,' and you forgave me! All my guilt is gone."

UNDERSTANDING THE PASSAGE
Psalm 32 is one of David's psalms of confession, written after a season of deep personal failure.

He likely wrote this psalm after his affair with Bathsheba and the murder of her husband Uriah (2 Samuel 11). David had finally had enough, and he was feeling the weight of his sin.

For the nation of Israel, psalms like this were both personal prayers and public songs. It was a way of teaching others about the seriousness of sin and the mercy of God. As king, David carried the responsibility of modeling faith. This psalm was a way for David to express his honesty through writing words that convey both the agony of guilt and the hope of forgiveness, for everyone to see.

Before his public confession, David had held back his sorrow and guilt, hiding them from everyone, including himself. He was avoiding the reality of his actions and their emotional cost. This silence led to an internal breakdown, both spiritually and emotionally. The turning point in this psalm comes when David acknowledges his sin and surrenders his feelings of sorrow he had kept hidden. When he confesses, he experiences both forgiveness and a release from the weight of sin that had been crushing him.

David's reflection in Psalm 32 reveals the deep toll his unacknowledged sorrow and sin took on him. He speaks of the silence he kept, which led to an internal struggle so intense it physically drained him. He said, "My bones wasted away, and my strength was gone." The weight of hiding sorrow and sin reveals itself in him groaning throughout the day, as well as in the heaviness of God's hand upon him. These words aren't merely poetic language, but a vivid description of the emotional and physical toll that buried grief and sin can have on our bodies and souls. David describes the oppressive feeling of sorrow like the heat of summer, symbolizing the relentless, inescapable nature of concealed sin.

It's important to note that David's sorrow in this passage is tied to his specific unconfessed actions surrounding Bathsheba and Uriah. This sorrow is different from the grief we experience from loss or death. While sorrow over sin involves a brokenness and guilt compelling us toward confession and reconciliation, sorrow from loss can feel like an aching emptiness, a longing for the person or thing we've lost. Both types of sorrow are valid but have different sources and results. Sorrow from sin is tied to the need for repentance and restoration, while sorrow from loss often requires mourning and time to heal.

This passage illustrates the difference between hiding sorrow and bringing it before God. When we bottle up sorrow resulting from sin, it can eat away at us, affecting not only our hearts but also our bodies and minds. However, when we bring our sorrow to God and speak it, feel it, and acknowledge it, it can lead to healing and restoration.

Like David, when we hide our anguish, whether from personal failures, loss, unresolved grief, or sin, it often shows up in ways we don't immediately recognize. It may manifest as irritability, anxiety, anger, or even emotional numbness. These are the ways emotions deeply buried within can surface. Emotions, especially sorrow, are not something we should avoid. We can move through them and find healing when we choose to understand and face them instead of pushing them aside. Just as David found freedom in confession, we, too, can experience healing when we acknowledge and process our sorrow with God.

REFLECTION QUESTIONS

- In this passage, David talks about how unconfessed sin and hidden sorrow affected him physically and emotionally. What does this passage show you about the connection between your emotional, spiritual, and physical well-being? How can this understanding help you today when you experience emotional or spiritual struggles?

- David describes how confessing his sin brought him healing. How is this moment of confession similar to other times in Scripture, such as when the prodigal son returns to his father in Luke 15:11–24, or when Peter confesses his denial of Jesus in John 21:15–19? What do these examples suggest about the connection between confession, emotional healing, and spiritual restoration?

FAITH IN ACTION

When sorrow feels intense and heavy, the instinct is often to push it away. But healing begins when we allow ourselves to notice it, name it, and bring it before God. The tools below are especially helpful when you feel weighed down by sorrow, but they can also be used with any emotion that feels overwhelming.

1. **Observe and Name**: When a strong emotion rises, take a moment to notice it. Say to yourself, "This is sorrow. This is fear. This is anger." Naming the feeling keeps you present instead of burying it.

2. **Validate the Feeling**: Tell yourself, "It makes sense that I feel this way after what I've walked through." Validation doesn't mean the feeling will last forever, but it honors its presence rather than fighting against it.

3. **Ground in the Present**: If an emotion begins to take over, use your senses to steady yourself: notice five things you see, four things you touch, three things you hear. For example, you might look around the room and name a picture on the wall, the color of a chair, the pattern on the floor, the book on the table, and the light coming through a window. This simple act helps bring you back into the moment.

4. **Breathe with Intention**: Place your hand over your heart and take slow, steady breaths, inhaling for four counts and exhaling for four. With each breath, imagine releasing part of what you're carrying into God's hands.

SEEING THE BIGGER PICTURE

Today, we explored how sorrow, whether rooted in sin or loss, can become overwhelming when left unacknowledged. Facing it honestly and allowing ourselves to process our feelings is a crucial part of the healing process, not a barrier to it. When we suppress our emotions, they don't disappear. They stay buried, smoldering while waiting for the right moment to surface. This kind of avoidance leads to emotional, spiritual, and even physical overload. It can be exhausting to keep our feelings and emotions hidden.

When we allow emotions to surface and give them a voice and ourselves space to feel them, we open the door to having a more intimate and authentic relationship with Christ. David's story shows how sorrow, though painful, can become a gateway to deeper intimacy with God. He stepped into a place of forgiveness and restoration by bringing his grief and guilt before the Lord.

Choosing to face our emotions rather than bury them takes intentionality and emotional strength. It also requires us to slow down and learn how to manage the intensity of what we're feeling. When we pause, breathe, and allow ourselves to feel without being overtaken, we shift from reaction to response.

Choosing to engage our emotions with honesty and intention moves us forward toward healing through the act of surrender.

In Matthew 11:28–30 Jesus said, "Come to me, all of you who are weary and carry heavy burdens, and I will give you rest. Take my yoke upon you. Let me teach you, because I am humble and gentle at heart, and you will find rest for your souls. For my yoke is easy to bear, and the burden I give you is light." When we invite God into our sorrow, we acknowledge the pain and allow him to step into it with us. He meets us there and takes the weight we have been carrying. Even in our brokenness, God shows up and transforms our hearts, leading us toward freedom.

CLOSING THOUGHT

Emotions are not obstacles to our well-being; they are guides pointing us toward what needs attention in our hearts and minds. Embracing our emotions isn't about indulging in them or allowing them to control us; instead, it's about honoring the truth they hold. When we sit with our emotions, we give ourselves permission to fully experience them, acknowledge their presence, and understand their deeper meaning. In doing so, we can invite God into those vulnerable spaces, where he can bring healing and renewal. By embracing our emotions, we step into the freedom of facing what we feel with courage rather than running from it, trusting we're not walking through it alone.

CLOSING PRAYER

God, you see the pain I carry and the parts I try to hide. Thank you for being near to me, even when I feel overwhelmed or worn down by what I'm holding deep inside. Help me stop running from what I feel and teach me how to face my emotions with honesty and courage. Please give me the strength to slow down, breathe, and bring my pain to you. Let this be the place where healing begins. I choose to trust you in the middle of my grief, and I surrender what I've been carrying.

In Jesus' name,
Amen

Day Two
What's Beneath the Surface

As we continue our journey through this week, today, we will take a deeper look into the emotional undercurrents in David's story. We will look at his reactions that bring to light the feelings he carried beneath the surface. Seeing David's emotions up close helps us recognize how our own unspoken feelings influence us more than we realize.

Today, we will see David in a moment of emotional intensity that doesn't quite match the outward offense. His reaction to a man named Nabal seems excessive, even violent. But when we look closer, we recognize what is actually happening beneath the surface: something deeper is fueling his reaction. This reaction is what I refer to as "smoke from a different fire." The situation sparks a buried emotion from the past, one that had been ignored but continues to smolder deep within, waiting for an outlet.

When we ignore our feelings and emotions, they don't just go away; they still exist, often reappearing in unexpected ways through uncontrolled reactions. Most of the time, we do not realize why we are reacting the way we are; it just seems to happen. Can any of you relate? When we find ourselves having what looks like an overreaction, it is good to take a step back and ask, *Is this smoke from a different fire?*

David was not alone in this struggle; Paul wrestled with it too. In Romans 7, Paul describes the exhausting back-and-forth between what he wants to do and what he actually does. His honesty gives language to the same inner conflict we feel when we are pulled in different directions, frustrated by our reactions, and confused by our impulses.

As we move into today's passages, remember the distinction we introduced earlier this week: emotions are automatic, rising without effort, while feelings evolve as we interpret and give meaning to those emotions. Holding onto that distinction helps us see that not everything we feel is rooted in the present moment.

So let's look beneath the surface to recognize the hidden fires that drive our emotional reactions.

SCRIPTURE REFLECTION 1

This story captures a heated moment between David and Nabal, and the wise intervention of Abigail. When Nabal refused David's request for provisions, David's anger flared:

1 Samuel 25:21–22

"'A lot of good it did to help this fellow. We protected his flocks in the wilderness, and nothing he owned was lost or stolen. But he has repaid me evil for good. May God strike me and kill me if even one man of his household is still alive tomorrow morning'!" (verses 21–22)

When Abigail intervened with humility and wisdom, David's response shifted:

1 Samuel 25:32–33

"'Praise the Lord, the God of Israel, who has sent you to meet me today! Thank God for your good sense! Bless you for keeping me from murder and from carrying out vengeance with my own hands'."

For the full account of this story, you may want to read 1 Samuel 25:2–35 in its entirety.

UNDERSTANDING THE PASSAGE

At this point in David's life, he is still waiting to become king and is living as a fugitive. Though he has been anointed by the prophet Samuel, Saul remains on the throne and sees David as a threat. David spends these years on the run, hiding in the wilderness, surrounded by loyal men, and constantly under the threat of being hunted down. His life is marked by exhaustion, fear, and a longing for God's promise to finally be fulfilled in his life by becoming King of Israel.

During this time, David and his men had protected the shepherds and flocks belonging to a wealthy man named Nabal. While camped nearby, they made sure nothing was stolen or harmed. When David sent messengers to request food and provisions, a gesture that would have been culturally expected in return for such protection, Nabal responded with insults and a harsh refusal.

David's response was immediate and intense. Enraged, he strapped on his sword and instructed 400 of his men to do the same. His plan wasn't simply to confront Nabal; it was to kill every male in his household. The intensity of David's reaction did not match the offense. His overreaction is a clear example of "smoke from a different fire." In David's defense, Nabal's refusal was uncalled for; at the same time, it was all David needed to react in anger. This spark stoked a fire that had already been burning. David's exhaustion, fear, and unresolved grief over his circumstances had built up beneath the surface, waiting for an outlet. His fury was real, but it was fueled by something deeper. This moment reveals how unprocessed emotion, particularly when ignored, can hijack our perception and lead us to create a narrative that fuels an existing emotional fire, resulting in a disproportionate reaction.

Abigail's intervention becomes the turning point. She meets David with humility and wisdom, helping him see what he could not in his emotional state. Her words break his emotional momentum, creating the space for David to reflect. David listens, and he chooses a different path. His emotional intensity doesn't disappear; however, he manages to regain clarity and surrenders his impulse for revenge.

This story gives us a biblical framework for recognizing when our own reactions might be connected to something deeper. When we find ourselves overreacting, shutting down, or feeling more than the moment seems to warrant, it's worth asking: *Where is this intense emotion coming from?* Sometimes, what we're feeling is grief or sorrow that hasn't been fully acknowledged. It hides in plain sight, driving our reactions before we even realize it. But, like David, we can learn to recognize those moments as opportunities to act differently. When we slow down and pay attention, we can choose to respond rather than react, demonstrating self-discipline and spiritual transformation, both of which are made possible through the power of the Holy Spirit living within us.

REFLECTION QUESTIONS

- What does David's initial reaction to Nabal's insult reveal about what might have been simmering beneath the surface emotionally? (Consider how his circumstances may have shaped his response.)

- How does Abigail's response shift David's behavior, and what can this teach us about the power of interruption in emotionally charged moments?

SCRIPTURE REFLECTION 2
Romans 7:15–25

"I do not understand what I do. For what I want to do I do not do, but what I hate I do. And if I do what I do not want to do, I agree that the law is good. As it is, it is no longer I myself who do it, but it is sin living in me. For I know that good itself does not dwell in me, that is, in my sinful nature. For I have the desire to do what is good, but I cannot carry it out. For I do not do the good I want to do, but the evil I do not want to do—this I keep on doing... What a wretched man I am! Who will rescue me from this body that is subject to death? Thanks be to God, who delivers me through Jesus Christ our Lord!"

UNDERSTANDING THE PASSAGE

Paul's words in Romans 7 are raw, honest, and quite familiar to anyone who has felt trapped in a cycle of conflicting thoughts, feelings, and behaviors. He is fighting the urge not to fall into familiar behavior patterns and is experiencing an inner battle between what he desires and what he actually does. It is clear to us he is frustrated and can't seem to figure out why he cannot break free from this pattern of behavior.

Paul wrote this letter to the church in Rome, a diverse group of Jewish and Gentile believers, during a time of growing tension and theological upheaval. Some clung to the law, while others were learning to walk in grace. Paul aimed to explain the power of the gospel and teach new believers that Christ's righteousness does not come from how well we follow the rules or how hard we try to do all the right things; instead, he explains, righteousness is a gift from God for all who accept Christ as their Savior.

To drive home his point, Paul uses himself as an example. He wants everyone to see the struggle we all have with sin and with our inner thoughts and outward behaviors. His explanation helps us understand our struggle is not only with sin but also with the spiritual tension of knowing what God would want for us to do. We have a desire to obey, yet we feel powerless over the pull of sin.

The intensity of his words, "I do not understand what I do," "What a wretched man I am!" candidly reveals how even those who walk closely with God are not immune to the battle we experience internally between our desires and our behaviors. Paul confronts the tension between human weakness, which can include emotional reactions, and his spiritual desires. By being honest about his own experiences, Paul brings out into the open the weight of our inner struggles with thoughts, feelings, and behaviors. He paints a powerful picture of what happens when emotions and feelings are left unattended.

Paul reacts to what has been building inside him, not just to the moment. His struggle involves more than controlling his behavior; it's about understanding what's underneath it. Without awareness of why we act as we do, lasting change is nearly impossible. As Christians, we have the Holy Spirit who provides us insight to see the root causes of our actions and the strength to change.

In this passage, Paul is giving us permission to take a moment and ask ourselves, *What am I actually feeling beneath this reaction? What is this emotion telling me, and what deep-seated belief might be fueling it?*

When the tension feels unbearable, Paul shifts the focus by asking his own question, "Who will rescue me?" His answer is, "Thanks be to God, who delivers me through Jesus Christ our Lord!" His struggle doesn't end in despair but leads to surrender. That surrender becomes the bridge between reaction and response, between emotional distress and peace, between inner conflict and spiritual strength. Just as Paul surrendered his inner struggle, we, too, must consciously choose to release our battles to God, allowing him to strengthen our faith.

As we continue to reflect on Paul's words, it is clear that surrender is less about achieving perfection or escaping struggle and more about recognizing the depth of our inner conflict and bringing it to God. Paul's shift from frustration to surrender shows us we don't have to fight our battles alone. His honesty is a reminder that surrender is the place where God meets us to heal the broken places and to give us the strength to keep moving forward.

Understanding the difference between our emotions and our feelings helps us examine what fuels our reactions. Beneath many of our responses are deeper beliefs or unmet needs. When we acknowledge both and bring them into God's presence, we surrender not only the struggle itself but also what lies beneath it, allowing him to guide us toward peace and strength.

It's not about having the perfect amount of emotional control; instead, it is about learning to sit with our emotional experience long enough to let God meet us in it.

REFLECTION QUESTIONS

- What does Paul's description of his internal struggle in Romans 7 reveal about the tension between our desires and our actions? How does this struggle mirror your own experiences with inner conflict?

- In Romans 7:24–25, Paul asks, "Who will rescue me?" and then gives thanks for deliverance through Jesus Christ. How does this moment of surrender shift Paul's perspective on his struggle, and what does it teach us about finding freedom in surrendering our own battles?

FAITH IN ACTION

The next time you feel a strong reaction like anger, sadness, irritation, or even numbness, take a moment and try this practice:

1. **Take a slow, steady breath in**, then let it out.

2. **Place your hand on your chest or stomach** and notice the rise and fall of your breath.

3. **Name what you feel in one word**: anger, grief, fear, fatigue

4. **Ask yourself:** "Is this about what's in front of me, or is this smoke from a different fire?"

5. **Check the facts:** Ask yourself: *What happened? What do I know to be true? What might I be assuming?*

6. **Stay with the feeling** instead of pushing it away or clinging to it. Think of it like a surfer riding a wave; you need to stay with the feeling long enough for the wave to complete its motion for a safe, steady landing. Notice how it rises, builds to a crest, and then begins to fall back until it settles. Allow the feeling to move through you in the same way.

SEEING THE BIGGER PICTURE

Not all emotional reactions are about what is happening right in front of us. Sometimes, our feelings are tangled up in something deeper and unresolved. It can be something we haven't given ourselves the time or space to acknowledge. That is why some situations hit harder than they should or why we find ourselves shutting down, lashing out, or feeling out of control in the moment.

David's reaction to Nabal went beyond the insult; it was influenced by the weight of unresolved issues lurking underneath. His response was real, but it wasn't entirely about Nabal.

In Romans 7, Paul's internal wrestling reminds us that emotional and spiritual struggle is not a sign of weakness but an essential part of emotional and spiritual growth. Paul felt the tension of wanting to do one thing and then doing another. That conflict is familiar to many of us, especially when our feelings have been shaped by deeper emotional patterns we haven't fully processed.

This inner battle is why understanding the difference between emotions and feelings matters. When we identify what we're feeling, where it's coming from, and how it might be connected to something deeper, we begin the process of learning how to respond rather than react. Emotional intensity doesn't disappear overnight. Learning to hold space for unresolved feelings helps us stop assigning meaning to every reaction and start uncovering what we are actually trying to express.

When we learn to hold this space for the feelings that usually get swept aside, we begin to build emotional resilience. Over time, resilience grows as we pay more attention to our emotions and start working through them, rather than reacting or trying to shut them down.

It is important to fully understand emotions are the messengers, and feelings are the interpreters. Remember, emotions are biological responses that show up quickly, often without warning, to signal something within us needs attention. Feelings are how we perceive and make sense of those emotions once we're aware of them. They help us interpret what our emotions mean in the context of what is happening around us. Both our emotions and our feelings matter. Without emotions, we would not know what needs to be addressed, and without feelings, we would not understand how those emotions are affecting our reactions. When we are aware of both of them, we can bring them before God so he can help heal our hurts and guide our response.

CLOSING THOUGHT

Struggling with our emotions is part of the journey, not a detour. When we choose to face them rather than avoiding them, we open the door for God to transform our pain into purpose and our weakness into strength.

CLOSING PRAYER

Lord, thank You for being present in my struggles. Help me to embrace my emotions with honesty, recognizing them as opportunities for growth. Teach me to surrender my inner conflicts to you, trusting in your strength to guide me toward healing and peace. Thank Holy Spirit for giving me the courage and strength to take this next step toward healing and freedom.

In Jesus' name,
Amen.

Day Three
Feelings : Fact or Fiction

As we continue this journey through David's life, today we will look back at him as a young shepherd boy. By examining his early years, we will see how false beliefs could have taken hold early on and caused him to draw wrong conclusions about his worth. In 1 Samuel 16, David was overlooked and ignored by his father, set aside in favor of his older brothers. He likely felt as though he was overlooked because he was not good enough for his father. His feelings of being unloved and undervalued were real to him, but these feelings were not based on truth; they were rooted in a false belief that told him he had no real value or worth.

The conclusion David most likely drew was based on a lie that made him feel insignificant. David's story illustrates how false beliefs and tainted perceptions of reality can lead to feelings that mislead us about our identity.

Today, we will examine how David's perceptions of his worth impacted his feelings. We will learn how distorted thoughts and beliefs affect our emotions, and we will discover how to reject these lies and align ourselves with the truth of God's Word.

SCRIPTURE REFLECTION 1
1 Samuel 16:6-13
"When they arrived, Samuel took one look at Eliab and thought, 'Surely this is the Lord's anointed!' But the Lord said to Samuel, 'Don't judge by his appearance or height, for I have rejected him. The Lord doesn't see things the way you see them. People judge by outward appearance, but the Lord looks at the heart.' Then Jesse told his son Abinadab to step forward and walk in front of Samuel. But Samuel said, 'This is not the one the Lord has chosen.' Next Jesse summoned Shammah, but Samuel said, 'Neither is this the one the Lord has chosen.' In the same way all seven of Jesse's sons were presented to Samuel. But Samuel said to Jesse, 'The Lord has not chosen any of these.' Then Samuel asked, 'Are these all the sons you have?' 'There is still the youngest,' Jesse replied. 'But he's out in the fields watching the sheep.' 'Send for him at once,' Samuel said. 'We will not sit down to eat until he arrives.' So Jesse sent for him. He was dark and handsome, with beautiful eyes. And the Lord said, 'This is the

one; anoint him.' So as David stood there among his brothers, Samuel took the flask of olive oil he had brought and anointed David with the oil. And the Spirit of the Lord came powerfully upon David from that day on. Then Samuel returned to Ramah."

UNDERSTANDING THE PASSAGE

In 1 Samuel 16:6-13, we witness a beautiful and profound moment in David's life. Samuel, who was a prophet sent by God to anoint the next King of Israel, arrives at Jesse's house and is presented with each of Jesse's sons. Samuel is captivated by the oldest son, Eliab, and assumes he is the one God has chosen to be the next King of Israel. However, God corrects Samuel on his assumption that Eliab must be the chosen one based on his "good looks," saying, "People judge by outward appearance, but the Lord looks at the heart." Samuel faces each son one by one, but God rejects them all. Puzzled by this outcome, Samuel asks Jesse if all of his sons are present. Jesse says no and then calls his youngest son, David, who was in the fields tending sheep.

Jesse hadn't even considered David as an option for the next King. After all, David was just a lowly shepherd. The fact that David was overlooked while his older brothers were deemed worthy speaks volumes about how perception shapes feelings. David's circumstances could have easily skewed his perception of his worth.

It is easy to conclude David most likely felt rejected, unimportant, and overlooked. Yet, God's view of David was radically different. While David's father saw him as unworthy, God saw him as the future King of Israel. Feelings are not facts. Just because David may have felt like he didn't measure up didn't mean he was less valuable in God's eyes. This truth is crucial for all of us. We often place expectations on ourselves based on our feelings. But feelings cannot be relied upon.

While Scripture doesn't explicitly tell us David's feelings in this specific moment, we do know from his psalms that he wrestled with feelings of being forgotten and abandoned. In Psalm 13:1, he cries out, "O Lord, how long will you forget me? Forever?" And in Psalm 27:10, he writes, "Even if my father and mother abandon me, the Lord will hold me close." These honest expressions reveal that David knew what it felt like to question his worth and wonder if he mattered.

Yet, God's view of David was radically different from any human perception. While David's father may not have seen his value, God saw him as the future King of Israel. This contrast reveals a powerful truth: our circumstances and how others view us do not determine our worth; God's perspective does.

Are you beginning to see how all of this fits together?

CIRCUMSTANCES (what happens)
↓
EMOTIONS (automatic biological response)
↓
PERCEPTION (how I see the circumstance - filtered through core beliefs)
↓
BELIEFS (what I conclude is true)
↓
THOUGHTS (what I tell myself about it)
↓
FEELINGS (my interpretation of my emotions)
↓
BEHAVIORS (how I act)

REFLECTION QUESTIONS

- According to 1 Samuel 16:6–13, how does God's view of David differ from Samuel's and Jesse's initial perceptions? What does this reveal about how God sees you compared to how others or even you see yourself?

- Describe David's circumstances in this passage. How might his experience of being overlooked have shaped his feelings, and how does God's response challenge those feelings?

SCRIPTURE REFLECTION 2

Romans 8:16-17

"For his Spirit joins with our spirit to affirm that we are God's children. And since we are his children, we are his heirs. In fact, together with Christ, we are heirs of God's glory. But if we are to share his glory, we must also share his suffering."

UNDERSTANDING THE PASSAGE

In the Book of Romans, Paul wrote to believers who were trying to navigate their faith while living under Roman rule. In the preceding chapters, he grapples with the tension between life in the flesh and life in the Spirit, gradually building toward the confidence believers have in their relationship with God. Romans 8 marks a shift. Instead of ignoring suffering, Paul acknowledges it, yet anchors the church's identity in Christ. What gave them strength wasn't a change in circumstances but the confidence they belonged to God and their identity, worth, and future in Christ were secure, no matter what came against them.

In these verses, Paul speaks to our identity as God's children. Through the Holy Spirit, God affirms our worth and belonging. When sorrow or rejection presses in, it's easy to let feelings taint or even completely distort how we see ourselves. We may feel overlooked, unloved, lost, unimportant, damaged, or abandoned (the list goes on; each of us can fill in the blank). But feelings can't be trusted or have the final say in who we are. Paul points us back to what is true. God's Word says we are his children, co-heirs with Christ, deeply loved and valued, even when our emotions and feelings suggest otherwise.

This passage places identity and suffering side by side. Sorrow and hardship may shape how we experience life, but they don't get to define who we are. Only God does. Even in our struggles, his truth about our worth remains unchanged. Feelings, however, come and go and are constantly changing. They are like the waves of the ocean, rushing in and moving out with the tide, carried by currents beyond their control. Similarly, our feelings often move in the same way. They ebb and flow as our circumstances change, some of which we can't always see or control, but they never alter how God sees us.

When our feelings seem overwhelming, we can trust God understands and is not making any judgments. He will always give us the space to feel as deeply as we need, and we can trust he will give us the courage and strength to release the tension of what we are experiencing, just as David did.

REFLECTION QUESTIONS

- Describe the relationship between identity and suffering in this passage. How does understanding your identity as God's child impact the way you interpret difficult emotions?

- What does this passage reveal about God's perspective of your worth, even when your feelings tell a different story?

FAITH IN ACTION

When feelings of being unworthy or unseen arise, take some time to think about and challenge the belief behind your feelings and emotions.

1. **Name What You Feel**: Say it to yourself or write it down: "I feel overlooked," "I feel unimportant." Naming the feeling helps create space between what you feel and how you respond.

2. **Check the Facts:** Ask: *What do I know is true about this situation, and what am I assuming?* Notice if the feeling is being fueled by an old belief that doesn't match the present moment.

3. **Anchor in Truth**: Open God's Word and let what he says about you speak louder than the false beliefs trying to define you.

Examples:
Ephesians 1:4–5
"Even before he made the world, God loved us and chose us in Christ to be holy and without fault in his eyes. God decided in advance to adopt us into his own family by bringing us to himself through Jesus Christ. This is what he wanted to do, and it gave him great pleasure."

→ **This counters the belief** "I have to earn my worth." You were chosen and loved before you ever did anything to deserve it.

1 Peter 2:9
"But you are not like that, for you are a chosen people. You are royal priests, a holy nation, God's very own possession. As a result, you can show others the goodness of God, for he called you out of the darkness into his wonderful light."

→ **This counters the belief** "I don't belong" or "I am insignificant." You are chosen, set apart, and deeply valued by God.

Psalm 139:13–14
"You made all the delicate, inner parts of my body and knit me together in my mother's womb. Thank you for making me so wonderfully complex! Your workmanship is marvelous—how well I know it."

→ **This counters the belief** "I am a mistake" or "I have no value." You were intentionally created, and God delights in his design of you.

4. **Practice Opposite Action**: Opposite action means choosing to act in alignment with what is true, even when your feelings tell you otherwise. Choose one small act that reflects the truth of your worth—text a friend who encourages you, step outside and breathe deeply as you thank God for making you, or speak this aloud: *"I am chosen. I am loved. I belong."*

Even if you don't feel it yet, acting from truth helps your heart catch up to what is real. Feelings matter, but they are not facts. When we notice them rising, we can pause, examine them, and choose a response shaped by God's perspective. As you acknowledge your emotions and your feelings and challenge the intensity, you're opening space for clarity, peace, and healing.

Remember, feelings are not facts. While your feelings are valid, they need to be examined through the lens of truth. When we notice our emotions taking over, we can pause, challenge them, and realign with God's perspective. As you acknowledge your emotions and your feelings and challenge the intensity, you're opening space for clarity, peace, and healing.

SEEING THE BIGGER PICTURE

Feelings can be strong enough to convince us of things that are not true. They can draw us into a narrative to support what we think is happening without us checking the facts or taking the time to see if our feelings line up with the truth of God's Word.

When we experience feelings like sorrow, frustration, or rejection, it's easy to believe the narrative our minds want to spin. We assume things about our circumstances or about other people's intentions without ever considering whether our thoughts are actually true. Often, we jump to conclusions because it's just easier, and over time, it becomes our natural default.

The real trouble comes when our feelings start calling the shots. Hurt, fear, and shame creep in, clouding our view. Before we know it, we're drawing conclusions that do not match reality. When our feelings cloud our view, sorrow can weigh the heaviest. It becomes the lens through which we see everything else. When grief or hardship settles in, life itself can start to feel empty. Hope thins out and the future starts to feel elusive. Even the smallest steps feel impossible. But right there, in the heaviness, God is present, and he is the one who steadies us and invites us to take one more breath and one more step.

Here's the good news: our story doesn't have to be held hostage by our feelings. We can turn our focus back to God's perspective. His truth reframes the narrative in our minds. And as that happens, our feelings begin to change as well.

As we continue exploring how feelings impact our experiences, remember that sorrow, rejection, or pain do not have to write the story of our lives. When we surrender our perspective, thoughts, and beliefs to God, we can clearly see he is the one writing our story. When we choose to see ourselves through his eyes, he brings clarity and changes how we perceive what's in front of us. That is how transformation happens, and negative feelings and the inaccurate conclusions we draw from them are replaced with peace, hope, and security in our identity in Christ.

CLOSING THOUGHT

Feelings come and go, but God's truth does not. When we lean on him, he reminds us of who we are and anchors us in his truths.

CLOSING PRAYER

Father God, thank you for being with me through every emotion I experience. Help me see my feelings through your eyes and remember they don't define me. When sorrow, frustration, or confusion rise within me, prompt me to take time to reflect and align my heart with your truth. Give me the strength to challenge the lies I have believed and replace them with your promises. Guide me to move forward with peace, clarity, and faith in your unshakable love.

In Jesus' name,
Amen

Day Four
Spiraling Thoughts

Some days, it feels like sorrow takes over everything. Your thoughts start to race, your feelings become too heavy to carry, and even the simplest tasks suddenly seem impossible. You might find yourself staying in bed with the covers pulled over your head or staying so busy that you don't have time to feel anything at all. Whether you shut down or keep going on autopilot, the result is the same: your emotions begin to dominate your life. You're no longer responding, just reacting.

In today's study, we'll explore again what it looks like to be emotionally hijacked and how spiraling thoughts can keep us stuck in sorrow. We'll look at David's cry for help in Psalm 143 and how Jesus speaks peace into our pain in John 16. More importantly, we will continue to learn how to hold space for our emotions without letting them completely take over, and learn how to take small, steady steps forward in the middle of the struggle.

SCRIPTURE REFLECTION 1
Psalm 42:5
"Why am I discouraged? Why is my heart so sad? I will put my hope in God! I will praise him again—my Savior and my God!"

UNDERSTANDING THE PASSAGE
Psalm 42 is believed to have been written during a time of great emotional distress for David, possibly while he was fleeing from Saul or facing another period of exile. This psalm reflects David's emotional struggle, in which he feels overwhelmed by sorrow, confusion, and a profound sense of longing. The opening verses capture a season where sorrow feels heavy, memories feel painful, and God's presence feels harder to grasp.

David shares the pain of feeling spiritually disconnected: "Why am I discouraged? Why is my heart so sad?" His question isn't merely an intellectual inquiry; David is genuinely feeling discouraged, and his emotions are surfacing. His intense feelings overpower his thoughts, leading him into despair and doubt. He feels as if God has forgotten him, and it seems as though his sorrow and despair are completely taking control.

This emotional response illustrates the point that raw, unchecked feelings can distort our perception, leading us to a false narrative, one that clouds our view of God's truth. Feelings take over, causing our thoughts to spiral and disconnect us from reality.

David's sorrow created a narrative in his mind in which he told himself he had been abandoned and God was no longer with him. These feelings, although real, were not the truth. David's emotional hijacking wasn't just a reaction to his circumstances, but a result of how he interpreted them. His perception of being alone and forsaken wasn't based on God's truth about him. But in the very next line, David begins to shift his focus. He says, "I will put my hope in God! I will praise him again—my Savior and my God!"

David actively chooses to challenge his feelings. He acknowledges his sorrow but refuses to let it define him or his reality. Instead, he turns to God's truth about who God is and what he has promised.

This moment is a clear example of how our feelings can hijack us by taking over our rational thoughts. But it is also a strong reminder of how we don't have to let our feelings take over our perceptions and behaviors. Just as David surrendered his feelings and turned his mind to the things of God, we, too, can choose to replace them with God's promises by checking the facts and recognizing we are not seeing things through the lens of truth, but believing the lies the enemy tells us.

David disciplined himself to stop spinning and asking why. Then, he turned his thoughts to God, and his perspective instantly changed. He went from feeling discouraged to praising God.

When our emotions and feelings begin to take control, we can stop and, like David, deliberately make a different choice. As we learned in yesterday's Faith in Action, this choice is called opposite action. We take the time to reflect and reset. Instead of being overwhelmed by our feelings, we can choose to break the cycle and allow room for God's peace to replace our turmoil. Our feelings may seem overwhelming, but we have the power through the Holy Spirit living within us to ground ourselves in God's love and his promises.

REFLECTION QUESTIONS

- In Psalm 42:5-6, David addresses his emotional turmoil and chooses to hope in God. What does this reveal about the role of personal choice in managing emotions according to the psalm? How does this align with the overall message of the psalm?

- How does David's shift from sorrow to hope in Psalm 42 illustrate the difference between feelings and faith? What does this passage suggest about the relationship between emotions and God's truth in shaping our responses to difficult circumstances?

SCRIPTURE REFLECTION 2

1 Samuel 27:1-4

"But David thought to himself, 'Someday Saul is going to get me. The best thing I can do is escape to the Philistines. Then Saul will stop hunting for me in Israelite territory, and I will be safe.' So, David took six hundred men and went over to Achish son of Maoch, the king of Gath. David and his men settled in Gath with Achish. Each man had his family with him, and David had his two wives, Ahinoam of Jezreel and Abigail of Carmel, Nabal's widow. When Saul was told that David had fled to Gath, he stopped searching for him."

UNDERSTANDING THE PASSAGE

In 1 Samuel 27, David, exhausted from years of fleeing Saul, begins to spiral into a state of fear and hopelessness. His feelings take the lead, and he makes a decision based on his feelings of abandonment and fear, not on what he knows to be true about God.

I can imagine David's thoughts racing through his mind like a bullet train leaving the station, "Saul's going to kill me eventually. I can't keep running forever. I'll never be safe. If I stay here, he'll find me. The Lord hasn't delivered me, and I'm all alone. I need to do something before it's too late. The Philistines are my only option. At least I'll be safe there."

His mind is overwhelmed by fear and uncertainty. David's feelings are valid, but his thinking is distorted by the belief God is no longer with him, a deception Satan persistently reinforces. In that moment, he doesn't stop to evaluate the truth of his situation, nor does he take time to reflect on God's faithfulness in the past or remember how God has guided him through numerous challenges. Instead, his thoughts escalate, and he concludes that the best course of action is to leave the land of Israel, seeking refuge among those who are enemies of his people.

We do this, too. When faced with uncertainty or fear, we often forget God's faithfulness, losing sight of all the times he has proven himself true in our lives. Like David, we get caught in a spiral of thoughts, allowing our emotions to cloud the truth.

This passage illustrates how feelings, when left unchecked, can quickly accelerate into distorted thoughts. David's fears about Saul's pursuit cloud his perception, and he makes a decision that goes against God's guidance. His emotions create a false narrative that justifies his decision to act on fear instead of trusting in God's promises.

David's experience demonstrates how feelings can distort our thinking, leading us to perceive the worst in our situation and make unwise decisions. The lesson for us is clear: When we allow our feelings to take the lead, our thoughts can quickly spiral out of control. We can convince ourselves our feelings define the truth of our situation, but the reality is feelings are not facts, and they cannot always be trusted. When we stop to examine them through God's lens, we can reframe our thoughts and avoid making decisions based on distorted perceptions.

REFLECTION QUESTIONS

- What feelings surface for David in 1 Samuel 27, and how do those feelings begin to influence his thinking?

- Which feelings most often rise for you during seasons of waiting or uncertainty, and how do they tend to shape your responses?

FAITH IN ACTION

When your thoughts begin to spiral and your feelings start to take over, pause and use the simple acronym of the word STOP to help you steady your heart and mind:

1. **S — Say Stop:** When you notice your thoughts racing and your feelings rushing in, gently tell yourself "Stop." You don't have to solve everything right now. You're just pressing pause so you can breathe before reacting.

2. **T — Take a Breather:** Slow your pace. Inhale gently, then exhale fully. Let your shoulders drop. This simple pause signals to your mind and body that it's safe to slow down.

3. **O — Open Your Eyes**: Turn your attention inward. Notice what you're thinking and feeling, and how your body is responding. Ask: *What emotion am I experiencing? What feelings are rising with it? What belief might be fueling this?* Naming what's happening gives you clarity and creates space between the emotion and your next step.

4. **P — Pray and Proceed**: Invite God into the moment. Ask him to steady your heart and guide your next step. Then, move forward gently, not in reaction to what you feel but with intention rooted in God's presence with you.

SEEING THE BIGGER PICTURE

When emotions run high, even a single thought can set off a spiral. It might be something small, like a flash of disappointment, or something big, like a surge of fear, but once it is sparked, our minds can take off, spinning thoughts of how things could go wrong. As those thoughts build, our feelings intensify. Left alone, they can distort what we see and feel, making things seem heavier and more hopeless than they really are.

Spiraling thoughts thrive in the space between what we feel and what is actually true. They build momentum quickly, feeding on half-formed assumptions and imagined outcomes. Before long, we're convinced our fears are facts. But, again, feelings are not facts. They are messengers.

When our thoughts start to spin, it helps to take some time and name what we're feeling, then bring it to God before our feelings take over. God can anchor us when our thoughts and feelings are moving too fast to catch. His truth steadies our minds and reminds us that our feelings and emotions do not get to write our story.

CLOSING THOUGHT
It's easy to get lost in the spiral of emotions and thoughts that overwhelm us, but the truth is, we have the power to shift our thinking to create a different feeling. Like David, when we slow down and reflect, we can realign ourselves with God's truth and step out of the cycle of negative thinking. Our feelings are valid, but they don't always reflect the truth. By choosing to trust in God's promises and take control of our thoughts, we create space for healing and peace.

CLOSING PRAYER
Father,
Thank you for the reminder that my feelings do not define me. Help me to recognize when my thoughts are spiraling and to pause long enough to reflect. When I feel overwhelmed, guide me back to your truth. Strengthen my ability to respond thoughtfully, not react blindly. Help me remember your faithfulness and the promises you've made to me so I can shift my perspective and regain peace. In moments of uncertainty, help me to have clarity. Thank you for your constant presence.

In Jesus' name,
Amen.

Day Five
Letting Go

Letting go can be one of the most complex parts of the healing process. Unfortunately, when we hear letting go, we often think it means not allowing ourselves to feel at all. We often mistakenly think it is simply a way to try to feel better. But letting go involves learning how to move through our feelings rather than being driven by them.

Sorrow and grief have a way of settling in and becoming something familiar, and in a weird way, that familiarity brings comfort. The heartache starts to feel like a companion we have grown used to, even though it hurts.

It might feel disloyal to release what you've carried for so long. Maybe you believe holding onto your pain honors what was lost or protects you from future heartache. But holding on too tightly can keep you from moving forward.

Today, we will follow David's lead as he models how to bring sorrow into God's presence honestly and vulnerably.

We'll explore what it means to loosen our grip on grief, not by pretending it's gone, but by allowing God to carry us through it.

SCRIPTURE REFLECTION 1

Psalm 31:1–3, 9–10

"O Lord, I have come to you for protection; don't let me be disgraced. Save me, for you do what is right. Turn your ear to listen to me; rescue me quickly. Be my rock of protection, a fortress where I will be safe. You are my rock and my fortress. For the honor of your name, lead me out of this danger…. Have mercy on me, Lord, for I am in distress. Tears blur my eyes. My body and soul are withering away. I am dying from grief; my years are shortened by sadness. Sin has drained my strength; I am wasting away from within."

UNDERSTANDING THE PASSAGE

Psalm 31 was written during one of the most difficult seasons of David's life, likely while he was fleeing from King Saul or facing betrayal during Absalom's rebellion. Absalom was one of David's older sons who believed he was next in line to be King. Though we don't know the exact moment, the intensity of his words reveals a man overwhelmed by fear, sorrow, and immense pressure.

David's words in this psalm again show us what it looks like to bring raw, honest emotion into the presence of God. He doesn't hold back when he describes his anguish and deep sorrow. His grief is consuming, his body worn out from pain. And yet, even in this place of deep distress, he anchors himself in one powerful truth: God is his refuge.

David doesn't wait until he feels better to cry out; he calls on God in the middle of the storm. He trusts God will be his rock and fortress, the one who will lead and guide him through what feels unbearable. Bringing your raw emotion before the Lord unedited is the first step of letting go and surrendering.

What makes David's cry so compelling is it doesn't come from a shallow place but from a deep well of personal pain and a series of traumatic experiences. At different points in his life, David was hunted by Saul, betrayed by his son Absalom, and forced to face the devastating fallout of his failures. He knew what it meant to hide in caves, to feel cut off, to grieve the loss of a child, and to wrestle with regret. His words, "I am dying from grief... my years are shortened by sadness," aren't poetic exaggerations. They reflect real pain.

Even so, David knew where to carry his pain. He didn't bury it or try to pretend it wasn't there; he brought it straight to God. He didn't polish it or water it down. He let the mess show. And still, in the same breath, he called God his rock and his fortress. This moment in David's story invites us to stop hiding our pain and bring it to God in its raw and honest form. He shows us what it looks like to fully embrace our feelings and then let them go, placing the weight of our grief in God's hands.

Letting go starts with honesty. It's not a one-time act; instead, it's a process of surrendering piece by piece. By watching David bring his pain to God, we see how healing begins when we stop hiding and start allowing ourselves to feel fully in God's presence.

The turning point is not when the pain ends but when we stop carrying it by ourselves. Surrendering your feelings to God does not mean forgetting the people or experiences we have encountered; it means we stop letting pain be the lens through which we view everything else. It means we trust God enough to hold what we can't, to lead us through what feels impossible, and to carry us through grief until we begin to feel whole again.

REFLECTION QUESTIONS

- What does Psalm 31 reveal about how David brings his grief, fear, and anguish before God, and how does his response challenge the way you usually handle your own pain?

- In this passage, David names his suffering honestly while still calling God his refuge and fortress. What pain have you been carrying alone, and what might it look like to place that weight into God's hands, one piece at a time?

SCRIPTURE REFLECTION 2

Psalm 91:1–2

"Those who live in the shelter of the Most High will find rest in the shadow of the Almighty. This I declare about the Lord: He alone is my refuge, my place of safety; he is my God, and I trust him."

UNDERSTANDING THE PASSAGE

In the previous psalm, David cried out from a place of deep sorrow, pleading for rescue and describing God as his refuge in the middle of overwhelming pain. Psalm 91 continues the theme, but with a change in tone. It moves from a cry of desperation to the peace that comes from abiding in God's presence. "Whoever dwells in the shelter of the Most High will rest in the shadow of the Almighty." These words do not come from someone who has escaped pain, but they come from someone who has learned where to place it. In this psalm, we see David bringing his pain into the shelter of God's presence, and over time, his presence became David's place of rest. As we slowly loosen the hold we have around our heartache, we, too, can experience what it means to be held emotionally and spiritually in the refuge of the Almighty.

These verses also offer us a picture of what it means to live from a place of spiritual security. The words "dwell" and "rest" suggest something more than a temporary escape; they point to a way of living. David is not describing a one-time cry for help but a continual choice to remain close to God. Dwelling in the shelter of the Most High means we change our priorities and place God's presence in the center of our lives. This keeps us anchored in his love and grace. In this psalm, David teaches us that a relationship with God at the center isn't just about finding refuge in crises; rather, it involves prioritizing God in every season of our lives, whether we are on the mountaintop or in the valley.

While David cried out in desperation, he pointed to something we often overlook in sorrow: our deep need for stability. Emotional pain can leave us feeling disoriented, untethered, and reactive. But the "shadow of the Almighty" offers a different rhythm. He provides a rhythm of rest. It is here, in this quiet place with God, where letting go becomes possible.

Letting go, in light of this passage, isn't passive. It's an act of faith. To rest in God's shadow is to trust his nearness even when answers haven't come and healing still feels far away. It declares we no longer need to hold onto sorrow so tightly to prove love or loyalty. Instead, we can choose to believe beyond all doubt that God holds us and everything that burdens us with strength, compassion, and unconditional love; he surrounds us within his presence as he tucks us into the shadow of his wings.

REFLECTION QUESTIONS

- What does Psalm 91:1–2 reveal about the kind of rest God offers to those who choose to dwell in his presence?

- According to these verses, how does abiding in God provide a sense of stability and refuge in the middle of sorrow or uncertainty?

FAITH IN ACTION

1. **Read Psalm 91:1–2 slowly**, letting the words settle over your heart.

2. **Open your hands and pray**:

    "Lord, I place _____ in your hands."

3. **Sit quietly for two minutes**, resting in his presence. If your mind begins to wander, gently come back to this truth: "You are my refuge."

4. **When you're ready, take a deep breath** and picture God holding the weight of what you've placed in his hands. Whisper, "It belongs to you now."

5. **If you have something tangible** tied to your sorrow (a photo, letter, or keepsake), place it in a safe spot where you won't see it every day. As you set it down, say, "God, I trust you to carry this for me."

SEEING THE BIGGER PICTURE

Sorrow doesn't disappear when we ignore it. It finds other ways to surface through spiraling thoughts, emotional intensity, or reactions that feel bigger than the moment deserves. This week has been about paying attention to those moments and learning how to stop long enough to ask: *What am I feeling, and where is it coming from?*

David's life was more than a sequence of triumphs and failures. It was an unfolding narrative that offers a window into the complexity of the human heart. David was a man who felt deeply, with emotions that ran extremely high and low. Due to these emotional highs and lows, he experienced emotional extremes, which occasionally led to his actions being out of range for the circumstances he found himself in. David teaches us not to let our circumstances outweigh our faith, but instead to make our faith central to our thinking and be the overcomers God has destined us to be.

David's emotional complexities are what make his life so relatable. Like us, David carried sorrow, frustration, and fear; some of which were on the surface and some buried deep within. His life gives us a framework for recognizing what we feel and understanding where those feelings come from. His example teaches us the importance of learning to respond rather than react. David's life shows us again and again what we bring into the presence of God doesn't need to be filtered, fixed, or figured out. It just needs to be honest and real.

David's willingness to name his sorrow and bring it before God gave him the resilience to keep going. His life wasn't free from grief, but it was marked by something deeper. David knew where to go with his pain. That's the bigger invitation this week: to stop avoiding sorrow and instead allow it to become a place where we meet God more intimately.

Understanding the difference between emotions and feelings has helped us begin to untangle what we're carrying. When we recognize emotions are automatic and feelings are shaped by our thoughts and perceptions, we create room to slow down. That moment of space between what we feel and how we respond is where emotional regulation begins.

These are not only spiritual concepts; they are tools for emotional health. Learning to interrupt spiraling thoughts, to ground ourselves in the truth, and speak honestly with God equips us to move forward, even in seasons of pain. Each time we take a moment to reflect instead of react, we build strength. Each time we tell God the truth about what we feel, we create space for healing. Each time we let go of what we have had to bear on our own, God is there to help us carry the emotional weight of our pain.

David's story shows us we don't have to be fearless to be faithful. We just need to be willing to show up, with sorrow in hand, and trust God will meet us there.

CLOSING THOUGHT
Letting go doesn't mean erasing the past. It means letting go of what weighs you down, freeing your hands to hold onto God. He won't rush your steps, but he will steady them as you walk with him.

CLOSING PRAYER
God, you see the parts of me I've tried to hide. The grief I've buried, feelings I've avoided, and the thoughts I can't seem to silence. Thank you for meeting me in the middle of it all. Teach me how to release what I've been holding and trust you to carry what I can't. When I feel overwhelmed, help me breathe, slow down, and remember I am not alone. You are my refuge. You are my strength. Keep leading me one step at a time.

In Jesus' name,
Amen.

WEEK SIX

GROUP DISCUSSION

Begin by watching the Week Six video together. Afterward, ask the group, "What stood out to you most from the video?"

After one or two participants have shared, take time to review last week's study. As a group, flip through each day's reading, briefly noting the Reflection Questions and Faith in Action prompts. Allow time for participants to share their responses to each prompt. If you finish early, use the Group Discussion Questions below to encourage deeper connection.

1. How does David's honesty in the Psalms encourage us to bring our emotions to God without holding back?

2. Why is naming an emotion an important step in processing it, and how might this practice help us engage with God more honestly?

3. How does the idea of "smoke from a different fire" help explain why reactions sometimes feel stronger than expected?

4. In 1 Samuel 30:1–6, David found strength in God during a painful experience. What does his response teach about turning to God in difficult moments?

5. How does understanding our identity as God's children, as described in Romans 8:16–17, bring hope when emotions feel heavy or confusing?

Week Seven

A Cup of Freedom

We have made it to the final week! Take a moment to recognize the significance of getting this far in our journey together. It marks your commitment and courage to deepen your spiritual walk toward inner healing. These past six weeks have been filled with deep reflection and emotional excavation. We have confronted our fears, wrestled with sorrow, and learned to identify the lies buried beneath the surface. This final week is not the end of our journey; it's the beginning of walking in freedom, knowing God's truth is what anchors our mind, body, and spirit.

But let's take a minute and clarify what freedom means. Freedom isn't the absence of hard things or the sudden disappearance of pain. Freedom is found when we stop striving and start aligning our thoughts, beliefs, and perceptions with the truth in God's Word, the truth about who he is, who we are, and the power we have through the Holy Spirit to walk in that truth. Freedom isn't about perfection or performance. It isn't about living free from painful feelings or avoiding difficult and challenging circumstances. It's about learning to experience peace and joy even in the midst of them.

Freedom means acknowledging our feelings without giving them the authority to lead us. It reflects a life aligned with God's nature, where truth, not emotion, sets the pace. It is about anchoring ourselves to the personhood of God and his unchanging character, which gives us hope because we know he is faithful, loving, present, all-knowing, all-powerful, and fully in control. Freedom rests in trusting his plan even when we do not understand it.

In the previous weeks, we have discussed the war within our minds, the moments when our inner world feels divided, when our faith says one thing but our thoughts and feelings say another. We've explored fear, shame, sorrow, and the distorted perceptions that shape our feelings and influence our reactions. This week, we shift the focus. Rather than focusing on the tension between our thoughts, feelings, and reactions, we will explore how the deeper work of transformation unfolds. We will examine how our spirit leads, our soul responds, and how our body reflects what's happening within.

A key part of this transformation comes from something many overlook: the power of the Holy Spirit living within us. Too often, we assume knowing Scripture should be enough to change us. But our minds can hold truth without our souls receiving it. That's why so many feel stuck. Truth cannot set you free without power. In this week's study, we will explore how the Holy Spirit becomes your power source. He's the one who activates the truth and makes it real and personal.

In addition, we will take a deeper look at our inner design: our body, soul, and spirit. These are not disconnected parts. They are all connected and influence one another in profound ways. When they're not aligned, it can feel emotionally overwhelming, lead to impulsive reactions, and create a sense of spiritual disconnection. But when the Holy Spirit aligns our spirit and soul, everything changes. We are supernaturally enabled through the power of the Holy Spirit to move from anxiety to peace, from confusion to clarity, from striving to surrender.

Freedom is not something we can force. It's something we receive. And it often starts by recognizing we were never meant to do this alone. We are created to be connected to a power source stronger than our strength. This power can absorb our sorrow and strengthen us in our weaknesses. Our power source comes from the Holy Spirit who lives within us.

As we step into this final week, I encourage you to stay open. Let the truths we have uncovered settle deeper. Let your heart soften to receive love that has no conditions. And let the Holy Spirit illuminate the path ahead toward freedom.

Day One

From Knowledge to Power

Many of us have learned to rely on what we know. We trust our intellect, memorize scripture, and exercise the spiritual disciplines, but there are times when, despite all these things, we still feel stuck. The truth is, knowing God's Word isn't the same as living in its power. It's possible to have the correct answers and still feel disconnected, confused, or spiritually empty. Why? Because transformation doesn't begin with knowledge; it starts with the Holy Spirit working within the depths of our souls.

Today, we'll examine what Jesus and Paul said about the role of the Holy Spirit in activating our knowledge and revealing what we've yet to receive.

SCRIPTURE REFLECTION 1
Acts 1:8
"But you will receive power when the Holy Spirit comes upon you. And you will be my witnesses, telling people about me everywhere—in Jerusalem, throughout Judea, in Samaria, and to the ends of the earth."

UNDERSTANDING THE PASSAGE
These were some of Jesus' final words to his disciples before ascending to heaven; they were words spoken to a group of ordinary people who had just experienced extraordinary events. They had followed Jesus, learned from him, and witnessed miracles with their own eyes. Yet, as they stood on the edge of what would become the early Church, Jesus didn't tell them to rely on their experience or knowledge. He told them to wait for power from the Holy Spirit. The Greek word for 'power' here is *dynamis,* the root of our English word dynamite. It indicates supernatural strength. It is a strength beyond human effort. Jesus was preparing them to carry out a mission far bigger than themselves, and he knew they would need more than courage and knowledge. They needed the power of the Holy Spirit living within them.

The power Jesus promised wasn't only for courage or miraculous signs. It was divine strength that would sustain them through everything they were about to face. It was the kind of power that would carry them through persecution and extreme hardship.

The same is true for us. We can study Scripture and attend church every Sunday, but if we're not walking in the power of the Holy Spirit, we will eventually hit a wall. The truth might live in our minds, but without the power of the Holy Spirit, it cannot take root in our hearts.

This passage reminds us that we are not meant to navigate life alone. When the Holy Spirit empowers us, we shift from depending on knowledge and willpower to living with supernatural strength. True freedom begins when we stop trying to force change through effort alone and instead surrender to the Holy Spirit, trusting him to activate the living truth of God's Word in our body, soul, and spirit.

REFLECTION QUESTIONS

- According to Acts 1:8, what kind of power did Jesus promise his followers, and how does this shape our understanding of how the Holy Spirit works in our lives today?

- Describe the difference between relying on your own strength and receiving power from the Holy Spirit, as reflected in this passage.

SCRIPTURE REFLECTION 2

1 Corinthians 2:12-14

"And we have received God's Spirit (not the world's spirit), so we can know the wonderful things God has freely given us. When we tell you these things, we do not use words that come from human wisdom. Instead, we speak words given to us by the Spirit, using the Spirit's words to explain spiritual truths. But people who aren't spiritual can't receive these truths from God's Spirit. It all sounds foolish to them and they can't understand it, for only those who are spiritual can understand what the Spirit means."

UNDERSTANDING THE PASSAGE

Paul wrote these words to the believers in Corinth, a city known for its intellect and competing philosophies. Many in the culture took pride in their human wisdom and reasoning. This mindset had begun to influence the early church. Paul wanted all the new believers to understand spiritual truth doesn't come through intellect alone. We receive truth from the Word of God revealed to us through the power of the Holy Spirit. The message Paul delivers in this passage remains relevant today. We live in a world that values knowledge and credentials, but these are not the things that will give us freedom.

The freedom we receive when we walk with peace, hope, and purpose comes through the power of the Holy Spirit. He supernaturally transforms our thinking and heals our hurts. He helps us see the bigger picture and view our circumstances through the lens of his promises in his Word. And as Philippians 4:7 says, he gives us peace that goes beyond our understanding and guards our hearts and minds as we walk with Christ Jesus.

Have you ever read a verse so many times, but then one day it suddenly leaps off the page, speaking directly to you in a moment when you needed it most? In my book *Drinking the Cup You're Served*, I share a story about visiting Disney World with my family and riding a 3-D attraction at Animal Kingdom. When we walked in, they handed us a pair of 3-D glasses. Without them, everything looked flat and blurred. The moment we put them on, the scene burst with color and depth, and we felt pulled into the story. The Holy Spirit works in much the same way.

Scripture can shift from ordinary words on a page to vivid, personal truth, opening our eyes to see and understand things from a completely different perspective. We have more clarity and are able to see things we couldn't see before. This isn't a coincidence. This awareness is supernatural, and it comes through the power of the Holy Spirit, revealing what our minds may have known but our hearts have not yet received.

Paul tells us we've been given access to supernatural power from the Holy Spirit to understand what God freely offers us.

REFLECTION QUESTIONS

- According to 1 Corinthians 2:12–14, what role does the Holy Spirit play in helping us understand spiritual truth? How does this help you interpret times when Scripture has felt confusing or distant?

- Paul contrasts human wisdom with the wisdom of the Spirit in this passage. In what ways are you tempted to rely on human reasoning, and how might inviting the Holy Spirit into your understanding lead to deeper clarity and peace?

FAITH IN ACTION

Today, we learned that inner freedom begins when we let the Holy Spirit transform what we know in our minds into what we believe in our hearts. This supernatural shift from our minds to our hearts changes our core beliefs and reshapes our thoughts.

Today, take a few minutes to engage your heart, mind, soul, and spirit in a way that invites the Holy Spirit to work within you:

1. **Pause and Pray: Invite the Holy Spirit into Your Space**: Find a quiet place to be still with God. Rather than jumping into requests, simply pray:
"Holy Spirit, I invite you to show me what I haven't yet received. Help me move from knowing to believing, from effort to surrender."

Allow a few moments of silence and stillness. Don't rush. Take a deep breath and then listen.

2. **Identify What You've Been Carrying On Your Own**: *Where have I been trying to rely on willpower? What have I been trying to fix, change, or force on my own?*

Write down one area where you've felt spiritually stuck. Be honest. Then, write this phrase next to it: *"I surrender this to the power of the Holy Spirit."* This process is not a one-time act but a posture of release.

3. **Anchor Yourself in a Promise:** Choose one verse from today's study—Acts 1:8 or 1 Corinthians 2:12–14—and write it somewhere visible: a note card, your mirror, your lock screen. But don't simply read it. Ask the Holy Spirit to reveal something personal to you through it. You may even find yourself drawn to one specific phrase. Sit with that. Let it take root.

4. **Pay Attention to the Shift**: Over the next 24 hours, notice any moments where you feel clarity, unexpected peace, or a change in your response. These are signs the Holy Spirit is doing the work. Don't dismiss any thought or feeling as insignificant. Recognize the Holy Spirit is working in you and through you.

SEEING THE BIGGER PICTURE

If you've ever felt frustrated by your lack of progress, you are not alone, even when you're doing all the right things. Many Christians find themselves asking, *Why am I still stuck?* Or *why doesn't this truth feel real to me?* That tension between what you believe in your mind and what you experience daily can feel defeating. But today's study reveals something deeper: we cannot just think our way to a better space; we have to allow the Holy Spirit to activate supernatural power in our body, mind, and spirit. With the Holy Spirit working in our lives, we can move further in our journey toward emotional and spiritual freedom.

When Jesus told the disciples to wait for power, he wasn't giving them a strategy; he was inviting them into a relationship. He knew they would need more than conviction and confidence. They would need the Holy Spirit to empower, sustain, and guide them. And so do we.

Today's study offers an opportunity to invite the Holy Spirit to become more active in our lives. By meditating on his Word, we will sense the prompting of the Holy Spirit in our hearts. These promptings are how we start to recognize his voice, discern his will, and receive courage to move forward.

CLOSING THOUGHT

Freedom doesn't always feel like a breakthrough. Many times, bits of freedom come in our quiet times with the Lord. Meditating on his Word and surrendering our will draws us into deeper intimacy with the Holy Spirit, where true transformation begins.

CLOSING PRAYER

Dear Jesus,

Thank you, Holy Spirit, for living within me. Teach me how to respond to your promptings. I want to recognize your voice and respond with faith, even when I don't understand or when it feels uncomfortable or uncertain. I lay my heartache and pain at the foot of your cross. I no longer want to bear the suffering alone. I trust you will guide my every step, but I need your strength to follow your lead. Thank you, Holy Spirit, for peace beyond my understanding. I am grateful I don't have to see all the pieces to know you are working on a masterful plan in my life.

In Jesus' name,
Amen

Day Two
The Anatomy of the Soul

If you've ever felt like your heart believes one thing but your thoughts tell you another, you're not imagining it. A real battle is happening within your soul. According to Scripture, we are made up of three distinct parts: body, soul, and spirit. It is essential to understand the role and function of each part. Our body is the physical vessel that carries us through life, allowing us to respond and experience the world around us. Our spirit is the place where God dwells, and our soul houses our mind, free will, and heart.

For those who belong to Christ, the soul becomes the very place where the Holy Spirit steps in with discernment, empowering us to know and understand the promises of God. However, our soul is also where most of our inner struggles take place. It's where lies get planted and feelings get twisted and magnified. Our soul also contains our flesh or our fallen nature. The flesh is the part of us that resists God and pulls us toward sin. It's where selfish desires, pride, and cravings for control take root.

It is in our soul where truth and deception collide. One part of us recognizes the lie, while the other part wholeheartedly convinces us the lie is actually the truth, leaving us in this tension of knowing what is true and what is false. On our own, it is nearly impossible to overcome the lies of the enemy, which is why we must understand the power we have been given by the Holy Spirit to identify and take captive every thought that does not align with Christ.

To break free from the battle within our soul, we must understand how each part of the soul operates. Again, our soul encompasses our mind, free will, and heart. Our minds hold our thoughts, beliefs, and perceptions; our hearts contain our emotions and feelings; and our free will manages our flesh and guides the choices we make.

Our past experiences, current circumstances, and relationship with Christ impact each part of our soul. Our mind, which carries the thoughts and beliefs we hold, is deeply influenced by our wounds. Our will, which reflects the choices we make, is often pulled by old patterns, and our heart, which holds our feelings and desires, is influenced by our beliefs and perceptions of our past and current circumstances.

When past wounds or false beliefs take root in our minds, it causes us to drift from truth, which makes it harder to discern God's voice. But when we invite the Holy Spirit into the inner workings of our soul, he brings clarity to our thoughts, healing to our emotions, and courage to make decisions that align with the heart of God.

Today, we'll take a deeper look at the anatomy of the soul, not from a clinical perspective but through a spiritual lens. We will see how the Holy Spirit strengthens each part of our soul and brings it into agreement with our spirit.

SCRIPTURE REFLECTION 1
Hebrews 4:12
"For the word of God is alive and powerful. It is sharper than the sharpest two-edged sword, cutting between soul and spirit, between joint and marrow. It exposes our innermost thoughts and desires."

UNDERSTANDING THE PASSAGE
While the author of Hebrews remains unnamed, many scholars throughout church history have believed the apostle Paul may have written it. Regardless of authorship, the message is clear. The book was written for early Jewish believers facing pressure, persecution, and the temptation to revert to familiar religious traditions. The writer urges them to stay anchored in the authority of God's Word, reminding them Scripture is not passive or distant but alive and active.

The metaphor of the two-edged sword is especially important to understand. In ancient times, a double-edged sword was known for its precision and power. The sword could cut cleanly in either direction, making it a highly effective weapon in battle. The author uses this image to describe how the Word of God operates within us. Scripture doesn't strike randomly. On the contrary, it cuts with intention and immaculate precision. It divides the lies from the truth.

The comparison to joints and marrow emphasizes both the depth and sharpness of God's Word. Just as it takes a skilled hand to separate things as closely connected as joint and marrow, it takes the power of God's Word to reveal the different beliefs between the soul and the spirit to precisely separate what is temporary from what is eternal, what is distorted from what is grounded in Scripture, and what is self-driven from what is Spirit-led.

This verse offers one of the most apparent distinctions in Scripture between the soul and the spirit. It tells us God's Word not only speaks to us, but it pierces us. It reaches into the deepest parts of who we are, places we may not understand or even recognize. The Word of God doesn't stay on the surface. It cuts through the noise and the layers of deception, exposing the lies the enemy tells us, bringing us face-to-face with the truth that will set us free.

This passage plays a crucial role in helping us understand the inner struggle that occurs within our soul. Our mind, heart, and will are the parts of us where sin dwells, where false beliefs are formed, and where Satan seeks to insert lies that distort our perception. Our spirit, however, is where God resides. It's pure, holy, and untouchable by sin. When the writer of Hebrews says the Word "cuts between soul and spirit," it's showing us how Scripture helps us discern what's true from what's distorted; what's rooted in God and what's been shaped by deception.

Through the power of the Holy Spirit, God's Word becomes a discerning tool, exposing the thoughts and feelings often suppressed or overlooked. As the Holy Spirit brings those hidden places into the light and we receive his promptings with a pliable heart, we begin to shift. We stop reacting from a place of pain or distorted beliefs; instead, we respond to the truth the Holy Spirit reveals within our souls. It's here, in this divide between soul and spirit, where transformation happens.

REFLECTION QUESTIONS

- According to Hebrews 4:12, what does it mean for the Word of God to divide between soul and spirit, and how does this help us recognize what is true in our lives?

- How does the image of a double-edged sword help you better understand the way Scripture works in your heart and mind? What might God be trying to bring into the light through his Word?

SCRIPTURE REFLECTION 2
Ezekiel 36:26-27

"And I will give you a new heart, and I will put a new spirit in you. I will take out your stony, stubborn heart and give you a tender, responsive heart. And I will put my Spirit in you so that you will follow my decrees and be careful to obey my regulations."

UNDERSTANDING THE PASSAGE

These verses are part of a prophetic promise God gave to the people of Israel through the prophet Ezekiel. At the time, Israel was in exile because of their long pattern of rebellion against God. For generations, they had turned to idols, ignored the prophets, and refused to obey God's covenant. After repeated warnings, judgment came through defeat at the hands of the Babylonians. They were no longer in the land God had given them.

As a consequence, they felt disconnected and far away from God. Disappointment and displacement had worn them down. Their hearts, once tender, had become calloused. Worship became nothing more than a ritual, and over time, their identity as children of God faded beneath the weight of exile. Yet, amid the spiritual and emotional dryness, God speaks words of hope. He promises to change their hearts.

This passage declared what God would one day do through the new covenant. He would send the Holy Spirit to dwell within us, making it possible for us to hear his voice and discern the lies the enemy tries to tell. Having the Holy Spirit dwell within us enables our souls to align with God's will.

During Old Testament times, the Holy Spirit did not reside within God's people. He would only ascend upon them for a specific task or season. We see this when the Holy Spirit came upon Samson, filling him with strength to fight the Philistines (Judges 14:6). The Holy Spirit also rested on David after Samuel anointed him as king, yet later departed from Saul when his heart turned away (1 Samuel 16:13-14). Daniel was given wisdom and insight to interpret dreams because the Holy Spirit was upon him (Daniel 4:8-9). These passages demonstrate how the Holy Spirit's presence in the Old Testament was powerful, yet temporary.

Because the Holy Spirit did not dwell within his children when Ezekiel spoke these words, this prophetic promise foreshadowed the coming of the Holy Spirit after Christ's death, resurrection, and ascension. It was a promise that was fulfilled at Pentecost, recorded in Acts 2.

Although Ezekiel's message was originally a promise of future renewal for the people of Israel, its meaning goes far beyond their return from exile. The restoration God spoke of wasn't limited to a physical homecoming; it was about an internal transformation. And that promise is just as relevant today.

We may not live in exile as Israel once did, but there are times when we feel distant from God. We still go through the motions and pray, but it seems as though nothing is happening and nothing is changing.

The weight of our circumstances leaves us weary, and our faith shaken. Over time, our hearts grow distant. In those seasons, it can seem as if God is far away. Ezekiel 36 speaks into that place with a promise of renewal, assuring us the Holy Spirit can breathe life into what feels empty and restore the places that seem numb and unresponsive.

This passage captures the heart of what it means to experience inner transformation. Transformation is a supernatural experience that comes from the power of the Holy Spirit working to align our soul and spirit. Transformation does not come through striving or self-improvement; it can only come through the power given to us through the Holy Spirit.

This promise of transformation unfolds within the framework of how God created us with a body, soul, and spirit. Here, Ezekiel uses the terms "heart" and "spirit" to reflect two parts of that design. The heart represents a part of the soul, which encompasses the mind and free will, where sin, emotional wounds, and false beliefs often live. The spirit, on the other hand, is the part of us where God dwells, where sin cannot exist, and where truth has already been established. As the Holy Spirit works within us, He aligns our soul with our spirit, enabling transformation by helping us see and understand the truth of God's Word and discern thoughts, beliefs, and perceptions that do not align with his promises.

In these verses, Ezekiel also uses the imagery of a "stony heart," depicting a soul shaped by pain and suffering, describing a person who is resistant and spiritually disconnected. This separation may result from disappointment due to unanswered prayer or a deep loss that can never be replaced. Whatever the cause, when we have been hurt and conditioned to believe God does not care or is unable to give us what we think we need, our heart hardens. Over time, we develop a deep-rooted belief that God does not consider us worthy of his love.

This passage of Scripture speaks directly into our brokenness and feelings of hopelessness. When hope becomes elusive and our hearts begin to shut themselves down to avoid further pain, God offers something entirely new. He will give us a new heart, one no longer hardened by pain or guarded by fear, but tender and responsive to his healing touch. Through the power of the Holy Spirit living within us, our souls can be transformed into his likeness.

The Holy Spirit becomes the internal power source who enables us to follow God and to think, feel, and choose what honors him. Having your thoughts, feelings, and behaviors align with the truth of God's Word is what transformation looks like. It's not about suppressing emotions or pushing past negative thoughts. It's about letting the Holy Spirit reshape us from within.

REFLECTION QUESTIONS

- According to Ezekiel 36:26–27, what does God promise to change within us, and how does that shift impact the way we respond to him?

- What does the image of a "stony heart" reveal about the condition of the soul, and how does this passage invite us to experience God's renewal through the Holy Spirit?

FAITH IN ACTION

Today, we have learned our soul is the place where the real battle begins. God placed his Spirit within us so we would never have to fight the battles of the soul by our own strength. We have the Holy Spirit to help us. He gives us the power we need to overcome the temptations and lies the enemy tries to use to keep us out of sync with God's will and purpose in our lives.

When our thoughts and feelings align with his, freedom and healing follow, enabling us to walk in obedience to his Word. Transformation starts when we slow down and pay attention to what is happening inside our souls.
Here's how to align yourself with God today:

1. **Map the Movement of Your Soul:** Take a moment and write down three areas of your life where you feel stuck, triggered, or conflicted. Then, beside each one, label whether it is primarily rooted in a distorted thought, a feeling, or a behavior. This

simple exercise will help you recognize which part of your soul is most affected and is not aligned with God's truth. Is it your mind, heart, free will, or all three that is out of alignment?

  1)

  2)

  3)

2. **Let the Word Speak to Your Soul:** Read Hebrews 4:12 and Ezekiel 36:26-27 again, slowly. This time, ask: *What does the Holy Spirit want to reveal in my thinking? Where is he inviting me to shift or surrender?* Write down a short phrase from either passage that stands out. Ask the Holy Spirit to use it like a sword to precisely divide what is true from what is not.

3. **Practice Spirit-Led Decision-Making:** Think of one small choice you need to make today. It can be something that involves your will. Before you act, pause and ask: *Am I making this choice from a place of surrender and peace?* Let the Holy Spirit lead you in that moment. This is where transformation becomes real: not in theory, but in practice.

4. **Close with a Prayer of Surrender**

SEEING THE BIGGER PICTURE

The real battle doesn't begin with our circumstances; rather, it starts in the soul. Our thoughts, feelings, and decisions are often shaped by past pain and distorted beliefs. But when the Holy Spirit steps into those deep, broken places, he helps us see more clearly and from a different perspective, allowing transformation to follow. It is not something we force; it's something that flows when our souls are brought back into alignment with our Spirit, where God's truth lives within us.

CLOSING THOUGHT

Healing begins when our soul comes into agreement with the truth that resides within our spirit. The pain that once silenced you can now become a place where God speaks. In his presence, even sorrow finds meaning, and freedom takes root where wounds once lived.

CLOSING PRAYER

Father,

Thank you for loving me as I am. I come in complete surrender and lay the broken places of my soul before you. Help me let go of lies and embrace your truth, soften my heart to receive your voice, and give me the courage to choose what honors you. I trust the work you have begun in me will lead to lasting freedom.

In Jesus' name,
Amen.

Day Three
Love Unlocks the Door

Yesterday, we explored the inner workings of the soul and how the Holy Spirit aligns each part of our soul with our spirit. However, it is vital we acknowledge and receive the unconditional love of God before we can fully align ourselves with the truth of God's Word and gain complete access to the supernatural power of the Holy Spirit.

Unconditional love is what softens the hardened places in our hearts, revealing the lies and broken places we have hidden deep within our souls. It isn't until we fully receive God's unconditional love that we can experience genuine transformation; otherwise, it remains just out of reach. This kind of love from our Heavenly Father opens the door for us to experience freedom and healing by creating a pathway from our soul to our spirit.

His love for us is unlike anything we have ever experienced. It is the kind of love that remains unwavering and unchanging, even when we fail or fall short. It is not a love we can earn. It is a love that is freely given because we belong to Christ. Scripture reminds us in Ephesians 3:16–19 that as we trust in Christ, "he will empower you with inner strength through his Spirit… your roots will grow down into God's love and keep you strong." It is through this deep and personal experience of his love that the Holy Spirit's power strengthens us from within, transforming not only our minds and hearts but also our capacity to live in freedom.

When we embrace God's love for us, transformation naturally unfolds. The walls we've built begin to fall, and the door between our soul and spirit opens.

Today, we'll explore how God's unconditional love unlocks the door from our soul to our spirit, making true freedom possible.

SCRIPTURE REFLECTION 1
Romans 5:8
"But God showed his great love for us by sending Christ to die for us while we were still sinners."

UNDERSTANDING THE PASSAGE

Paul wrote this letter to the believers in Rome, helping them grasp the depth of salvation and the assurance of God's love and grace. In the surrounding verses, Paul explains God's love is unlike human love. His love doesn't wait for us to be worthy. In fact, this statement comes in the middle of a discussion about how Christ died for the ungodly and the undeserving.

This one single verse is a simple yet profound reminder of how God doesn't wait for us to get it right before he loves us. His love is extended in the middle of our mess, while we are still far from him, still broken, still unsure. This kind of love is difficult for the soul to receive on its own, especially when pain and rejection have shaped how we perceive ourselves and how we believe others perceive us.

The moment God's unconditional love meets us in our brokenness is when our souls are met with the kind of love that doesn't waver or demand anything from us. His love causes our heart, mind, and free will to realign. With this realignment, the door between our soul and spirit begins to open. Satan's influence begins to weaken, and the walls we have built start to crumble as we surrender our fear and shame. God's love doesn't simply comfort us; it unlocks the deeper places of our souls so truth can enter, transform our hearts and minds, and tear down the strongholds that once held us captive.

Take a moment to read Romans 5:6–11 to see how Paul builds this profound picture of God's love, a love that pursues us before we ever invite him into our hearts.

REFLECTION QUESTIONS

- How does this verse challenge any beliefs you may hold about needing to be "worthy" of God's love before receiving it?

- If you allowed yourself to fully receive the love described in Romans 5:8, how might it begin to reshape the way you think, feel, or respond?

SCRIPTURE REFLECTION 2

Ephesians 3:16-19

"I pray that from his glorious, unlimited resources he will empower you with inner strength through his Spirit. Then Christ will make his home in your hearts as you trust in him. Your roots will grow down into God's love and keep you strong. And may you have the power to understand, as all God's people should, how wide, how long, how high, and how deep his love is. May you experience the love of Christ, though it is too great to understand fully. Then you will be made complete with all the fullness of life and power that comes from God."

UNDERSTANDING THE PASSAGE

Paul wrote these words to believers in Ephesus, a city renowned for its rich culture. The people of Ephesus were spiritually diverse, encompassing a range of ideologies. His prayer wasn't for outward success or protection, but rather for something far deeper. It was for inner strength, rooted in love. Paul knew a personal experience of Christ's love was essential because without it, believers would remain spiritually weak, even if they appeared outwardly strong and faithful.

This passage speaks to the deepest parts of the soul. Paul's prayer is not merely for knowledge but for a personal encounter with Christ's love. The kind of love that stretches far beyond what the natural mind can grasp. That love, he says, is what grounds us. It's what builds trust. It's what makes room for Christ to dwell within us in a lasting way.

When we receive this kind of love, it restores us from all our shortcomings and brokenness. It settles our souls and quiets the noise of the enemy's lies. Healing flows into the inner workings of the soul, where shame and fear once ruled. As our worth is restored and our fears are replaced with the assurance of God's provision and protection, our perspective changes.

REFLECTION QUESTIONS

- According to verse 17, what happens as we trust in Christ?

- According to verse 19, what is the result of experiencing Christ's love, and how does that connect to the idea of being made complete?

FAITH IN ACTION

1. Identify the Barrier: Take a moment to notice a recurring thought you have about yourself when it comes to receiving love. Ask yourself: *Does this thought reflect God's love, or is it a distorted belief rooted in fear or shame?*

2. **Challenge the Distortion:** Write that thought down. Beneath it, write a truth from Scripture that contradicts it. *Example:*
"I have to earn love." → "While I was still a sinner, Christ died for me" (Romans 5:8).

3. **Dispute the lie:** If love had to be earned, Jesus would have waited until I was worthy. This verse shows he loves me at my worst, which means my worth isn't based on performance but on who I am to him.

4. **Reframe with Truth:** Speak what is true aloud. Ask the Holy Spirit to renew your mind, settle it in your heart, and bring your will into agreement with God's Word. Speak this reframed truth aloud.

5. **Practice Receiving:** Slow your breath. Quiet your mind and pray:

Jesus, help me receive your love where I've been closed off. Let it reshape how I think, what I feel, and how I respond.

SEEING THE BIGGER PICTURE

Understanding who God is changes how we interpret what we're walking through. His faithfulness isn't proven by easy circumstances; it's revealed in his unwavering presence through every season. His love isn't conditional on our performance or dependent on our feelings; it remains constant even when we can't sense it. When we anchor our hearts in these truths, that God is both loving and faithful, we stop measuring his goodness by our current situation. Instead, we begin to see his character as the foundation that holds us steady when everything else shifts. Knowing who God is doesn't eliminate the weight of the cup we're carrying, but it transforms how we carry it. We're no longer walking alone or wondering if he cares. We're held by a love that never ends and a faithfulness that begins fresh every morning.

CLOSING THOUGHT

The truth in your spirit is constant, even when your thoughts and emotions are not. That is why the Holy Spirit must lead the soul. Otherwise, the soul will continue to believe the lies the enemy tries to tell, which damages your mental filter. God's unconditional love for you will trap those lies and cast them out of our soul. When you receive the promised Holy Spirit, you receive power to tear down the strongholds that keep you from freedom. Freedom is your destiny. Practice taking your thoughts captive today and allowing God's love to fill your soul and align it with the power of the Holy Spirit.

CLOSING PRAYER

Dear Lord,

Thank you for loving me with your unconditional love. You know how easily I get pulled into lies that aren't true about me. Help me believe your love is real and personal. Lead my soul back to what's already true in my spirit. I want to live from that truth, not from shame.

In Jesus' name,
Amen

Day Four
When the Spirit and Soul Merge

Today, we'll take a closer look at how God's Word becomes personal for us, moving from something we read to something we live. If you've ever read a verse that seemed to speak directly to your situation or felt like God highlighted something just for you, you've experienced what Scripture calls a *rhema* word, which is a specific, Spirit-breathed word that brings supernatural clarity in the moment you need it most.

This kind of word doesn't just inform you; it transforms you. It settles your fears and calms your thoughts. Instead of spiraling, you begin to think with clarity and respond with faith. The *rhema* Word of God is how the Holy Spirit takes what is already true in Scripture and makes it personal to your life circumstances. His *rhema* word becomes the anchor for your soul and the fuel for your faith.

Today is about learning how to live guided by God's voice, not by your feelings, doubts, or circumstances. We'll explore what it means to live a Spirit-led life.

SCRIPTURE REFLECTION 1
John 10:27
"My sheep listen to my voice; I know them, and they follow me."

UNDERSTANDING THE PASSAGE
This verse is part of a larger conversation in John 10, where Jesus describes himself as the Good Shepherd. Using a Shepherd metaphor was an ideal illustration for his audience, one he knew would connect with Jewish culture. Shepherding was a common occupation in ancient Israel, and throughout the Old Testament, Christ is often shown as a shepherd who lovingly cares for his people (see Psalm 23 and Ezekiel 34). Jesus uses this rich imagery to teach his followers that he was the Messiah, the Son of God, who would care for and protect them as a shepherd tends his sheep.

At the time, religious leaders were questioning Jesus' authority and challenging his claim to divine identity. In response, Jesus draws a clear distinction between those who are part of his flock and those who are not. He said his sheep will recognize his voice.

Sheep listen, trust, and follow their shepherd. Jesus was telling his listeners to not only listen to his words but to take action.

Jesus knows us personally and intimately, and his voice becomes our guide amid all the noise, confusion, and heartache.

To be known by the Shepherd is about having a deep and intimate relationship with him. Jesus describes a relationship where his followers recognize his voice and respond to it. This kind of relationship helps us understand how God's Word becomes personal. In Greek, the New Testament uses two primary words for "word": *logos* and *rhema*. *Logos* refers to the written Word of God, which is timeless and unchanging. His Word is true for all people. *Rhema* refers to a specific, Spirit-breathed word that speaks directly to us about something specific in our lives. Jesus says his sheep listen to his voice. This is the kind of listening that opens the door to a *rhema* word. A *rhema* word is when the Holy Spirit highlights a passage of Scripture, brings a timely word to mind, or stirs something within you so personally that you know God is speaking to you. A *rhema* word doesn't simply give information; it brings transformation. It aligns your thoughts with truth, strengthens your faith, and leads you forward, giving you strength and hope in a way only God's voice can.

REFLECTION QUESTIONS

- According to John 10:27, what do Jesus' sheep do in response to his voice, and what does this reveal about their relationship with him?

- What does this verse show us about how Jesus relates to his followers, and how might recognizing his voice impact the way you respond to him in your daily life?

SCRIPTURE REFLECTION 2
Jeremiah 1:4–5
"The Lord gave me this message: 'I knew you before I formed you in your mother's womb. Before you were born, I set you apart and appointed you as my prophet to the nations'."

UNDERSTANDING THE PASSAGE

Jeremiah was young when God called him, possibly still a teenager, and the responsibility placed on him would have most likely felt heavy. He lived in Judah during a time of national unrest and spiritual decline. God was appointing him as a prophet during this tumultuous time. Jeremiah was called to speak hard truths, often standing alone as he warned the people and their leaders of the consequences of turning away from God. Jeremiah did not feel qualified. His immediate response was full of hesitation and self-doubt. Yet before he could speak a word of protest, God interrupted him with a deeply personal message: "I knew you."

This is more than a simple word of reassurance. It is a *rhema* word. It was a timely, Spirit-breathed truth spoken directly into Jeremiah's fear and shame. God doesn't start by telling him what to do; he starts by reminding him who he is. He affirms Jeremiah's worth, identity, and purpose before Jeremiah even raises a concern. "I knew you before you were formed," God says. "I set you apart. I appointed you." Those three statements dismantle every internal narrative Jeremiah might have believed about being too young or unqualified.

Although these words were originally spoken to Jeremiah, they still speak to us today. The way God's Word is both transcendent and deeply personal reveals the beauty of a *rhema* word. When the Holy Spirit takes something written thousands of years ago and breathes it into our present lives, it becomes a living word that speaks directly to our situation, shifting our perception. A *rhema* word helps us see as God sees. It moves us beyond what is directly in front of us and expands our vision to see the bigger picture.

We may not be called to be prophets to the nations, but we are called as his children to fulfill a specific purpose. We are set apart and chosen. There may be moments when God brings this exact passage to mind, not as a general encouragement but as a personal reminder of who he says we are. And when he does, the same Spirit of God who inspired these words in the Old Testament uses them to bring transformation to our lives today. When God speaks to us this way, when the Holy Spirit breathes life into Scripture, we are empowered to break through Satan's lies and tear down his strongholds. Aligning our souls with God's truth changes our perception about ourselves, God, and our circumstances.

Our thoughts are renewed, and our feelings become anchored in his promises. Without the power of the Holy Spirit, our minds are easily influenced, and our feelings are quick to follow. Through the power of the Holy Spirit, a *rhema* word brings truth forward and confronts the lies rooted in our souls. Shame tries to close the door by telling us we are disqualified. Shame tells us the promises of God are for someone else. But when we receive God's love, shame loses its power, and the door remains open, allowing the truth of God to penetrate our minds, hearts, and wills.

When we feel disqualified by our past or unsure of our worth, this passage reminds us God has called out our purpose and has secured us in who he created us to be. This passage declares we are known and set apart because he has called us.

In this scripture, God cuts straight through the lies we carry about ourselves. Shame tells us we're not enough. Fear says we're not ready. Insecurity insists we've been overlooked. But when the Holy Spirit speaks, these lies are completely wiped out and destroyed. When God speaks truth, it becomes the anchor that secures us in his Word.

REFLECTION QUESTIONS

- According to Jeremiah 1:4–5, what did God say to Jeremiah before giving him an assignment, and what does that reveal about how God views us?

- Who gave Jeremiah his assignment, and what does that tell you about the source of his calling?

FAITH IN ACTION
1. **Take a moment today and ask God** what he sees in you.

2. **Sit with Jeremiah 1:5 and read it slowly**, as if it were spoken directly to you.

3. **Write down any words, phrases, or thoughts** that stand out. If shame or doubt tries to dismiss them, pause and ask the Holy Spirit to help you receive what is true. Let this moment be less about what you feel and more about what God has said.

SEEING THE BIGGER PICTURE
The story of Jeremiah shows us God speaks with intention, not only to call us forward, but to anchor us in who we've always been in his eyes. When we receive a *rhema* word, it isn't just a moment of inspiration; it's a call to let truth transform our souls. We may wrestle with fear, inadequacy, or shame, but those struggles do not disqualify us from receiving a rhema word from the Holy Spirit. Those exact struggles may become the very place where God's personal word lands with the most power.

CLOSING THOUGHT
A rhema word is more than a moment of inspiration; it's the Holy Spirit bringing truth to life in the exact moment we need it. We may have read the words before, but when God speaks them directly to our souls, something shifts. Believing, receiving, and living out God's truth is how transformation happens. Freedom does not arrive through our own effort, but through surrendering and accepting the power of the Holy Spirit to give us supernatural wisdom and strength. When we learn to listen for his voice, we stop relying on what we feel and start responding to what God is actively saying. This is the difference between knowing Scripture and living within its truth.

CLOSING PRAYER
Dear Lord, thank you for speaking in ways that reach my soul. When I struggle to hear or believe, remind me you are near and still speaking to me. Help me respond to your voice with trust and a willing heart.

In Jesus' name
Amen

Day Five
Walking in Freedom

You've made it to the final day of the study, and my prayer is that you have gained an understanding of how our body, soul, and spirit work together to achieve wholeness and transformation. I hope you have been inspired to have a deeper relationship with Christ.

We've spent time exploring how truth resides in our spirit, but that truth can be blocked by lies that exist within our soul, encompassing our mind, heart, and free will, which influence our thoughts, perceptions, emotions, and choices. We have learned the Holy Spirit not only informs us, but more importantly, he empowers us.

Today, we will shift our focus from receiving freedom to walking in it. Freedom is not a one-time thing; it is a way of living. It's not the absence of difficulty or painful emotions; rather, it is the presence of the Holy Spirit, leading our souls to receive and respond to the truth of God's Word.

Earlier this week, we discussed how knowledge without power cannot transform us. Just as a light bulb cannot illuminate a room unless it is connected to electricity, its power source, we also cannot walk in freedom without staying connected to our power source, the Holy Spirit. We might have the right beliefs, the right practices, or even the right intentions, but without the Holy Spirit's power, we are left trying to handle life with limited strength. When our thoughts start to spiral and our emotions escalate, even our most sincere efforts cannot break through the internal chaos. The noise is overwhelming, and despite our best efforts, we cannot silence it. When we attempt to do so without the Holy Spirit's help, it rarely results in peace and freedom.

Today, we will explore how to stay connected and live plugged into our source of power by allowing the Holy Spirit to guide our thoughts, feelings, and choices. Having an intimate relationship with God is how we stay connected to our source of power and how we walk in freedom, one step, one day, or even one moment at a time. We become grounded in truth and empowered by God our Father, Son, and Holy Spirit.

SCRIPTURE REFLECTION 1
John 14:16–17

"And I will ask the Father, and he will give you another Advocate, who will never leave you. He is the Holy Spirit, who leads into all truth. The world cannot receive him, because it isn't looking for him and doesn't recognize him. But you know him, because he lives with you now and later will be in you."

UNDERSTANDING THE PASSAGE

Jesus spoke these words to his disciples during the Last Supper, one of his final conversations before his arrest, crucifixion, and death. In this moment, Jesus prepares them for what is to come. He knows they're about to face uncertainty, and instead of giving them a strict formula to follow, he promises to send the Holy Spirit, who will walk alongside them. The Holy Spirit had been with the disciples, but not living inside them. Jesus reassured the disciples that the Holy Spirit would soon dwell within them, offering them a power that would carry them through any hardship, ensuring they would never face any situation alone. To help them understand the importance of this promise, Jesus refers to the Holy Spirit as "another Advocate." The Greek word used here, *paraklētos*, means comforter, counselor, helper, and one who comes alongside. This promise wasn't just reassurance; it was a strong declaration they would never walk alone again.

This moment marks a turning point in how God's presence dwells within his people. Throughout Scripture, the Holy Spirit has been active, resting on prophets, guiding leaders, and moving among God's people. But Jesus describes something entirely new. Soon, the Holy Spirit will no longer just come alongside God's people, but he will live within them. God's presence will no longer dwell in specific places like the tabernacle or temple, but within the hearts of those who belong to him. This promise isn't symbolic; it is real and lasting. Through the indwelling of the Holy Spirit, God establishes a new level of closeness, one that brings about change at the deepest level, within the soul, where beliefs are formed, emotions are felt, and decisions are made.

Jesus states the Holy Spirit will lead us into all truth. He's not talking about intellectual understanding. He is promising us spiritual discernment and clarity. This truth has the power to transform the soul as it connects with the undeniable truth secured in the spirit.

The Holy Spirit is not distant or passive. He is active within us, guiding our thoughts, softening our hearts, and helping us make decisions that align with God's Word.

This passage also explains why truth often seems elusive when we rely on our own understanding. The world does not recognize the Holy Spirit, nor can it receive what it is not looking for. When we live disconnected from the Holy Spirit, we rely on our own efforts and reasoning. But when the Holy Spirit is present and active, he brings clarity and peace that cannot come from anywhere else. He changes how we think, what we believe, and how we choose to respond.

Walking in freedom means learning to recognize the Holy Spirit not as a force, but as a friend. A helper. A counselor. A steady presence in your life who speaks into your thoughts, renews your mind, and helps you live in alignment with God's promises, connecting your body, soul, and spirit.

REFLECTION QUESTIONS

- According to John 14:16–17, how does Jesus describe the Holy Spirit, and what does this reveal about the kind of relationship we are meant to have with him?

- Jesus says the world cannot receive the Holy Spirit because it isn't looking for him. What might it look like in your life to stay open and attentive to the Holy Spirit's presence?

SCRIPTURE REFLECTION 2

Joel 2:28–29

"Then, after doing all those things, I will pour out my Spirit upon all people. Your sons and daughters will prophesy, your old men will dream dreams, and your young men will see visions. In those days, I will pour out my Spirit even on servants—men and women alike."

UNDERSTANDING THE PASSAGE

Joel spoke these words hundreds of years before Jesus walked the earth, during a time when God's people were facing devastation and drought. The land was dry, the people were weary, and the spiritual climate felt barren. But in the middle of that dryness, God spoke a promise. It was a promise for a future moment when his Spirit would be poured out on all people.

This prophecy was revolutionary. In the Old Testament, the Holy Spirit would come upon specific individuals for specific tasks, like prophets, kings, and judges. But Joel prophesied something new. A time was coming when the Holy Spirit would no longer be reserved for the few but would be available to all. Sons and daughters. Young and old. Men and women. The Spirit of God would no longer dwell among his people; he would dwell within them.

This promise was fulfilled after Christ's resurrection and ascension, when the Holy Spirit arrived at Pentecost (Acts 2). Peter cited this exact passage in Acts 2:16-21 to show how the prophetic word was being fulfilled at that time. They were not witnesses to chaos or confusion, but to the fulfillment of the prophetic outpouring of the Holy Spirit.

Joel 2 reminds us that God's plan was always to dwell with his people. His plan wasn't to be an observer from afar but to live within each of his children. This passage reaffirms a critical aspect of our freedom. This passage tells us the Holy Spirit is not a gift for a select few, but for everyone who belongs to Christ. His presence enables us to drink the cup we never wanted to drink, the cup that seems too bitter to swallow. Through the power of the Holy Spirit, we are able to rise above every storm and experience peace that surpasses understanding. It is a supernatural peace that enables us to truly walk in freedom.

When the Holy Spirit lives within us, we no longer have to rely on emotional willpower, spiritual performance, or striving to maintain our connection to God. We walk in freedom by surrendering to him and abiding in his presence. The Holy Spirit anchors our souls, clarifies our thinking, and empowers our will. He doesn't just walk beside us; he lives in us, transforming our souls, our minds, hearts, and free will.

REFLECTION QUESTIONS

- According to Joel 2:28–29, upon whom does God promise to pour out his Spirit?

- Why was this prophecy about the Holy Spirit so significant for God's people then, and what does it reveal about how God relates to us now?

FAITH IN ACTION

1. **Take a few minutes today** to pause and reflect on how far you've come. Look back over the Faith in Action sections from each week. Determine which practices helped you slow down and listen more closely. Maybe it was naming distorted thoughts and aligning them with truth. Maybe it was learning to sit with your feelings without being ruled by them. Maybe it was recognizing the difference between your soul and your spirit and inviting the Holy Spirit to lead both. Which ones brought clarity or peace to your soul?

2. **Choose one or two practices** that helped you most and write them down where you'll see them regularly. Let these become part of your daily rhythm, not just something you tried for a season.

3. **As you walk forward**, let these Scriptures speak fresh hope into your heart:

- Isaiah 41:10 – "Don't be afraid, for I am with you. Don't be discouraged, for I am your God. I will strengthen you and help you. I will hold you up with my victorious right hand."

- Galatians 5:25 – "Since we are living by the Spirit, let us follow the Spirit's leading in every part of our lives."

- Psalm 73:26 – "My flesh and my heart may fail, but God is the strength of my heart and my portion forever."

- Romans 15:13 – "I pray that God, the source of hope, will fill you completely with joy and peace because you trust in him."

SEEING THE BIGGER PICTURE

Throughout this study, we've held many cups. Some cups were filled with fear, others with sorrow or shame. Each one revealed something deeper beneath the surface. We uncovered distorted perceptions, false beliefs, and emotions we didn't always know how to manage. We saw how our thoughts, feelings, and reactions are shaped by past pain, internal narratives, and the unspoken stories we carry.

We've learned what it means to name the lies, sit with the pain, and invite truth into places we've long tried to manage on our own. As we allow those deeper parts of the soul to surface, we begin the process of transformation. True freedom comes when we walk in step with the Holy Spirit, even when the path is difficult. He lives within you now. He knows the weight you carry, the thoughts that swirl, and the emotions that don't always make sense. And he's not overwhelmed by any of it. He offers wisdom when yours run dry and strength that doesn't depend on your feelings. The same power that raised Christ from the dead is now at work in you, leading your soul to respond to the promptings of your spirit. As you move forward, there's no need to perform or push your way through. You've already been invited to live free, day by day and moment by moment, walking in step with the Holy Spirit who dwells within you.

CLOSING THOUGHT

You didn't choose the cup life served you, but I hope you have learned how to embrace it and sit with it long enough to stop running from the pain or numbing the feelings. Throughout this study, you have been willing to face what may have felt overwhelming and met God in places you once avoided. You have allowed his presence to touch the parts of your soul that have longed for relief but didn't know where to find it. I hope you have learned the Holy Spirit has been there through all of it. He is the source of peace when your path feels uncertain, and he is the source of strength when you feel too weak and beaten down to move forward.

Receiving God's unconditional love opens the door between your soul and spirit. When that door opens, something shifts. The noise silences, and you begin to recognize the voice of the Lord speaking in real time, offering exactly what you need in the moment you need it.

Whatever cup comes next, you won't face it empty-handed. You now know God's truth runs deeper than your feelings, and you have tools to anchor yourself when your soul begins to spin.

But more than anything, you carry a relationship with Christ that will not fail. Christ himself will walk with you into whatever comes next. He's not asking you to ignore the places that hurt. He is inviting you to move through the territories of your soul with him, trusting the Holy Spirit to lead you into freedom from the bondage of lies.

CLOSING PRAYER

Dear Lord,

Thank you for walking with me through every page of this study and helping me see your hand in every part of my story. Thank you for recognizing what I've carried, for sitting with me in the pain I didn't want to face, and for speaking truth into the places I didn't know how to reach. I receive your unconditional love, and I ask for the courage to keep opening that door between my soul and spirit. Teach me to listen for your voice. Help me live from the truth you've planted within me. Remind me that I don't have to perform or strive. I just need to stay close to you. I trust your Spirit to lead me forward, one step at a time, into the freedom you've already made mine.

In Jesus' name,
Amen

WEEK SEVEN
GROUP DISCUSSION

Begin by watching the Week Seven video together. Afterward, ask the group, "What stood out to you most from the video?"

After one or two participants have shared, take time to review last week's study. As a group, flip through each day's reading, briefly noting the Reflection Questions and Faith in Action prompts. Allow time for participants to share their responses to each prompt. If you finish early, use the Group Discussion Questions below to encourage deeper connection.

1. How does the Holy Spirit bring clarity or peace into our lives as we grow in our faith?

2. In what ways do passages like Romans 5:8 or Ephesians 3:16–19 help shape a deeper understanding of God's love?

3. What rhythms or habits support a life that stays aligned with the Holy Spirit's guidance?

4. How does the idea of a "rhema word" encourage us to stay attentive to God's voice in our daily life?

5. What's one area of your life, your mind, heart, or will, where you'd like to invite the Holy Spirit to bring transformation and why?

ABOUT THE AUTHOR

Connie Hagen is an ordained minister through Christ for the Nation's Institute in Dallas, Texas. For ten years, she was a private practice licensed professional counselor who worked with women recovering from trauma. Through her ministry, she has cultivated a unique ability to connect with women who have experienced suffering, loss, brokenness, grief, and shame. Connie received her undergraduate degree in psychology from Evangel University as well as her Master's of Education degree in marriage and family counseling from the University of North Texas. She obtained her LPC license and specialized in post-traumatic stress disorder, depression, and anxiety in women. In 2004, she made the decision to devote herself to her growing family—Christopher, Tori, Maddie, and her husband, Jeff. Her husband left a large OB/GYN Medical Group in the DFW area to establish a private practice in the small town of Bastrop, Texas. For the following fifteen years, she dedicated herself to raising her children and managing her husband's medical practice. Their shared vision to provide medical care to the underserved and economically disadvantaged was a natural progression of Connie's passion to serve women in need. She currently serves as director of the women's ministry at her local church, where she uses her gifts of teaching and public speaking on a regular basis.

OTHER BOOKS BY AUTHOR

Order copies of *Drinking the Cup Your are Served* – The Bible Study
Or *Drinking the Cup Your Are Served* – The Book
at Amazon.com

GET IN TOUCH WITH CONNIE

 @ConnieHagen

 @ConnieLHagen

 @ConnieHagenAuthor

 ConnieHagenAuthor.com

STREAMING VIDEOS ACCESS

Here's your video access:

To stream teaching video sessions for
Drinking the Cup You Are Served – The Bible Study
please follow these steps:

1. Go to https://ConnieHagenAuthor.com/DTCvideos - OR -

2. Scan the QR code below

QUESTIONS? If you are having any problems with video access reach out to Thrilling Life Publishers Tech Support Team at 214-257-8716.

This video access entitles you to one non-transferable license with no expiration date. Please do not share the QR code or link with others or post them on any online services or social media platforms for any purposes, as that would be copyright infringement and is prohibited.

www.ingramcontent.com/pod-product-compliance
Lightning Source LLC
Chambersburg PA
CBHW081208170426
43198CB00018B/2884